THE SPIRIT OF POLYPHONY

T&T Clark New Studies in Bonhoeffer's Theology and Ethics

Series editors
Jennifer McBride
Michael Mawson
Philip G. Ziegler

THE SPIRIT OF POLYPHONY

Dietrich Bonhoeffer's Musical Pneumatology

Joanna Tarassenko

LONDON • NEW YORK • OXFORD • NEW DELHI • SYDNEY

T&T CLARK
Bloomsbury Publishing Plc, 50 Bedford Square, London, WC1B 3DP, UK
Bloomsbury Publishing Inc, 1385 Broadway, New York, NY 10018, USA
Bloomsbury Publishing Ireland, 29 Earlsfort Terrace, Dublin 2, D02 AY28, Ireland

BLOOMSBURY, T&T CLARK and the T&T Clark logo are
trademarks of Bloomsbury Publishing Plc

First published in Great Britain 2024
Paperback edition published 2025

Cover image: Dietrich Bonhoeffer (1906–45) photographed in the
late 1930s. Photo by ullstein bild via Getty Images.

A catalogue record for this book is available from the British Library.

Library of Congress Cataloging-in-Publication Data
Names: Tarassenko, Joanna Catherine, author.
Title: The spirit of polyphony : Dietrich Bonhoeffer's musical
pneumatology / Joanna Catherine Tarassenko.
Description: New York : T&T Clark, 2024. | Series: T&T Clark new studies in
Bonhoeffer's theology and ethics | Includes bibliographical references and index.
Identifiers: LCCN 2023038137 (print) | LCCN 2023038138 (ebook) |
ISBN 9780567713575 (hardback) | ISBN 9780567713940 (paperback) |
ISBN 9780567713582 (pdf) | ISBN 9780567713599 (epub)
Subjects: LCSH: Music–Religious aspects–Christianity. | Music–Philosophy and aesthetics. |
Spirit christology. | Bonhoeffer, Dietrich, 1906-1945–Criticism and interpretation.
Classification: LCC ML3921.2 .T37 2024 (print) | LCC ML3921.2 (ebook) |
DDC 781.1/2–dc23/eng/20230829
LC record available at https://lccn.loc.gov/2023038137
LC ebook record available at https://lccn.loc.gov/2023038138

ISBN: HB: 978-0-5677-1357-5
PB: 978-0-5677-1394-0
ePDF: 978-0-5677-1358-2
eBook: 978-0-5677-1359-9

Series: T&T Clark New Studies in Bonhoeffer's Theology and Ethics

Typeset by Integra Software Services Pvt. Ltd.

For product safety related questions contact productsafety@bloomsbury.com.

To find out more about our authors and books visit www.bloomsbury.com
and sign up for our newsletters.

CONTENTS

PREFACE

A small corner of specialist Bonhoeffer scholarship has long recognized that the musico-theological discussions in his prison letters go beyond simple musings written to a like-minded soul. In recent years Bonhoeffer's creative use of musical terminology has even sparked a highly constructive resurgence of interest in this adumbrated theology of music. Yet, the full significance of Bonhoeffer's musical thinking has not been sufficiently actualized. In this context, this study offers a reexamination of how Bonhoeffer employs musical patterns of thought and language to a theological end. First outlining Bonhoeffer's musico-theology and how it has been understood up until now, I set the stage for a closer examination. Through an analysis of Bonhoeffer's musical metaphor of polyphony as he applies it to the Chalcedonian definition, I am able to demonstrate how his account of Christian formation which is so intimately connected to this Christology, and which polyphony helps to articulate, also contains a latent pneumatology. Showing that the relationship between Christology and Christian formation in his theology is most fully realized by incorporating a pneumatology I argue that his appeal to polyphony in effect articulates this pneumatology, as an indirect but nevertheless exceedingly successful means of contouring an account of the Spirit's work.

This interrogation of Bonhoeffer's musico-theology has two main benefits. First, my clarification of Bonhoeffer's use of polyphony with respect to the Christology it expresses helps to disclose a pneumatology. While only nascent in Bonhoeffer, this pneumatology is arguably vital to understanding his theology of Christian formation in Christ. Second, this examination of Bonhoeffer's musico-theology opens the way for me to make some suggestions with regard to what musical metaphors, with their capacity to convey dual agency, can offer a theology of the Holy Spirit with respect to Christology.

ACKNOWLEDGMENTS

I should like to thank the following people (and the organizations which represent them) for helping me on the journey from beginning this research to its completion:

Cambridge Faculty of Divinity (The Hedley Lucas Trust), Ridley Hall, and the Diocese of Oxford for collaborating financially to enable me to undertake this work.

Members of the International Bonhoeffer Society and fellow conference attendees whose engagement with Bonhoeffer stimulated my own, and whose friendship was sustaining.

My supervisor, Jeremy Begbie, for his unerring alacrity, attentiveness, and patience and, above all, his humanity. It is one of my life's greatest pleasures and privileges to have worked with Professor Begbie.

The women who, by their example, words, prayers, and practical efforts, cheered me on: Alice, Amy, Beki, Lizzie, Rachael, Sarah; Anne Tarassenko, Catherine Wright, Christie Gilfeather, Christiane Simon, Christine Torrance, Clare Backhouse, Debbie Ford, Ellie McLaughlin, Johanna Harris-Tyler, Judith Gretton-Dann and Nessa Watts.

My parents, Stuart and Alison, for their many sacrifices, seen and unseen.

My dearest daughter, Bianca, and my beloved son, Benjamin, who disrupted everything and, in so doing, provided me with the most life-giving counterpoint of all.

Finally, and above all, my husband, Luke, who has been my theological inquisitor and best friend for over thirteen years; and whose own academic travails were not sufficiently off-putting; and who kept believing.

INTRODUCTION

> "it's strange how music, when one listens with the inner ear alone and gives oneself up to it utterly, can be almost more beautiful than when heard physically. It's purer, all the dross falls away, *and it seems to take on a 'new body*.'"[1]

With these words Dietrich Bonhoeffer presents us with an arresting possibility. He likens the act of recalling a piece of music, specifically Beethoven's "Sonata in C Minor," op. 111, to the "new [resurrection] body" of Christ.[2] From a theological perspective, the comparison is evocative.[3] As Bonhoeffer does not trouble to explain the allusion, we cannot easily say what he means by it. We are left to wonder how music can be heard "with the inner ear"; how music, thus remembered, is "almost more beautiful" than when it is "heard physically"; and, most tantalizingly of all, in what ways it might be similar to Christ's post-resurrection state. By the end of this book, I hope to have shown that, for Bonhoeffer, the way music transfigures existence is an especially apposite metaphor for the way the Holy Spirit transforms the Christian life.

In what follows I examine Dietrich Bonhoeffer's musico-theology; that is, how his musical patterns of thought and language, especially the metaphor of polyphony, are employed to a theological end. In particular, I show that the relationship between Christology and Christian formation in Bonhoeffer's theology is realized in an implicit pneumatology in which the dual agency of Christ and the Spirit are conceived through musical metaphors.

While the polyphony of Bonhoeffer's own life is often discussed in biographies, anecdotally, his theological appeal to musical metaphors was for a long time an outlying area of Bonhoeffer studies, receiving specialist attention from only

1. Bonhoeffer, *Letters and Papers from Prison*, 8:332. In a letter to Eberhard Bethge, dated March 27, 1944, which Bonhoeffer calls his "Easter letter." Emphasis mine.

2. We know this to be the meaning of the statement "new body" because of how the letter proceeds to focus on Christ's resurrection body.

3. Of course, the comparison works both ways. We could also ask what it means from a musical perspective: that is, how our musical understanding can benefit from being likened to the resurrected form of Christ.

a few scholars.[4] More recently this circle of interest has widened, leading to a number of constructive interpretations which make use of Bonhoeffer's appeal to polyphony but move beyond Bonhoeffer himself.[5] All of these accounts correctly note the Christological relevance of Bonhoeffer's musico-theology. However, no one has yet recognized the full significance of these metaphors for conceptualizing a pneumatology. By interrogating Bonhoeffer's use of musical metaphors, I show that they help him to reimagine how Christians should live before Christ in the world today and, upon further examination, I find that his account of Christian formation is ameliorated by appeal to the agency of the Holy Spirit. This pneumatology, I contend, is not only concealed in the use of musical terms in his late theology but, moreover, upon being disclosed, it is seen to be a potent means of articulating a theology of the Holy Spirit. That is, by full and careful examination of Bonhoeffer's appeal to musical metaphors for a theology of Christian formation, it is possible to identify a theology of the Holy Spirit which is being conveyed through them.

Therefore, this work, I believe, offers an important addition to studies of Bonhoeffer's musical imagination and, furthermore, it also seeks to contribute to a growing body of research on Bonhoeffer's pneumatology; a subject which has, until very recently, been largely overlooked. I draw two related conclusions: the first for Bonhoeffer studies and the second for Christian theology more widely.

4. The primary expositor of Bonhoeffer's theological musings on music to date is: Andreas Pangritz, *The Polyphony of Life: Bonhoeffer's Theology of Music*, first published in German in 1994. John W. de Gruchy has examined Bonhoeffer's relationship with aesthetics focusing on his theological appeal to music in his important work: de Gruchy, "Restoring Broken Themes of Praise." His interest in this subject was revived in an essay on Bonhoeffer's love of Beethoven for Andreas Pangritz's Festschrift. See: de Gruchy, "The Search for Transcendence in an Age of Barbarism: Bonhoeffer, Beethoven, Mann's Dr Faustus and the Spiritual Crisis of the Present Time."

5. Two highly constructive readings of Bonhoeffer's appeal to polyphony demonstrate the potency of the metaphor for theology by creatively developing it beyond Bonhoeffer's own use. They are: Harvey, *Taking Hold of the Real: Dietrich Bonhoeffer and the Profound Worldliness of Christianity*; and Gardiner, *Melodies of a New Monasticism: Bonhoeffer's Vision, Iona's Witness*. There have also been several important essays which examine Bonhoeffer's appeal to polyphony within the parameters of wider explorations of theology and music. See, especially: Begbie, "Music in God's Calling"; Moseley, "'Parables' and 'Polyphony': The Resonance of Music as Witness in the Theology of Karl Barth and Dietrich Bonhoeffer." In a notable exception to the foregoing, Lisa Dahill comes to the metaphor by an alternative route to that of a theology of music: by examining Bonhoeffer's theology of spiritual formation. It is, therefore, with considerable acuity that Dahill observes: "For Bonhoeffer, the image of polyphony evokes our participation in Christ whose resurrection draws us into the heart of the world … a lovely and authentically Lutheran image of Christian conformation to the Risen One." Dahill, Lisa E., *Reading from the Underside of Selfhood: Bonhoeffer and Spiritual Formation*, 98.

First, an examination of musical metaphors in Bonhoeffer offers new ways of understanding his theology of Christian formation by unearthing and giving expression to an underdeveloped pneumatology. Second, the musical language and thought I explore in Bonhoeffer provides especially valuable ways of understanding the Holy Spirit's work, as it can help to imagine the dual agency of the Spirit and the Son in a way that upholds a Chalcedonian Christology.

Overview of Chapters

This work is divided into three parts. The first part analyzes "Dietrich Bonhoeffer's Musico-Theology"; the second part focuses on "The Polyphonic Shape of Christian Formation"; and the third examines "Space for the Holy Spirit."

In Part I, I provide a survey of Bonhoeffer's musico-theology, examining evidence of musical ideas and language operating theologically for him. In Chapter 1, "A Musico-Theological Life," I explore Bonhoeffer's musical backstory before turning to his explicit musico-theological reflections in *Letters and Papers from Prison*. I set the scene for his musical engagement with theology by focusing on two experiences prior to his imprisonment in which Bonhoeffer's Christian formation is either informed by, or informs, his engagement with music: his experience of African American spirituals in New York in 1930, and Nazi propaganda music in Germany five years later. Narrowing in on these musical experiences provides snapshots of Bonhoeffer's life in which his engagement with music influences his resistance to racism. Turning to *Letters and Papers from Prison*, I proceed to explore three letters in which music is discussed at length in relation to theology. In these letters I identify an emerging musico-theology as Bonhoeffer examines: (1) the relationship between "aesthetic existence" and being a Christian; (2) the music of Heinrich Schütz and the Irenaen view of recapitulation; and (3) J. S. Bach's *Art of Fugue* and eschatological hope. These musico-theological sketches form the prelude to his most explicit musical metaphor, which is the subject of the next chapter.

Chapter 2 is entitled "A Musico-Theological Invention" and focuses on Bonhoeffer's so-called "little invention" (*Fündlein*) polyphony. After briefly outlining the musical understanding of the term, I focus my examination of polyphony on Bonhoeffer's understanding of it. I identify the term in Bonhoeffer's prison letters before analyzing its two main uses, namely to articulate (i) the relationship between loving God and "earthly loves"; and (ii) more broadly, the Christian's relationship with God and the world. This will show that polyphony helps Bonhoeffer to imaginatively describe the Christian life as interrelating God and the world in a way that maintains the discrete integrity of each. At this juncture I observe some enticing, but rather loose, ties between pneumatology and music: first, Bonhoeffer himself alludes to the role of the Holy Spirit in forming "New Creations" in one of the musico-theological letters discussed in Chapter 1; second, in Chapter 2, we see that two commentators associate polyphony with a pneumatology in their discussions of Bonhoeffer, though without elaboration.

These observations, while easy to overlook, are early indicators of the pneumatology which is deeply embedded in Bonhoeffer's musico-theology.

Part II addresses "The Polyphonic Shape of Christian Formation." Here I deepen my exploration of the musico-theological term "polyphony" by clarifying how it is used by Bonhoeffer to articulate both Christology and Christian formation. "The Polyphony of Christ" is the subject of Chapter 3, in which I attempt to elucidate Bonhoeffer's use of polyphony as a metaphor for the Chalcedonian Definition. I first examine Bonhoeffer's Christology lectures which are characterized by the idea of a personal encounter with the composite Christ, the Counter-logos. In agreement with Rowan Williams, I detect a form of kenosis in Bonhoeffer's emphasis on Christ's "promeity": Christ's mode of being, which is radically hospitable in its other-directedness, correlates with an ontology of Christ in which the divine nature, displayed through the composite person of Christ, is supremely *for* the human. On this basis, I argue that polyphony is a telling metaphor for the union of the divine and human natures: it conveys the "interpenetration" of distinct natures, their capacity to resonate with each other while each also retains its full integrity, as well as the "attunement" of the human nature to the divine.

Chapter 4, entitled "The Contrapuntal Christian," examines the "participative ecclesiology" and ethics entailed by Bonhoeffer's Christology, with its emphasis on a personal encounter with Christ. I first locate Bonhoeffer's use of the term "Christian formation" in *Ethics* and examine the "tri-formative" pattern of conformation to Christ incarnate, crucified, and resurrected which directly forms the Christian as human, judged, and renewed. This raises a critical problem concerning what is, at times, a vagueness in the distinction Bonhoeffer makes between Christ and the Church. With this in mind, second, I examine Bonhoeffer's participative ecclesiology more closely, turning to *Sanctorum Communio*. I demonstrate that Bonhoeffer guards against an overidentification of Christ with the Church and effectively secures the integrity of each through an implicit pneumatology. By distinguishing between the work of the Holy Spirit and that of the risen Christ, Bonhoeffer can differentiate an established ontological situation, in which the Church is grounded in Christ, from a socio-temporal situation, in which it is actualized, at present only partially, by the Holy Spirit.

The subject of Part III is "Space for the Holy Spirit." In Chapter 5, "A Musico-Pneumatology," I thread together the arguments of the previous four chapters by demonstrating how Bonhoeffer's pneumatology coheres with his use of musical metaphors. I analyze David Ford's account of Bonhoeffer's pneumatology in *Ethics*, which I find can be strengthened by acknowledging that there is more evidence of a pneumatology in that text than he notices. I argue that Bonhoeffer's concept of "reality" (*Wirklichkeit*), in *Ethics*, is of something established by Christ and actualized by the Spirit; a similar distinction to the one made in *Sanctorum Communio*. However, in *Ethics* this work of Christ and the Spirit is presented as constituting reality itself, encompassing the whole world rather than being limited to the Church. This is a subtle, but important, shift in Bonhoeffer's thinking. It introduces a tension for him between conveying the relationship between God and the world in Christ, on the one hand, and the difference between them, on the other, in such a way that Christ's work is not undermined. This tension is maintained by the Spirit.

I argue that the metaphor of polyphony as Bonhoeffer employs it in *Letters* is the means by which he conceptualizes reality as he has come to view it in *Ethics*. Polyphony, and musical casts of mind more generally, helps Bonhoeffer reimagine reality with the kind of nuance his theology requires, expressing the relationship between God and the world in Christ and the Church, as well as the distinction between them. They provide him with a means of contouring reality which correlates with his understanding of the work of the Spirit. I find further support for my argument in Bonhoeffer's own critique of the inadequacy of static spatial images for expressing his account of reality.

In the final chapter, "A Spirit Christology Acoustically Defined," I move beyond an exclusive examination of Bonhoeffer in order to demonstrate how the implicit pneumatology which can be detected in his thought could be further developed, though with recourse to the musical casts of mind he so creatively employs. In Chapter 6 I propose that an orthodox Spirit Christology as per Ian McFarland's "pneumatic Chalcedonianism" is both broadly consonant with Bonhoeffer's Christological commitments and also offers a means of strengthening his account of the Holy Spirit by positioning it in the life and work of Jesus of Nazareth. While such an account lends greater depth to pneumatology, in particular by providing it with a Trinitarian context, I show that Bonhoeffer's musico-theology itself has much to offer this Spirit Christology. The musico-pneumatology which we have seen at work in Bonhoeffer offers a means of recasting the dual agency of the Spirit and the Son without either being neglected or undermined and this, in turn, provides the basis for the church's life in the Spirit.

In this way we see that our examination of polyphony not only throws light onto Bonhoeffer's pneumatology, suggesting that the musical metaphor rests on and, consequently, discloses what is, admittedly, only a nascent theology of the Holy Spirit; but, furthermore, the musical metaphor is a highly potent way of articulating and imagining the agency of the Holy Spirit. Not only does it help to shape a pellucid account of the involvement of the Spirit in a Chalcedonian Christology but it also provides a potent means of articulating the Christian formation which rests on this Christology. The Spirit who causes God and the world to resonate in Christ by attuning the human nature to the Son and, through the Son, to the Father, also attunes us to God through Christ.

A Few Notes on Methodology, Style, and Terminology

An immediate methodological concern for all interdisciplinary research is the need to retain the integrity of each discipline. This is particularly relevant with respect to the term "polyphony," which, it will be noted in Chapter 2, I analyze as a musical term *prior* to my analysis of Bonhoeffer's theological use of it. At the same time, I am not attempting an evenly weighted dialogue between theology and music, although such dialogues are necessary and highly valuable. This is a theological work which focuses on the musical imagination and language of Dietrich Bonhoeffer for theological purposes.[6] I intend to unearth greater insights regarding Bonhoeffer's theology through my exposition of his musical casts of mind.

In this respect, musical language is being understood as metaphorical in this project, providing new theological insights.[7] Before we can analyze these new insights, it is important to realize that the musico-theological casts of mind and language which Bonhoeffer uses both rely on and disclose a different kind of spatial thinking to that which is employed in the use of "receptacle" or "container" metaphors.[8] Whereas visually informed perceptions of space from which container metaphors are derived reinforce boundaries, musical metaphors are capable of conveying "edgeless difference."[9] This is because the perceptual phenomenon of musical space is highly distinct from the visual perception of space on which a very large part of our conceptual thought depends.

So vital to my argument is this conceptual difference, and so deeply entrenched are these habits of thought which over-rely on visual perception, that it is worth

6. The following is an example of the kind of problems faced by treating music with theology, and also discloses how, in this book, it is resolved by prioritizing Bonhoeffer's own preference for privileging theology. In presenting for the Noesis seminar series in the Cambridge Divinity Faculty, a music student in attendance responded that Bonhoeffer's view of polyphony, which (as we discuss in Chapter 2) likens the *cantus firmus* to love of God and proceeds to emphasize the role of the *cantus* in "anchoring" the whole composition, was "highly romanticized." While bearing in mind, then, that a theological appeal to the musical concept of polyphony might jar with the term as understood next door in the Music Faculty, this is not to say that Bonhoeffer's understanding of polyphony is necessarily inaccurate, or that a musico-theological exploration of the kind we are pursuing is invalid. This is a matter of emphasis and Bonhoeffer's emphasis is firmly on Christian theology.

7. As Janet Soskice puts it, "not as an ornament to what we already know but as an embodiment of a new insight." Soskice, *Metaphor and Religious Language*, 48.

8. Lakoff and Johnson describe "container metaphors" as fundamental to humans, even across cultures, because of the basic human instinct for territoriality. They write: "But even where there is no natural physical boundary that can be viewed as defining a container, we impose boundaries—marking off territory so that it has an inside and a bounding surface—whether a wall, a fence, or an abstract line or plane. There are few human instincts more basic than territoriality. And such defining of a territory, putting a boundary around it, is an act of quantification." See: Lakoff and Johnson, *Metaphors We Live By*, 29. The inadequacies of "container," or "receptacle," metaphors for theology, are rightly criticized by T. F. Torrance See: Torrance, *Space, Time, and Incarnation*; Torrance, *Space, Time and Resurrection*.

9. Imogen Adkins makes this point extremely well. She argues that musical space generates a conceptuality which can overcome some of the issues related to container metaphors for kenosis, for instance the harmful effects of receptacle metaphors as observed by T. F. Torrance. See: Adkins, "Sound, Space and Christological Self-Giving."

underscoring here the distinction between visual modes of thought and those which rely on an acoustic environment. Underlining the negative impact of the conceptual habits which arise from visual-spatial patterns of thought in theology, Jeremy Begbie describes how visually informed modes of thought entail perceiving space as "an aggregate of place," with "bounded locations" of distinct objects; "discrete zones that cannot overlap" without their integrities being "threatened."[10] The problematic theological tendencies which arise from such habits of thought includes zero-sum thinking which apportions space to God and the world in competitive terms or presents "immanence" and "transcendence" as being in opposition.[11]

Acoustic space is strikingly different. In our aural field of perception space is not boundaried.[12] Sounds are capable of interpenetrating, so that multiple sounds can simultaneously be heard as full and distinct.[13] With musical space there is no magnitude of elements, in the sense that more of one does not equate to less of another. At the same time, there is what Begbie calls a "resonant order" to this space; when the appropriate notes are played, the more a lower string sounds, the more the upper string will vibrate.[14]

The salient point is this: musical casts of mind overcome some of the limits of visually informed concepts and make it possible to imagine God and creation as interpenetrating, in the closest possible relationship, while also remaining

10. Begbie, "Room of One's Own? Music, Space and Freedom," 142. Begbie gives the example of different colors which cannot overlap without changing: "We cannot see a patch of red and a patch of yellow in the same space *as* red and yellow. We see either red *or* yellow; or (if the colours are allowed to merge) we see a mixture of the two—orange." Ibid. See also: Begbie, "'A Semblance More Lucid'? An Exploration of Trinitarian Space."

11. "God's 'thereness' and 'hereness' will tend to be understood against the background of a 'hyperspace', discrete portions of which both God and the world inhabit. It is not hard to see how this can encourage and support a philosophy of univocity—ontological and linguistic—in which God and created world are regarded as belonging to the same genus." Begbie, "Room of One's Own? Music, Space and Freedom," 144.

12. Unlike a visual construal of space, "there is no clear orientation of sounds in auditory space: no way of assigning faces, ends, boundaries, and so on to them, so as to introduce those topological features which help us to make sense of the idea of 'occupying' a place … the acousmatic experience offers a world of objects which are ordered only *apparently*, and not in fact." Scruton, *The Aesthetics of Music*, 14.

13. "The tones can 'sound through' one another, interpenetrate. They can be in one another, while being heard as two distinct tones." Begbie, "Room of One's Own? Music, Space and Freedom," 159.

14. "The lower string enhances the upper string, brings it to life, frees it to be itself, compromising neither the integrity of the upper string nor its own. We hear the resonant order of musical space." Begbie, "'A Semblance More Lucid'? An Exploration of Trinitarian Space," 25. Here Begbie draws on the work of Victor Zuckerkandl. See: Zuckerkandl, *Sound and Symbol: Music and the External World.*

distinct.[15] According to my argument, these metaphors not only offer a fitting way of imagining the "spatiality" of the God–world relation, or the relationship between the divine and human natures in Christ which resists the kind of zero-sum thinking of container metaphors; they especially assist in conceptualizing the Holy Spirit's work in the Christian life and in Jesus' own life.

Something should be said about my use of the term "Christian formation," not only because Bonhoeffer resolutely rejects programs of Christian formation, but also because I do not seek to construct one myself based on Bonhoeffer's thought. By focusing more on the "upstream" doctrinal commitments of Christology, pneumatology, and ecclesiology, rather than "downstream" human practices, I privilege the former as determinative of the pattern of Christian formation; that is, I focus on the work of Christ and the Spirit.[16] In so doing, I employ the term as Bonhoeffer does in his description of formation; it is the *a priori* action of Christ and the actualization of this by the Spirit which forms the Christian.[17] While the practical outworkings of these doctrinal commitments are not my primary focus, they arise almost ineluctably and so are also addressed, albeit to a lesser extent.[18]

My shorthand name for the way Bonhoeffer adopts musical language for theological purposes is "musico-theology"; and specifically for a pneumatological purpose, "musico-pneumatology."[19]

15. This is similar to the Trinitarian metaphor of the perichoretic dance, except with musical metaphor there can be a stronger emphasis on interpenetration; the interpenetration of musical notes in our aural perception can help us to imagine more emphatically the extent of the relationship.

16. The elegant distinction between Bonhoeffer's "upstream" commitments to pneumatology, Christology, ecclesiology, theological and philosophical anthropology, and sanctification, and the "downstream" theology of how these matters are worked out in Christian formation, is made by Joseph McGarry. See: McGarry, "Christ among a Band of People: Dietrich Bonhoeffer and Formation in Christ," 1. I largely agree with McGarry when he suggests that by clarifying doctrine (an upstream focus) the correct ordering of practices (downstream) will emerge.

17. Bonhoeffer writes about formation on only one occasion, in the manuscript "Ethics as Formation". Bonhoeffer, *Ethics*, 6:76–102. This is discussed in detail in Chapter 4.

18. In this respect my argument is quite different from Lisa Dahill's study of Bonhoeffer and "spiritual formation," which gives more attention to the role of human action. In assessing Bonhoeffer's theology of formation alongside the experiences of female abuse victims, Dahill's project poses an important challenge to the idea of putting too much stock in Bonhoeffer's theology without giving sufficient voice to those in the Church who might suffer as a result of harmful practices which an imbalanced reading of Bonhoeffer might seem to endorse. See: Dahill, *Reading from the Underside of Selfhood: Bonhoeffer and Spiritual Formation*.

19. Though she does not widely employ the expression, these are notably distinct from Catherine Pickstock's category of "theologico-musical" which she uses to refer to music as a metaphysical category. See: Pickstock, "Soul, City and Cosmos after Augustine." Bonhoeffer's theological appeal to music occurs in personal letters and, therefore, is not so developed an account that he directly addresses metaphysical claims about music, though they are implied.

Letters and Papers from Prison as a Text

It will also be prudent at the outset to describe my use of the prison letters as a theological text.[20] Deciphering the significance of theological ideas in *Letters* is somewhat complicated by the epistolary format, censorship issues, and circumstances around preservation of material. Additionally, the interweaving of theological material with other affairs (traumatic and mundane) means that judging Bonhoeffer's musical discussions for their theological insights must be approached with care. Of all Bonhoeffer's writings, *Letters* has proven most slippery; as evidenced by the multivalent interpretations, especially those of the 1960s which include finding in *Letters* inspiration for the Death of God movement or a case for Christian secularism.[21]

In my view the prison letters should be treated as an essential part of Bonhoeffer's theological corpus which demonstrate the ongoing development of his thought, without being over-privileged as the hermeneutical key to all

20. A limited collection of Bonhoeffer's more "theological" letters was first published in German in 1951, followed by somewhat expanded editions in 1967 (in German) and 1971 (in English). The Fortress Press editions, *DBW 8* (published in German in 1998), and its English translation *DBWE* 8 (published in English in 2010) used here arrange the prison letters chronologically and biographically in keeping with Bethge's intended structure of 1971. There are four parts: "Part 1: The Interrogation Period (April–July 1943)"; "Part 2: Awaiting the Trial (August 1943–April 1944)"; "Part 3: Holding Out for the Coup Attempt (April–July 1944)"; "Part 4: After the Failure (July 1944–February 1945)". Letters conveyed through the proper channels during this time were all censored. However, on November 18, 1943, Bonhoeffer began an uncensored correspondence with Bethge, made possible by the illegal smuggling of letters. When Bethge was conscripted in January 1944 for ten months on the Italian front, his correspondence was less strictly guarded and access to a typewriter meant that some of Bonhoeffer's letters, especially his theological reflections, could be preserved. This structure is described in more detail in the editor's introduction. Bonhoeffer, *Letters and Papers from Prison*, 8:11–18. The majority of the material I examine in this book is from Parts 2 and 3, according to the editor's divisions of the text and I adopt the abbreviations *DBWE* (*Dietrich Bonhoeffer Works,* English edition) and *DBW* (*Dietrich Bonhoeffer Works*, German edition).

21. The most prominent of which was Robinson's *Honest to God* which influenced a whole generation of Bonhoeffer scholars. See: Robinson, *Honest to God*. The potential for such a reading was surely in view when Karl Barth cautioned that Bonhoeffer's enigmatic statements in the *Letters* could not be entirely understood and recommended sticking with the early Bonhoeffer. See: Editor's Afterword. Bonhoeffer, *Letters and Papers from Prison*, 8:591–2. With respect to the multivalent interpretations of theological formulae in *Letters*, Peter Selby argues convincingly in defense of a moderate reading of Bonhoeffer which recognizes new developments in his thought but no drastic departures from core doctrinal beliefs. Selby, "Christianity in a World Come of Age," 228.

his works.[22] There are three reasons for this. First, it is clear that Bonhoeffer continued to pursue his vocation as a theologian and pastor in prison. He adopted a strict regime;[23] he avidly consumed reading material to assist his theological production (Dilthey, Hartmann, Kant) as well as non-theological material (Weizsäcker, Stifter, Paul de Kruif).[24] He also took seriously his role as a pastor in prison, maintaining spiritual disciplines, reading the daily texts and the Old Testament, in particular, voraciously;[25] he penned liturgy for fellow inmates[26] (some of whom intentionally sought out his counsel),[27] and was even entreated to pray by prison officers.[28] His life's purpose did not end with his imprisonment, and although he acknowledged that the lives of his generation were "unfinished and fragmentary," he also recognized that they "may point to a higher fulfilment."[29]

Second, in addition to this pattern of life his writing is self-consciously theological. Viewed collectively together with his fiction, the prison writings are the product of a mind which continues to be motivated by the desire to make a theological response to the problems of his country and the Church, a mind which ventures widely and experimentally but is also markedly consistent and focused in its output. As an example, he tries his hand at fiction and poetry in prison (perhaps taking the opportunity to do so while deprived of music) but the ideas he expresses betray his theological preoccupations.[30] As a result, the Tegel writings as

22. Unlike, for instance, Ernst Feil who reads the idea of a "world come of age" in the *Letters* as the theme of Bonhoeffer's life. For a helpful discussion of reception of Bonhoeffer's *Letters* and issues of continuity and discontinuity see: Nickson, *Bonhoeffer on Freedom: Courageously Grasping Reality*, 1–6.

23. "I am reading, studying, and working a great deal systematically." Bonhoeffer, *Letters and Papers from Prison*, 8:70.

24. In prison he is apparently still researching with the completion of his magnum opus, *Ethics*, in view as he writes of de Kruif: "One often learns more for 'ethics' in such places than in textbooks." Bonhoeffer, 8:128.

25. Bonhoeffer, 8:213.

26. Bonhoeffer, 8:194–6.

27. Bonhoeffer, 8:233.

28. Bonhoeffer, 8:214.

29. Bonhoeffer, *Letters and Papers from Prison*, 8:301. As Heinrich Ott puts it: "What Bonhoeffer here says expressly about his life must also be true of his work, which was so closely bound up with that life. For interpretation of his work the basis must be to recognise 'how the whole was planned and thought out' or at least 'what material was used here for the building.'" Ott, *Reality and Faith: The Theological Legacy of Dietrich Bonhoeffer*, 65. Bonhoeffer's life and work were so closely bound that we must look for the purpose and plan in the fragments of what he wrote.

30. A strong case for viewing the Tegel writings as theology has recently been made by Eleanor McLaughlin, who connects the concept "unconscious Christianity" to Bonhoeffer's thinking in *Ethics*. See: McLaughlin, *Unconscious Christianity in Dietrich Bonhoeffer's Late Theology*.

a whole—which in addition to the letters include fiction (often overlooked because of its being published separately), poetry, notes, "Outline for a Book," as well as the circular he writes to his co-conspirators, and the baptism sermon—share common theological themes, especially the letters from April 30, 1944, onward. These letters are dubbed "theological" by the editors of the recent collected works of Bonhoeffer because Bonhoeffer himself names them as such, expressing his wish that Bethge find a way to preserve them.[31]

Third, *Ethics* (widely taken to be Bonhoeffer's magnum opus) is unmistakably theological and yet it is also fragmentary, written as a series of manuscripts of which the intended order is unknown. Furthermore, like *Letters*, it was produced under pressure. In the same way that the fragmentariness of *Ethics* and the circumstances surrounding its creation are not sufficient reasons to discount its theological worth, the same can be said of *Letters*.

While the texts are, of course, vastly different, and the theological argument much easier to follow in *Ethics*, I am of the opinion that the dialogical character of *Letters* even has certain advantages. Immediately following Bonhoeffer's request that Bethge preserve his theological letters, he states: "One writes things in a more uninhibited and lively way in a letter than in a book, and in a conversation through letters I often have better ideas than when I'm writing for myself."[32] Bonhoeffer's theology was highly collaborative long before his isolation in prison; produced in conversation with influential teachers and peers, it was demonstrably a theology formed in and through community.[33] In the *Letters* this dialogical element is simply more explicit.[34]

As such, I view *Ethics* and *Letters* together as belonging to a late stage in his theology, one which is still under development in the *Letters* as evidenced by the

31. "By the way, it would be very nice if you didn't throw away my theological letters but, since they are surely a burden for you to keep there, send them off to Renate from time to time. I might perhaps life to read them again later for my work." Bonhoeffer, *Letters and Papers from Prison*, 8:458.

32. Bonhoeffer, 8:458.

33. The voices of Reinhold Seeberg in *Sanctorum Communio*, Karl Barth throughout his dialectical approach to "religion," Jean Lasserre in *Discipleship*, and Bishop George Bell on the subject of "culture" in *Ethics* have long been recognized. We will identify additional voices, especially those of the gospel choir of Abyssinian Baptist Church, Albert Frank Fisher, Adam Clayton Powell, and other Black friends in Harlem, as well as the intonations of Søren Kierkegaard.

34. A major advantage to students of Bonhoeffer is the published account of Bonhoeffer's main interlocutor, Eberhard Bethge, which will be important for interpreting theological formulations in *Letters*. See: Bethge, *Dietrich Bonhoeffer: Theologian, Christian, Contemporary*. This brings with it a shadow side: the interpretative weight given to Bethge on the basis of friendship must be counterbalanced by other accounts which could expose blind spots or an uncritical eye. I, therefore, make use of additional biographies, such as: Marsh, *Strange Glory: A Life of Dietrich Bonhoeffer*; Schlingensiepen, *Dietrich Bonhoeffer 1906–1945: Martyr, Thinker, Man of Resistance*.

new theological formulations he adopts there (suggesting a "new theology" in the making). Situating *Letters* with *Ethics*, as the closest possible academic writing, provides a kind of anchor or plumbline by which we can ground or measure the ideas in *Letters*.

As a result of the fragmentary nature of the theological material in the letters, the arrangement this book takes with respect to Bonhoeffer's writings is thematic, as opposed to chronological: Part I focuses in the main on *Letters*, although I also appeal to Bonhoeffer's writings from New York in 1930 and, to a lesser extent, his writings at Finkenwalde (1935–7). In Part II, the Christology lectures and *Sanctorum Communio* are the main texts under discussion, though there is some recourse to *Ethics*, *Discipleship* and *Theological Education at Finkenwalde 1935–1937* (*DBWE 14*). In Part III I turn properly to *Ethics*. This will demonstrate both consistencies with Bonhoeffer's earlier arguments concerning Christology and ecclesiology, and also where his thought develops, particularly with respect to his views of reality and the relationship between God and the world.

Part I

Dietrich Bonhoeffer's Musico-Theology

Chapter 1

A MUSICO-THEOLOGICAL LIFE

Introduction

Dietrich Bonhoeffer's musicality is widely appreciated and his appeal to musical ideas for theology has generated a laudable, if somewhat rarefied, degree of interest.[1] These accounts of Bonhoeffer's theology of music have, to date, tended to concentrate on his early education in the classical tradition, his strident views about music while running a seminary at Finkenwalde, and the more magnanimous statements appropriating music for theology in his prison letters. This chapter will, likewise, examine these while also redressing an oversight: Bonhoeffer's embrace of African American spirituals. By overlooking Bonhoeffer's time in Harlem, when his encounters with racial injustice and his musical tastes intersect, a musical experience which significantly influences his Christian practice is underplayed. A focused discussion of Bonhoeffer's engagement with the Harlem Renaissance, especially in the worship of Abyssinian Baptist Church, therefore fills a small, but significant, lacuna in erstwhile accounts of Bonhoeffer's musical background. I contend that this encounter with a specific kind of music and what this music represents, in New York in the early 1930s, was so formative for Bonhoeffer that it echoes and resounds in his support of the Jews after his return to Germany (in the period from 1934 to 1937).

Turning to *Letters and Papers from Prison*, in which musical reflections occur liberally, I examine three letters which particularly evince how Bonhoeffer's musical imagination informs his theological thinking. I contend that this emerging musico-theology gives a degree of formal expression to his previous experiences of music and their relation to his Christian formation. I conclude Chapter 1 by

1. The most detailed account of Bonhoeffer's theology of music remains that of Andreas Pangritz's *Polyphony of Life* (*Polyphonie des Lebens*), as mentioned in my Introduction; first published in German in 1994, the English translation appeared over two decades later in 2019. See: Pangritz, *Polyphonie Des Lebens: Zu Dietrich Bonhoeffers "Theologie Der Musik"*; Pangritz, *The Polyphony of Life: Bonhoeffer's Theology of Music*. Pangritz's will be an especially important voice in Part I of this study. For details of the other main interpretations of Bonhoeffer's theology of music, see the introduction to this book.

arguing that in prison Bonhoeffer begins to explicitly integrate musical patterns of thought with ideas about Christian formation, a synthesis which was already taking place in practice prior to his imprisonment.

Bonhoeffer's Musical Existence

Music-making came naturally to Bonhoeffer and was a vital part of his life. In the very first letter of the prison correspondence, Karl Bonhoeffer writes to his son of the last time they had been together, just five days before Dietrich's arrest, when he performed J. S. Bach's cantata *Lobe den Herren* with his siblings for his father's seventy-fifth birthday.[2] Six months later his mother writes to him on October 23, 1943: "That you have so little exercise in the fresh air and no possibility of music weighs on Papa and me very much."[3] Musical learning and performance were normative for a family such as the Bonhoeffers who belonged to the *bürgerlich* class.[4] He and his siblings played various instruments and singing together was common practice. Bonhoeffer's musical aptitude even surpassed that of his cultural inheritance; he played Mozart's sonatas by the age of ten and a career in musical composition was, at one time, a serious possibility.[5]

This only too brief account of Bonhoeffer's musical backstory already gives grounds for understanding the eloquence he displays in his appeal to musical expressions when he writes from prison. His musical acumen will be even more evident when we come to examine these. But before we do so, there is a further dimension to Bonhoeffer's musicality to explore which will better pave the way for an interrogation of his musico-theological patterns of thought in his last writings. By considering his engagement with music in two particular periods in the decade prior to his imprisonment (1930–1 in Harlem and 1934–7 in London and Finkenwalde) we will see that Bonhoeffer's musical tastes are notably influenced by his Christian practice and, vice versa, music also contributes to his formation as a Christian.

2. Bonhoeffer, *Letters and Papers from Prison*, 8:43.

3. Bonhoeffer, 8:171.

4. The educated middle class.

5. Bethge recalls that Bonhoeffer performed his own compositions as a child. See: Bethge, *Dietrich Bonhoeffer: Theologian, Christian, Contemporary*, 13. Bonhoeffer's twin sister, Sabine, is more sparing in her praise, admitting that while he considered a career as a professional pianist he was right to give this up because he "was not good enough." Leibholz-Bonhoeffer, *The Bonhoeffers: Portrait of a Family*, 34. With a slightly different inflection, Craig Gardiner suggests that he gave up musical composition *for* theology, citing a fascinating eyewitness account by Bonhoeffer's friend Johannes Goebel. Gardiner, *Melodies of a New Monasticism: Bonhoeffer's Vision, Iona's Witness*, 28–9. Although such a view is rejected by Andreas Pangritz who is adamant that: "Bonhoeffer's turn to theology never displaced music." Pangritz, *The Polyphony of Life: Bonhoeffer's Theology of Music*, 2.

Nine Months in Harlem (1930–1)

From 1930 to 1931 Bonhoeffer studied at Union Theological Seminary, New York. During this time, he attended Abyssinian Baptist Church in Harlem, worshipping alongside a publicly oppressed minority whose persecution was wrought out in "Negro spirituals."[6] His engagement with African American spirituals is not always acknowledged, let alone examined, by those who explore his theology of music. For instance, despite producing the most comprehensive account of Bonhoeffer's theology of music to date, Andreas Pangritz altogether overlooks the spirituals, even though he does address Bonhoeffer's musical biography and Bonhoeffer's engagement with this music is well documented.[7] Where scholars do account for this musical experience, they tend to do as an example of the breadth of Bonhoeffer's aesthetic taste and cultural openness. So, de Gruchy notes with interest: "It is remarkable that someone so deeply embedded in the classical traditions of European music should have responded so enthusiastically to the popular gospel songs of slaves and their descendants."[8]

The reasons for not discussing the spirituals at greater length are not entirely clear. Perhaps, as Ruth Zerner observes, it is because Bonhoeffer did not go into great descriptive detail about the music: "black worship, particularly in song, was so overwhelming and personal for [Bonhoeffer] that he found it difficult to analyse in writing."[9] Certainly, it seems that while Bonhoeffer was profoundly affected by the worship at Abyssinian Baptist and thought extremely highly of spirituals, calling them "some of the greatest artistic achievements in America," he did not describe the music or lyrics at great length.[10] That said, we know that he owned recordings of them which he played on the gramophone at Finkenwalde, as well

6. Where the term "Negro" is used in this chapter it will only be to accurately quote Bonhoeffer or his contemporaries.

7. This oversight is not replicated by Craig Gardiner, who at least notes in passing that Bonhoeffer's experience of racial segregation appalled him and his engagement with the spirituals deeply impacted him. Gardiner, *Melodies of a New Monasticism: Bonhoeffer's Vision, Iona's Witness*, 27.

8. de Gruchy, "Restoring Broken Themes of Praise," 139. De Gruchy comes closest to identifying the importance of the spirituals on Bonhoeffer's formation by describing his engagement with them as evidence of his cultural inclusivity (having famously used Bonhoeffer's writings more widely in support of reconciliation in the post-Apartheid South African Church). He does not, though, credit Bonhoeffer's engagement with this music as a motivating factor, in and of itself, in this cultural inclusivity, as I argue here.

9. Zerner, "Dietrich Bonhoeffer's American Experiences: People, Letters, and Papers from Union Seminary," 11.

10. Bonhoeffer, Dietrich, *Barcelona, Berlin, New York: 1928–1931*, 10:269.

as sheet-music for over sixty piano renditions, and a book on the subject.[11] It is also possible that there has been a general reluctance to discuss this music at any length in studies of Bonhoeffer's theological treatments of music because of a lack of knowledge about it or because he does not, himself, recollect this music from prison as he does other music. However, it is also almost certainly the case that this subject has received so little attention because of a greater blind spot with respect to this period in Bonhoeffer's life: a lack of appreciation for his engagement with the Black community in Harlem.[12] While Bonhoeffer's sojourns in New York (chiefly his first, longer visit of nine months) have long been regarded as formative, recent scholarship has illumined the extent of the significance of his experience of Black America.[13]

In the final report of his academic year in New York, Bonhoeffer writes of his experience of the Black Church in America:

> I heard the gospel preached in the Negro churches … Here one really could still hear someone talk in a Christian sense about sin and grace and the love of God and ultimate hope, albeit in a form different from that to which we are accustomed. In contrast to the often lecturelike character of the "white" sermon, the "black Christ" is preached with captivating passion and vividness. Anyone

11. Albert Frank Fisher, a contemporary at Union who was responsible for connecting Bonhoeffer with Abyssinian Baptist Church, gifted him James Weldon Johnson's *Book of American Negro Spirituals* and sixty pieces of music. See: Clifford Green's 'Editor's Introduction to the English Edition' Bonhoeffer, Dietrich, 10:30.

12. While Eberhard Bethge credits Bonhoeffer with a great capacity for making friends with social outcasts during his time in Harlem, we should not forget that this relationship was mutually impactful: standing and singing with those who were racially ostracized had a lasting effect on Bonhoeffer. Bethge, *Dietrich Bonhoeffer: Theologian, Christian, Contemporary*, 113–14. Charles Marsh's biography gives much more attention than previous biographies to Bonhoeffer's experience of Harlem, Abyssinian Baptist Church and his friendships with African Americans (especially Albert Frank Fisher).

13. Eberhard Bethge remarks that Bonhoeffer's friendship with "'Negro' Frank Fisher … played a big part" in his time in America, though he does not elaborate on this. Bethge, *Dietrich Bonhoeffer: Theologian, Christian, Contemporary*, 113–14. Clifford Green observes, with greater definition, that Bonhoeffer's experience of racial segregation in America and his time at Abyssinian Baptist were "formative." See: Bonhoeffer, *Ethics*, 6:3–4. Moreover, Green's introduction to the English translation of volume 10 of Bonhoeffer's works, which covers his time in New York, clearly draws attention to these experiences of America as formative for Bonhoeffer. See: Bonhoeffer, Dietrich, *Barcelona, Berlin, New York: 1928–1931*, 10:17–43. The most focused account of Bonhoeffer's immersion in the Harlem Renaissance is provided by Reggie Williams, who uncovers the extent to which Black theology influences Bonhoeffer while also exposing his scathing indictment of white liberal-American Christianity. See: Williams, *Bonhoeffer's Black Jesus: Harlem Renaissance Theology and an Ethic of Resistance*.

> who has heard and understood Negro spirituals knows about the strange mix of reserved melancholy and eruptive joy in the soul of the Negro. The Negro churches are proletarian churches, perhaps the only ones in America.[14]

As this extract suggests, Bonhoeffer's interest was not merely academic; he did not simply observe, dispassionately, a different culture which he was occasionally exposed to in New York. In actuality, a great deal of Bonhoeffer's stay in America was spent inhabiting the "hidden perspective" of the Black community.[15] For some six months he immersed himself in the Black church community. His engagement with the church community of Abyssinian Baptist was thoroughgoing, his report makes clear.[16] He was strongly impacted by the preaching (which he also took a turn at) and the congregations' participation in this;[17] he also taught in the Sunday school with and at a women's Bible study.[18] The extent of the impact of these experiences on Bonhoeffer can only be fully appreciated when we also take into account his criticisms of "white preaching"—including the theology he was exposed to at Union and his disgust at the racism he witnessed.[19]

14. Submitted to the Church Federation Office, August 25, 1931. These views conform to his earliest impressions, as he expressed them at the end of his first semester in a letter to Max Diestel on December 19, 1930: "As long as I've been here, I've heard only one sermon in which you could hear anything like a genuine proclamation [of the Gospel], and that was delivered by a Negro." See: Bonhoeffer, Dietrich, *Barcelona, Berlin, New York: 1928–1931*, 10:315; 266.

15. Not only did he seek to get to know "the Negro problem from every angle," he acknowledges, but he also, in turn, observed "white America from this rather hidden perspective." He also remarks, in the same report: "Through my friendship with a Negro student [Albert Frank Fisher] at the seminary I was introduced not only to the leaders of the young Negro movement at Howard College in Washington, but also in Harlem, the Negro quarter of New York." Bonhoeffer, Dietrich, 10:314.

16. In the same report he attests to the personal significance of his encounters with African Americans as among "the most important and gratifying events" during his trip. Bonhoeffer, Dietrich, 10:314–15.

17. Charles Marsh recalls a conversation between Bonhoeffer and Myles Horton, a friend from Union who he bumps into after attending a service at Abyssinian: "He conveyed the thrill of the flock voicing ascent [*sic*] with the preacher." Marsh, *Strange Glory: A Life of Dietrich Bonhoeffer*, 117.

18. Williams, *Bonhoeffer's Black Jesus: Harlem Renaissance Theology and an Ethic of Resistance*, 77.

19. In the same report he comments that American pastors are undignified in their servility and that the theology of Union is "accelerating the process of the secularization of Christianity in America." Bonhoeffer, Dietrich, *Barcelona, Berlin, New York: 1928–1931*, 10:309. In a letter to Karl-Friedrich Bonhoeffer written approximately in the middle of his stay, he writes of his "shameful impression" of racial segregation and the "repugnant" way southern Americans talk about African Americans, including the pastors. See: Bonhoeffer, Dietrich, 10:269.

By participating in the worship of African Americans Bonhoeffer shared in their experience, standing with them before the same Christ. In view of his criticisms of the theology, preaching, and practice of white Americans (which Williams describes as "the white liberal modernist hope for human achievement"), we can say that it was primarily, if not exclusively, among Black Christians that Bonhoeffer found a community centered on Christ in America. Reggie Williams underscores the importance of this experience for Bonhoeffer when he states:

> Bonhoeffer found that black Christians identified black suffering with Jesus' suffering. Bonhoeffer heard this connection in black preaching and in black Christian music. Historically, black Christian music emphasized that Jesus' work of redemption and deliverance demonstrated his solidarity with social outcasts, even unto death. That explains why the lived experience of Jesus' cross for black people in America was one of the most often repeated themes within the spirituals, as evidenced by the question in the spiritual "were you there?"[20]

It was in these sorrow songs, as Williams suggests, that the lived experience of Black Christians delivered up their theology, their faith in Jesus, and their experiences of oppression. In the spirituals "the strange mix of reserved melancholy and eruptive joy," which Bonhoeffer likened to the African American soul, could be experienced almost first-hand.[21]

Nine months in Harlem impacted Bonhoeffer beyond the borders of America. A well-documented feature of his time in New York is the stark pacifism which emerged from his friendship with Jean Lasserre and which had a salient influence on his exposition of the Sermon on the Mount in *Discipleship*.[22] But his experience

20. Williams, *Bonhoeffer's Black Jesus: Harlem Renaissance Theology and an Ethic of Resistance*, 25. In addition to "Were you there?" cited by Williams, Charles Marsh states, unreservedly but without pointing to his source, that Bonhoeffer had recordings of the following spirituals which he played to the brothers at Finkenwalde: "Go Down Moses," "Swing Low, Sweet Chariot," and "There is a Balm in Gilead." See Marsh, *Strange Glory: A Life of Dietrich Bonhoeffer*, 245. Bethge recalls only the second of these, "Swing Low, Sweet Chariot." We could speculate that he may also have worshipped to the words of "Steal away Jesus," a popular spiritual in the early 1930s in New York (it was featured in the Broadway production of *Run Little Chillun* in 1933 but predated the musical).

21. Bonhoeffer, Dietrich, *Barcelona, Berlin, New York: 1928–1931*, 10:315.

22. Bethge writes of this friendship: "His encounter with Lasserre, this first ecumenical confrontation, transformed his academic knowledge of Lutheran ethics into a committed identification with Christ's peace teaching." Bethge, *Dietrich Bonhoeffer: Theologian, Christian, Contemporary*, 113.

of Black America galvanized in him an empathy for the racial outcast, and this arguably had an even greater impact on Bonhoeffer in the end, as evinced by his support of the Jews.[23] Williams demonstrates that Bonhoeffer's preaching *prior to* his stay in New York displayed, on occasion, "*völkisch dissonance*";[24] thus exposing a fault line in some of Bonhoeffer's early thinking about the Jews. Following this line of inquiry, David Robinson and Ryan Tafilowski compare the early Bonhoeffer with Paul Althaus for displays of Christian antisemitism, especially citing Bonhoeffer's Barcelona lectures.[25] This ambiguity toward the Jews (which was by no means a staunch Nationalism or full-blown antisemitism) nevertheless perished following his time in America and ultimately led to a resolute opposition to the German Christians.[26]

In short, then, Bonhoeffer's experience of racism in New York became for him an analogue of the situation in his homeland, clarifying his perception of it and transfiguring it, so that an early ambivalence toward the Jews was all but transformed into a defense of them. This is all the more astonishing when we recall that, in April 1931, Bonhoeffer could write that there was no analogous situation

23. Bonhoeffer's involvement with the *Abwehr* and the coup attempt on Hitler's life show that he moved beyond Lasserre's pacifism and he explicitly modifies his position with respect to Lasserre in one of his letters. See: Bonhoeffer, *Letters and Papers from Prison*, 8:541–2. However, his defense of the racially segregated, especially the Jews, only deepens over time. In a separate article David Robinson demonstrates a convincing connection between the "race question" and the "Jewish question" for Bonhoeffer. Robinson puts it thus: "That black and Jewish struggles are linked in Bonhoeffer's mind seems evident in his reference to the black church under the *Rassenfrage*, 'the race question,' echoing his homeland construct of the *Judenfrage*." Robinson, "Confessing Race: Toward a Global Ecclesiology after Bonhoeffer and Du Bois," 126.

24. This can be perceived in the Barcelona lectures given in 1928, in particular in "Basic Questions of a Christian Ethic" (postponed until February 1929) in which he speaks about prioritizing loyalty to his own people as part of "a divine order of things." See: Bonhoeffer, Dietrich, *Barcelona, Berlin, New York*: *1928–1931*, 10:371–2.

25. In which he argues that defense of one's blood relations and fellow countrymen excuses acts of violence, sanctifying them; a position which causes him consternation, but one he expresses, nonetheless. Robinson and Tafilowski, "Conflict and Concession: Nationality in the Pastorate for Althaus and Bonhoeffer," 134.

26. Bonhoeffer's bold polemic at the 1934 ecumenical conference in Fanø, Denmark, made his position clear: for a Christian to go to war against another Christian is equivalent to going to war against Christ. See: "The Church and the Peoples of the World," Bonhoeffer, Dietrich, *London, 1933–35*, 13:307–10. See also: Robinson and Tafilowski, "Conflict and Concession: Nationality in the Pastorate for Althaus and Bonhoeffer," 137.

in Germany to that of the racial problems in the States.[27] Two years later he would face such a problem in his homeland and, we will see, this had a corresponding effect on his musical tastes.

Post-New York: London (1934) and Finkenwalde (1935–7)

We have seen, therefore, that during Bonhoeffer's time in New York his formation as a Christian was influenced by African Americans; a cultural openness which was expressed in his enjoyment of spirituals. By contrast, after Bonhoeffer leaves New York we find him cautioning *against* cultural assimilation, especially with respect to the power of music which was being politicized by the Nazis in their expurgation of the Jews.[28] Up to this time, Bonhoeffer had freely listened to Wagner and Beethoven but preferred "the classical works of Bach for their witness to the truth of the gospel."[29] Yet, in 1934 he began to apply restraint to music formerly deemed suitable in a Church setting, so that even Bach came to be "suspected of 'outward beauty' at the expense of true 'inner beauty.'"[30] In a sermon given in London on Cantate Sunday, April 29, 1934, preaching on the power of music and the danger of idolatry, he had declared: "This is why we listen to Bach in church, and not to Beethoven." While his personal engagement with art remained richly varied,[31] he began to draw a division between what was appropriate for the Church and what could only be enjoyed outside it (a division he would later reject). He goes on to comment on the sung worship at Finkenwalde (1935–7), that the beauty of harmony is to be resisted and that complete unison should be the aim.[32]

27. In a letter to his brother and sister-in-law, Karl-Friedrich and Margarethe Bonhoeffer. With a striking prescience which can only be gleaned with hindsight, he writes: "I don't quite know whether I have not perhaps spent too much time on this question here [regarding the situation with the Negroes], especially since we don't really have an analogous situation in Germany, but I've just found it enormously interesting, and I've never for a moment found it boring." Bonhoeffer, Dietrich, *Barcelona, Berlin, New York: 1928–1931*, 10:293.

28. The Aryanization of the arts under Joseph Goebbels as Reich Minister for Propaganda is well known. For a discussion of the impact of this on the legacy of three musicians (Mendelssohn, Mozart, and Handel), see: Levi, "The Aryanization of Music in Nazi Germany."

29. de Gruchy, "Restoring Broken Themes of Praise," 138.

30. de Gruchy, "Restoring Broken Themes of Praise," 139.

31. As de Gruchy points out: "At Finkenwalde … he showed his appreciation of the 'worldly art' of the Dutch masters, his love for the sacred sensuality of the music of Heinrich Schütz." de Gruchy, "Restoring Broken Themes of Praise," 140.

32. For sung worship he approves only of unison singing and rejects "the improvised second part"; bass, alto, or solo voices; and those who cannot sing or refuse to sing, for all detracts from the unity of the group around the Word. See: Bonhoeffer, *Life Together*, 5:66–7.

With the intensification of National Socialism, Bonhoeffer consolidated his political resistance in musical terms with the memorable phrase: "Only he who cries out for the Jews may sing Gregorian chants."[33] Gregorian chant should not be sung by those who would abuse God's creation: a clear reference to the propagandist efforts of the Nazis. By now entirely resolute in his resistance to the political agenda of his country, he expressed this through his rejection of any music that might be exploited to aid the Nazi regime.[34]

Curtailing his (and his church community's) musical pleasure, it is perhaps unsurprising that Bonhoeffer replays the spirituals at this time.[35] Music so unfamiliar to European ears and not generally available was above suspicion; it could not be tainted. But is there any more to it than that? Can we imagine, with David Robinson, that for Bonhoeffer, listening to the spirituals again in his homeland he would hear a "lament over his own country's ominous claims to exceptionalism"?[36] While we must admit, with Zerner, that the absence of more extensive reflections concerning this music in this period of Bonhoeffer's life prevents us from making any conclusive claims, we can, at the very least, make the following observation: there is a striking similarity between Bonhoeffer's experience of the spirituals sung in Harlem, created and performed in the furnace of oppression, and the parallel he draws between Gregorian chant and voicing support for the Jews. Whether worshipping through spirituals or Gregorian chant, true worshippers, Bonhoeffer seems to say, will stand with the marginalized as they look to the suffering Christ.[37]

Examining Bonhoeffer's musical imagination in these two very distinct cultural and Church settings—Abyssinian Baptist Church in Harlem, New York (1930–1) and the church community in Finkenwalde, Germany (1935–7)—it is plain that he understands music to be intimately connected to Christian living and

33. Bethge, *Dietrich Bonhoeffer: Man of Vision, Man of Courage*, ed. Edwin Robertson, trans. Eric Mosbacher, Peter and Betty Ross, and Frank Clarke, 512.

34. As Andreas Pangritz observes: "The radical intensification of Bonhoeffer's own position during the church struggle, as reflected in his book *Discipleship* (1937), is expressed in musical terms in the way he comes to suspect even Bach of superficial beauty." Pangritz, *The Polyphony of Life: Bonhoeffer's Theology of Music*, 8.

35. Bethge, *Dietrich Bonhoeffer: Theologian, Christian, Contemporary*, 348.

36. Robinson, "Confessing Race: Toward a Global Ecclesiology after Bonhoeffer and Du Bois," 124. Robinson also draws attention to Bonhoeffer's self-awareness when it comes to the dangers of white hypocrisy in appropriating Black art forms. Moreover, in my view, any possibility that Bonhoeffer played the spirituals to the brothers at Finkenwalde for cultural entertainment or dispassionate, academic observation is easily countered by recalling his participation in the church community in Harlem.

37. Or, as de Gruchy puts it: "Just as external beauty should not be allowed to take the place of internal beauty within the context of worship, so appreciation of the beauty of church music was contingent upon a commitment to justice. Only in this way could the broken themes of praise be restored." De Gruchy, "Restoring Broken Themes of Praise," 139.

action. Worshipping through spirituals in Harlem was a lived expression of his commitment to African Americans in racially segregated America; an experience which disabused him of an earlier "*völkisch dissonance*" and strengthened his support of the Jews. His strengthened commitment to the racially oppressed in his own country causes him to warn *against* music's exploitative powers, including music he had previously endorsed for a Church setting. Nevertheless, as he listens again to the soundtrack of a fringe movement of Harlem, he hears it as one who is now standing with the oppressed minority in his own country.

A complex picture, therefore, emerges in which music, on the one hand, has the power to help the struggling Church to engage with the suffering Christ and with the suffering of others but, on the other hand, has the potential to lead the Church astray. As Bonhoeffer's ethical resistance sharpens, we might expect his suspicions of musical beauty to grow. But, on the contrary, we find that when he is most outspoken against tyranny (in his final academic work, *Ethics*) he also envisions a recovery of aesthetics for the Church, in which art and culture are wrested from oppressive political control and restored to those who practice justice.[38] And when the possibility of playing and enjoying music is unattainable in prison, it is there we find Bonhoeffer eager to re-accommodate aesthetics into Christian life, including the music he held in suspicion for a time in Finkenwalde.

Bonhoeffer's Musico-Theological Imagination

In what follows we will see how, in prison, Bonhoeffer's musical imagination is directly applied to theological themes. Although these musico-theological discussions are marked by a conspicuous fragmentariness, derived as they are from letters, taken together they indicate that Bonhoeffer was beginning to creatively shape the relationship between music and Christian practice in more formal terms.

Bonhoeffer's musicality does not diminish in prison. On the contrary, music takes on an even greater significance for Bonhoeffer when he has least access to it himself. In the *Letters* he writes frequently about music, encouraging his interlocutors through the lyrics of hymns or recollecting important events through the music that had been playing.[39] At least part of the reason for these musical reminiscences can be explained by the nature of the material: personal

38. In a working note for *Ethics* he articulates what he had personally practiced in his time in New York: "It is uncultured to laugh at a film when negro dances are performed. It is uncultured to ridicule something merely because it is different from oneself. It is uncultured to parade one's 'culture.'" *DBWE* records the existence of the note but not the content. See: Bonhoeffer, *Ethics*, 6:218n162. The English translation of the second German edition of *Ethics*, which was arranged by Bethge, contains the note in full. See: Bonhoeffer, Dietrich, *Ethics*, 185.

39. See for example: Bonhoeffer, *Letters and Papers from Prison*, 8:68; 179.

correspondence covering a vast array of subjects. But without much opportunity to listen to music (apart from occasional songs on the wireless or Christmas carols), Bonhoeffer's musical acumen manifests itself in an incredible ability to recall music from memory, listening "with the inner ear" and noting down extracts from musical scores.[40]

In what follows, I will appraise three musico-theological discussions which stand out in Bonhoeffer's letters for the way that a musical (and, in the first instance, aesthetic) concept is used to frame and explore a theological idea. The fragmentariness of these accounts reflects not only the epistolary format (letters occasionally went missing or unanswered) but also Bonhoeffer's personal situation (a life that was being increasingly broken off from that which had given it coherence). The letters under discussion were written before the theological letters; the earliest of them in Advent 1943 (approximately five months before the first theological letter). Nevertheless, Pangritz argues that the themes explored in these earlier reflections on music are important precursors for his "revolutionary new formulas" in the theological letters.[41] Pangritz together with John de Gruchy will be the main interlocutors in this section, since they have provided the primary interpretations of these ideas to date.

Aesthetic Existence

Our first example of Bonhoeffer's musical imagination expressing itself in partnership with his theological ideas, as a musico-theology, comes from a letter to Eberhard Bethge on January 23, 1944, in which Bonhoeffer raises the idea of "aesthetic existence," a category which he takes from Kierkegaard. Although it only mentions music in passing, this letter reveals Bonhoeffer's interest in explicitly relating aesthetics to theology. It has also stimulated discussions of a new phase in Bonhoeffer's theological development, leading de Gruchy to go so far as to suggest that "aesthetic existence" was to be the next step in Bonhoeffer's theological development following single-minded discipleship and ethical responsibility.[42]

Bonhoeffer has been writing about the difficulty of defining "friendship" sociologically, following Bethge's observation in an earlier letter that friendship

40. For instance, as we saw in the introduction to this book, he appeals to Beethoven's "Sonata in C Minor," op. 111 as part of an extended Easter reflection. See above, p. 1 Bonhoeffer, 8:332. For a fascinating discussion of the "Sonata in C Minor," op. 111 which uses Bonhoeffer's reflections on it as a platform to examine a dialogue between Theodor Adorno and Thomas Mann, see: Pangritz, *The Polyphony of Life: Bonhoeffer's Theology of Music*, 41–51.

41. "Reflections on music prepare for and interpret Bonhoeffer's latest theological thinking and can thus be of help in understanding the revolutionary 'new formulas.'" Pangritz, "Point and Counterpoint—Resistance and Submission: Dietrich Bonhoeffer on Theology and Music in Times of War and Social Crisis," 29.

42. de Gruchy, "Restoring Broken Themes of Praise," 151.

is unequal to marriage in social status.[43] This causes him to consider where friendship would reside in the four divine mandates of "marriage," "work," "state," and "church." He suggests that it should, probably, "be understood as a concept subsumed within culture and education [*Bildung*]" (by contrast to "brotherhood" which "falls within the concept of church and 'comradeship' with the concepts of work and politics"). But he then asks: Where should culture and education be? Although tempted to locate these in the sphere of work, he thinks this is wrong and instead states: "They belong not in the sphere of obedience but rather in the sphere of freedom (*spielraum*), which encompasses *all three spheres* of the divine mandates."[44] He proceeds:

> I wonder whether—it almost seems so today—it is only from the concept of the church that we can regain the understanding of the sphere of freedom (art, education, friendship, play). This means that "aesthetic existence" (Kierkegaard) is not to be banished from the church's sphere; rather, it is precisely within the church that it would be founded anew. I actually believe this, and from here we could recover our connection with the Middle Ages! Who in our time could, for example, lightheartedly make music, nurture friendship, play, and be happy? Certainly not the "ethical" person, but only the Christian.[45]

This passage requires some explanation, and in what follows we will interrogate each of the terms in the order they appear: "church"; "sphere of freedom"; "aesthetic existence"; and "Middle Ages."

One could be forgiven for interpreting Bonhoeffer as suggesting a totalizing role for the Church here, to alarming effect. Indeed, this is how Hans Urs von Balthasar reads the passage, describing the Church as the "source" of a rediscovery for aesthetics.[46] Although Bonhoeffer clearly views the Church as having a significant part to play in regaining freedom for art, education, friendship, play (aesthetics, in short), this emphasis is not so acute as Balthasar makes out. Such an interpretation overlooks Bonhoeffer's views of organized religion at this time. For while Bonhoeffer's ecclesiology has earned him a reputation for paving the way for a possible *rapprochement* with the Roman Catholic Church, his wariness of the German Church makes him allergic to anything that might appear to be approaching clericalism, so that by the time he is in prison he even conceives of a "religionless Christianity" (discussed further in Chapter 2); and, as we have already seen, he is rightly cautious about art being employed in a coercive way.

43. Bonhoeffer, *Letters and Papers from Prison*, 8:248.

44. Bonhoeffer, 8:268. Italics mine.

45. Bonhoeffer, 8:268.

46. A misleading translation, as de Gruchy points out. De Gruchy, "Restoring Broken Themes of Praise," 147–8. See: Hans Urs von Balthasar, *The Glory of the Lord: A Theological Aesthetics*, ed. John Riches, trans. Brian McNeil, vol. 7, 20.

As such, Bonhoeffer cannot be viewing the Church as having solely a regulative function in relation to aesthetics.

How, then, does he understand the church's role here? To answer this, we need to examine Bonhoeffer's doctrine of the "divine mandates" and what he means by the *spielraum* ("the sphere of freedom"), because he links aesthetics to freedom as well as to the Church. The divine mandates of marriage and family, work, government and Church are drawn from the traditional Lutheran three estates (*Stände*) of government, household and Church, as well as the doctrine of the "order of creation" (*Schöpfungsordnung*). However, by the time of *Ethics* Bonhoeffer had long rejected the *Schöpfungsordnung* and its corollary, the order of preservation (*Erhaltungsordnung*), in clear opposition to their misuses by the Nazis.[47]

Yet, the flexibility with which Bonhoeffer treats the mandates goes beyond unhooking them from a political agenda. In *Ethics* the fluidity of the mandates is in evidence when Bonhoeffer writes about music under the divine mandate of "work" (*Arbeit*) in the manuscript "Christ, Reality and Good," but changes this to "culture" (*Kultur*) in the manuscript "The Concrete Commandment and Divine mandates"[48] out of an apparent desire for more aesthetic freedom. In the *Letters*, further reinvention occurs as Bonhoeffer anchors aesthetics to the sphere of freedom, instead of the sphere of obedience.[49] We see that he is gradually, cautiously even, giving greater freedom to aesthetics in his thought by these reinventions.

In answer to our earlier question of how Bonhoeffer understands the Church, then, we see that on the one hand, *contra* Balthasar, the Church is not the absolute foundation of the recovery of freedom for friendship, play and art, and so on, because it remains one of the four mandates. On the other hand, it is privileged beyond the other mandates: bound to the sphere of freedom, it embraces the other three mandates. Bonhoeffer wants the Church to retain a modulating role for aesthetics but only *up to a point*. This tension between being anchored in the Church and simultaneously being free is echoed in the relationship he apparently envisages between the Word and "free play," as we will see when we come to examine Bonhoeffer's discussions of specific music to theological ends (in points (2) and (3), below).

47. For a detailed account of Bonhoeffer's use of the order of preservation as a substitute for the order of creation, as well as his development of the divine mandates to replace the latter, see: Puffer, "Creation."

48. Bonhoeffer, *Ethics*, 6:71.

49. This leads Pangritz to suggest that Bonhoeffer's views here are the result of "an experimental flow" which emerges in the exchange of letters. Though, we might add that such a reworking is not untypical of Bonhoeffer and predates *Letters*. Pangritz, *The Polyphony of Life: Bonhoeffer's Theology of Music*, 30. As Matthew Puffer observes, Bonhoeffer displays a general openness to critically reconsider his convictions with respect to the orders of creation and preservation, and the divine mandates, in order to respond to the needs of the time. Puffer, "Creation," 179.

We come to Bonhoeffer's appeal to "Kierkegaard's aesthetic existence." Bonhoeffer's engagement with the work of Søren Kierkegaard (1813–55) is widely recognized, though, arguably, the extent of Kierkegaard's influence on Bonhoeffer has yet to be fully appreciated.[50] De Gruchy positions Bonhoeffer with Barth with regard to the impact of Kierkegaard; on the one hand, they resolutely reject bourgeois Christianity (with Kierkegaard), but, on the other, they ultimately resist existential angst (*contra* Kierkegaard).[51] He sees in Bonhoeffer's radical call to discipleship from the Finkenwalde period resonances with Kierkegaard's critique of the Danish Church,[52] and as Bonhoeffer's views evolve from pacifism in the early to mid-1930s to considering the ethical possibility of tyrannicide in an ethics of free responsibility, this aligns with Kierkegaard's "teleological suspension of the ethical."[53] But, according to de Gruchy, it is the relationship between being a cultured person and a Christian which lies behind Bonhoeffer's appeal to Kierkegaard's "aesthetic existence" in the letters.

In order to make sense of Bonhoeffer's reference to "aesthetic existence," as well as de Gruchy's claim, a brief explanation of Kierkegaard's three spheres of existence is required. The spheres of existence are a means of categorizing human existence and can be detected in Kierkegaard's writings as early as *Either/Or* (in which only the aesthete and ethical person are considered at length), but are most fully laid out in *Stages on Life's Way* and *Concluding Unscientific Postscript*.[54] The three spheres of possible existence (the aesthetic, the ethical, and the religious) interact dialectically throughout his pseudonymous authorship as he attempts to provoke the reader to reflect on their existence and consider what it means to become a Christian.

It is in this light that we can begin to make sense of the contrast Bonhoeffer draws between the "ethical person" and the "Christian" in our passage.[55] If taken at face value this could be misapprehended as a significant departure from his position as outlined in *Ethics* in which he is making the case that only the Christian can be truly ethical. By contrasting "ethical person" and "Christian," Bonhoeffer likely

50. Rowan Williams contends that a detailed examination of Kierkegaard and Bonhoeffer is still outstanding. See: Williams, *Christ the Heart of Creation*, 186. But this overlooks the direct examination made by Matthew Kirkpatrick. See: Kirkpatrick, *Attacks on Christendom in a World Come of Age: Kierkegaard, Bonhoeffer, and the Question of "Religionlessness Christianity."*

51. de Gruchy, "Restoring Broken Themes of Praise," 149.

52. "Just as Kierkegaard's aesthetics was taken up and transformed by the ethical and religious, so Bonhoeffer's costly discipleship was carried forward but expressed differently in the next phase of his life, that of worldly ethical engagement." de Gruchy, 150.

53. de Gruchy, 150.

54. Kierkegaard, *Stages on Life's Way*; Kierkegaard, *Concluding Unscientific Postscript to Philosophical Fragments*.

55. See above, p. 24.

has in mind the three spheres of possible existence as Kierkegaard understands them, in which only the religious sphere entails dependence on Christ and imitation of him; living in the religious sphere alone makes it possible to become a "Christian." In Kierkegaard's dialectical schema, the "ethical" together with the "aesthetic" are two other possible spheres of existence which are ultimately superseded by the religious (though in such a way as they are actually taken up into the religious).[56]

The picture is further complicated by two distinct ideas of the "aesthetic" throughout Kierkegaard's works. The first, as we have already described, is the explicitly negative presentation of the aesthetic as a way of life which conflicts with the religious ("Christian"); the second is a positive view of creativity which can be exercised by the Christian. "Aesthetic existence" is not, then, living as an aesthete (living without awareness of dependence upon Christ), nor is it an affirmation of Idealist aesthetics (which Kierkegaard countered vehemently) but is closer to Kierkegaard's "living poetically," in which Kierkegaard himself integrates his own aesthetic practice with being a Christian.[57]

On this reading, "aesthetic existence" equates with what is life-affirming. It is in no way opposed to ethical action but, rather, ethical behavior and aesthetic pursuits are integrated in the life of the Christian. As de Gruchy puts it, through his appeal to "aesthetic existence" Bonhoeffer is trying to "christen" the goodness of life itself.[58] Music, friendship, and play do not hold the status of being divinely commanded, as Bonhoeffer expresses in his poem "The Friend," likening friendship to the beauty of the cornflower rather than the toil of work for daily bread.[59] Nevertheless, they are necessary to life, and for this reason they are located in the "sphere of freedom." It can be no coincidence that the elements of life that pertain to freedom take on a greater importance for him while he is deprived of them in prison. "Without claiming that music has the *necessitas*

56. In *Either/Or Part II* Kierkegaard writes of the "harmonious unison of different spheres" and clearly values their distinctiveness as well as their interrelation, when he says: "If you cannot manage to see the esthetic, the ethical and the religious as the three great allies, if you do not know how to preserve the unity of the different manifestations everything gains in these different spheres then life is without meaning." Kierkegaard, *Either/Or Part II*, 60; 147. See also *Stages on Life's Way* in which he describes three existence-spheres and the progression to the religious: Kierkegaard, *Stages on Life's Way*, 476–7. See also: Kierkegaard, *Concluding Unscientific Postscript to Philosophical Fragments*, 501.

57. As de Gruchy has it: "His proposal is more akin to, though not to be equated with, Schiller's 'art of life', Nietzsche's 'fundamentalization of aesthetic activity', Kierkegaard's 'living poetically' or John Dewey's 'integration of art into life.'" de Gruchy, "Restoring Broken Themes of Praise," 151.

58. This affirmation of life was influenced by his reading, in prison, of Wilhelm Dilthey, which I examine further in Chapter 2.

59. See the second stanza especially for his comparison "what's necessary" and "what's free" and his allusion to the mandates. Bonhoeffer, *Letters and Papers from Prison*, 8:526.

of a divine commandment," says Pangritz, "Bonhoeffer now places it under 'the *necessitas* of freedom.'"[60]

This positive interpretation of "aesthetic existence" finds further support when we consider Bonhoeffer's engagement with Nietzsche on this subject. Bonhoeffer moves carefully between the extremes of some of Kierkegaard's explicit rejections of "the aesthetic" in favor of faith (in his dialectical method), on the one hand, and Nietzsche's rejection of Christianity in favor of the aesthetic, on the other. In *Letters* Bonhoeffer rejects the dualisms that Nietzsche's understanding of aesthetics seems to require, in which aesthetics must be unencumbered by Christianity.[61] De Gruchy puts it this way: "Bonhoeffer's response to Nietzsche was a rejection of the dualisms of both gnosticism and modernity which separate creation and redemption, body and spirit, earth and heaven, faith and politics, prayer and action, rationality and experience."[62] In place of the Apollonian (light, harmony, or balance) or the Dionysian (chaotic) Bonhoeffer affirms an alternative: earthly beauty.[63]

There is one more point to make about this letter which concerns the rather opaque allusion to the Middle Ages, a subject which preoccupies Bonhoeffer, to some extent, in prison.[64] No clear consensus has been reached about what Bonhoeffer means in our passage about a recovery of a connection with the Middle Ages, and speculation as to his precise meaning is beyond the scope of this work. He may have in mind the transcendentals in which aesthetic values are inherent to a unitary schema along with the ethical and theological, as de Gruchy notes.[65]

In this analysis of Bonhoeffer's first musico-theological letter we have seen his commitment to integrating art, education, friendship, and play into a Christian schema. To achieve this, he creatively experiments with the divine mandates, compelled by a double commitment to ground aesthetics in the Church while simultaneously ensuring it is liberated from the control of National Socialism. This commitment to root aesthetics in the Church makes sense when viewed in the

60. Pangritz, *The Polyphony of Life: Bonhoeffer's Theology of Music*, 30.

61. He writes: "We go along too easily with Nietzsche's primitive alternatives, as if the 'Apollonian' concept of beauty, and the 'Dionysian', the one we call demonic nowadays, are the only ones." Bonhoeffer, *Letters and Papers from Prison*, 8:331.

62. de Gruchy, "Restoring Broken Themes of Praise," 153.

63. Bonhoeffer cites, in particular, the beauty of the French Impressionists Brueghel and Velazquez, among others, saying: "They have a beauty that is neither classic nor demonic, but simply earthly in its own right; and I must say that this is the only sort of beauty that speaks to me personally." March 25, 1944 to Eberhard Bethge Bonhoeffer, *Letters and Papers from Prison*, 8:331.

64. As Bethge notes in Bonhoeffer, 8:337. Bonhoeffer himself is rather inconsistent in his discussions of the Middle Ages for although he speaks positively of a recovery here, elsewhere he remarks on "the *salto mortale* back to the Middle Ages" as though it were a kind of cop out in theological thinking in the face of modernity. Bonhoeffer, 8:478.

65. de Gruchy, "Restoring Broken Themes of Praise," 153.

light of Kierkegaard's spheres of existence and Nietzsche's aestheticism; without the Church, aesthetics is dialectically opposed to Christianity-proper, a reality Bonhoeffer had witnessed in the exploitation of art by National Socialism.

What, precisely, does Bonhoeffer mean by "aesthetic existence"? As it is not a term he uses again and again, his precise meaning in employing it evades a succinct summary and its importance should not be overplayed. But what is clear is that he attributes pleasure in life, such as nurturing friendship and play, but also the more explicitly aesthetic enjoyment of making music, to the lot of the Christian; an emphasis which is also at work in his embrace of worldliness through his appeal to polyphony (as we will see in the next chapter). This account of aesthetic existence also corresponds with Bonhoeffer's behavior in relation to his experiences of music, as discussed above, in which he demonstrates Christian freedom by worshipping in Church alongside an oppressed group, against the national grain in America, or, in Germany, resisting the church's form of worship when it aligns with the nation but contradicts Christian action. Apparently, Bonhoeffer's aesthetic existence was a pattern he reflexively lived by before he began to conceptualize it in something approaching a formal structure.

The Music of Heinrich Schütz and Recapitulation

The second musico-theological example concerns the seventeenth-century "father of German music," Heinrich Schütz (1585–1672), who is the subject of the vast majority of musical references in Bonhoeffer's letters.[66] Bethge introduces Bonhoeffer to the music of Schütz in Finkenwalde and it remains an accompaniment to their friendship into Bonhoeffer's final years,[67] when he writes to Bethge from prison that Schütz's music "has become one of the greatest enrichments of my life."[68] The influence is such that Bonhoeffer is unable to read the Psalms without hearing them in the musical setting of Schütz's compositions.[69] Schütz's *Kleine Geistliche Konzerte*, composed during Thirty Years War (1618–48),[70] was especially significant for Bonhoeffer's circle of friends due to the conditions of war under which it was composed, circumstances with which the friends were familiar.

On the Fourth Sunday in Advent 1943, not long before his reflection on Kierkegaard's notion of aesthetic existence, Bonhoeffer quotes the score of *Kleine Geistliche*. In the same letter he also reflects on the line from the hymn *Evangelisches*

66. In the words of Andreas Pangritz, Heinrich Schütz is "the musical authority Bonhoeffer quoted most during his imprisonment." Pangritz, *The Polyphony of Life: Bonhoeffer's Theology of Music*, 17.

67. In the letter in question Bonhoeffer also requests, parenthetically, the three Schütz pieces he wants played at his funeral. Bonhoeffer, *Letters and Papers from Prison*, 8:230.

68. Bonhoeffer, 8:81. The remark is addressed to Renate but intended for Eberhard Bethge.

69. Bonhoeffer, *Letters and Papers from Prison*, 8:81.

70. There were two sets, one published in 1636 and the other in 1639.

Gesangbuch no. 36 by Paul Gerhardt: "Calm your hearts, dear friends; /Whatever plagues you, /Whatever fails you, /I will restore it all."[71] He asks what "I will restore it all" means and finds comfort in the idea that because of Christ: "Nothing is lost; in Christ all things are taken up, preserved, albeit in transfigured form, transparent, clear, liberated from the torment of self-serving demands. Christ brings all this back, indeed, as God intended, without being distorted by sin."[72] He relates this to Irenaeus' doctrine of recapitulation: "[T]he doctrine originating in Eph 1:10 of the restoration of all things, is a magnificent and consummately consoling thought. The verse 'God seeks out what has gone by' [Eccl. 3:15] is here fulfilled."[73]

He proceeds by citing another Gerhardt hymn ("I stand here at your manger") which emphasizes the importance of Christ's relationship with the individual, in addition to his relationship with the community, and connects this to recapitulation.[74] Proceeding to discuss the "I and Christ" further, he turns from the Gerhardt hymn to Schütz's "O bone Jesu," an Augustinian hymn. At this point he even includes some musical notation.[75] He asks of the Schütz piece: "in its devotion—ecstatic, aching, and nevertheless so pure—isn't this passage something like the 'restoration' of all earthly desire?"[76] Pangritz here discerns the influence of the biography of Schütz by Hans Joachim Moser (given to him by Bethge) on Bonhoeffer's writing on recapitulation, even down to the language used by Bonhoeffer. When Bonhoeffer asks if the music he notates "in its ecstatic longing combined with pure devotion, suggests the 'bringing back' of all earthly desire?" he seems to be drawing on Moser's description of the piece in which it is said that a "transposed repetition of the melismatic motif" achieves an "ecstatic cry of longing" which forms the "'center and climax' of the composition."[77]

Pangritz presses this connection further. Helpfully discussing Schütz's setting itself, Pangritz tells us that "Bonhoeffer cites the ascending melodic figure of seven notes on occasion of the exclamation 'o', languishing for union with Christ, in the line 'o how my soul longs for you.'"[78] The effect of this (as "the melismatic figure on 'o' is repeated four times, each time a fifth higher (*e flat-b flat, b flat-f,*

71. Bonhoeffer, *Letters and Papers from Prison*, 8:229.

72. Bonhoeffer, 8:230.

73. Bonhoeffer, 8:230.

74. Bonhoeffer, 8:230. The importance of both the individual and the community is in view from his doctoral thesis *Sanctorum Communio* until his latest writings. For instance, he writes in his first dissertation: "The collective unit and the individual until have the same structure in God's eyes." Bonhoeffer, Dietrich, *Sanctorum Communio*, 1:81.

75. Bonhoeffer, *Letters and Papers from Prison*, 8:230. Although the reproduction of the musical notes at this point is not entirely accurate. My thanks to Andreas Pangritz for pointing this out to me in personal correspondence.

76. Bonhoeffer, *Letters and Papers from Prison*, 8:231.

77. Pangritz, "Point and Counterpoint—Resistance and Submission: Dietrich Bonhoeffer on Theology and Music in Times of War and Social Crisis," 32.

78. Pangritz, 32.

f-c, c-g)") is to bring the piece to an extreme musical intensity. The ecstatic cry for longing, the repetition of the "o," and the potent music together culminate in a kind of erotic fulfillment, a most earthly expression of human longing. Moser, says Pangritz, relates this composition to Schütz's motet on the *Song of Songs* and finds the language of the Augustinian hymn is, in turn, "coloured by erotic associations" (further underscoring its similarities to the composition on the *Song of Songs*), making allusion to sexual fulfillment here pertinent.[79] This, we will see, corresponds with Bonhoeffer's first appeal to the metaphor "polyphony," in which the subject is the "earthly [erotic] love" shared between a married couple (where Bonhoeffer mentions *Song of Songs* for its affirmation of the sensuous). Strikingly, this erotic and earthly longing is linked to a deep longing for Christ. Pangritz finds that this musical allusion only makes sense when conceived of in the context of recapitulation.[80] He says of Bonhoeffer's remarks on Schütz: "We already have here, in musical terms, Bonhoeffer's Christological concentration even before his theological question, "who is Christ really for us today" gains its full intensity and intimacy."[81] Additionally, he also views Bonhoeffer's appeal to Gerhardt's hymns as "a tendency towards Christ mysticism."[82]

Certain music, this letter indicates, provokes an intimacy with Christ for Bonhoeffer and an expectation of divine involvement; a belief which exists alongside a refusal to mollify his present desires by somehow redirecting them to Christ or denying that they exist. In short, his appeal to the promise of Christ's restoration via hymns and compositions which promote this is not a way of denying his present struggles. Bonhoeffer is resolute on this point, qualifying what the "'restoration' of earthly desire" is by stating what it is not: "By the way, 'restoration' is, of course, not to be confused with 'sublimation'! 'Sublimation' is σάρξ, [flesh] (and pietistic?!), whereas 'restoration' is spirit, meant not in the sense of 'spiritualization' (which is also σάρξ) but of καινὴ κτίσις [New creation] through the πνεῦμα ἅγιον [Holy Spirit]."[83] Restoration, he insists, is a work of the Holy Spirit in forming new creations (though he does not elaborate further on this). Bonhoeffer is further clear that there can be no substitutes for the losses inflicted by the war: "The substitute repulses us. We simply have to wait and wait; we have to suffer indescribably from the separation … Further, there is nothing more mistaken than to attempt to acquire for oneself in such times some sort of substitute for what is unattainable."[84]

79. "For without doubt the language of Augustine's hymn is also erotically charged." Pangritz, *The Polyphony of Life: Bonhoeffer's Theology of Music*, 20.

80. Pangritz, "Point and Counterpoint—Resistance and Submission: Dietrich Bonhoeffer on Theology and Music in Times of War and Social Crisis," 34.

81. Pangritz, "Point and Counterpoint—Resistance and Submission: Dietrich Bonhoeffer on Theology and Music in Times of War and Social Crisis," 33.

82. Pangritz, *The Polyphony of Life: Bonhoeffer's Theology of Music*, 20.

83. Bonhoeffer, *Letters and Papers from Prison*, 8:231.

84. Bonhoeffer, *Letters and Papers from Prison*, 8:227.

This warning against sublimation will be relevant to our discussion of polyphony for it suggests that Bonhoeffer neither sees earthly desire as a threat to loving God nor as something extraneous to the love of God. Instead, unfulfilled longing has a place in the "multidimensional" experience of life through Christ and the Holy Spirit. As he goes on to say, "'*I* will restore it all'—that means we cannot and should not take it back again ourselves but allow ourselves to be given it by Christ."[85] Thus, Bonhoeffer reads Irenaeus' doctrine of recapitulation as restoration by Christ at the eschaton of all that has been lost. As de Gruchy puts it: "In Christ everything is taken up and restored without the distortion of sin."[86]

There is one final point to note about the music cited in this letter, which is that it is entirely texted music. While in prison, Bonhoeffer shows a marked preference for music with text. This emphasis on the Word in relation to music is not untypical of Bonhoeffer's Lutheranism, but the concentration on such music in prison is more pronounced, causing Pangritz to remark that, for Bonhoeffer in prison, it is the music's connection with the Word which "determines the musical value of the compositions."[87] Interestingly, though, Pangritz understands the attachment to "the Word" via the text of Bonhoeffer's chosen hymns exclusively in terms of scripture. Despite the fact that he also explicitly relates Bonhoeffer's discussions of music in prison to his Christology, when it comes to Bonhoeffer's particular preference for texted music Pangritz only views this in terms of the relationship between the text and scripture. I would contend, however, that Bonhoeffer's preference for music with texts has a Christological significance, also. The same Bonhoeffer who writes in prison that he cannot read the Psalms without hearing them in Schütz's musical settings also interprets the Psalms as being prayed by the Son.[88] The texts interweave the word of God, the scriptures, with the Word of God, the Son. At times Christ is the object to whom the words are directed (as in the case of "O bone Jesu" which begins, "O you who are sweeter, kinder, O gracious Lord Jesus Christ, how highly have you loved us in misery,"); on other occasions his voice is represented by the lyrics (for instance, in the case of the hymn *Evangelisches Gesangbuch 36* by Paul Gerhardt "Calm your hearts, dear friends"). We can well imagine that Bonhoeffer's preference for texted music in prison arises from a desire to reach out to God, in which the hymns words are a vehicle for the words of scripture and the incarnate Word; but, ultimately, it is the Eternal Word of God, the Son, who undergirds them both.

In sum, in examining this second musico-theological discussion, we have seen that the music of Heinrich Schütz helps Bonhoeffer to describe both his present situation, which is one of desire, longing and suffering, and the presence of Christ

85. Bonhoeffer, 8:231. Italics original.

86. de Gruchy, "Restoring Broken Themes of Praise," 159.

87. Pangritz, *The Polyphony of Life: Bonhoeffer's Theology of Music*, 18.

88. In *The Psalms as the prayerbook of the bible* Bonhoeffer describes "how the Psalter is entirely taken up into the prayer of Jesus." Bonhoeffer, Dietrich, *Prayerbook of the Bible: An Introduction to the Psalms*, 5:162.

in it. The music of Schütz and Gerhardt gives expression to sheer, unqualified earthly desire while the text represents the Word of God, which we have here interpreted as pertaining both to the Son of God and to the words of scripture, the latter of which often form the text verbatim. Through his appeal to this music, Bonhoeffer argues that our earthly cries of longing are met by Christ, in whom we are new creations, through the Holy Spirit and are given a place in him; that Christ's coming gathers the threads of everything preceding it together, rather than ending all that has gone before.[89] Thus, Bonhoeffer appeals to the Irenaean view of recapitulation to emphasize that in Christ nothing is lost. As we will see in the next chapter, a focus on the importance of this world is an important theme in Bonhoeffer's appeal to the metaphor of polyphony.

Bach's Art of Fugue *and Eschatology*

The third musico-theological discussion concerns the *Art of Fugue*. J. S. Bach (1685–1750) composed *Die Kunst der Fuge*, BWV 1080, in the last decade of his life, although it was only published posthumously in the spring of 1751.[90] A monothematic cycle of approximately twenty fugues (the number and order of which remain controversial), Bach was unable to complete a copy of the final movement and, in order to mitigate the effect of this, the editors added the organ chorale BWV668, *Vor deinen Thron tret ich hiermit* at the end. The chorale was Bach's last piece of work and had remained under revision.[91]

A reputed masterpiece, the mathematical structure of the composition was revolutionary when it was composed; it displayed "musical erudition comparable with scientific scholarship."[92] What may sound rigid and austere to modern ears is, to Bonhoeffer's mind, evidence of "free play," as Bach's radical innovations in counterpoint reach their culmination with his final composition. The *Art of Fugue* becomes an anthem for the resistance movement, as Bonhoeffer draws on it to encourage his friends in their political resistance against the Nazis. Having attempted to attend a performance in Berlin which was canceled because of the war, he reflects on their own "cancelled" lives which have been irreversibly devastated.[93]

89. Bonhoeffer, *Letters and Papers from Prison*, 8:231.

90. The original score has been lost but an early surviving version containing fourteen movements dates from 1742. Wolff and Emery, "Bach, Johann Sebastian."

91. Wolff and Emery.

92. Pangritz, "Point and Counterpoint—Resistance and Submission: Dietrich Bonhoeffer on Theology and Music in Times of War and Social Crisis," 38.

93. There is an additional pathos to this analogy which he could not have foreseen: by the time the rescheduled performance took place, the resistance had failed, his involvement in it exposed and his execution carried out. See: Pangritz, "Point and Counterpoint—Resistance and Submission: Dietrich Bonhoeffer on Theology and Music in Times of War and Social Crisis," 40.

The analogy even extends to the conditions surrounding Bach's composition and the lives of Bonhoeffer and his fellow conspirators, leading Pangritz to inquire as to the extent to which art is imitating life or vice versa.[94] But it is the music itself which offers Bonhoeffer a theological analogy of almost lapidary brilliance; a means of illuminating the many facets of his distinct circumstances.

In the letter of February 23, 1944, precisely one month after he has written about "aesthetic existence," Bonhoeffer writes to Bethge:

> What matters, it seems to me, is whether one still sees, in this fragment of life that we have, what the whole was intended and designed to be, and of what material it is made. After all, there are such things as fragments that are only fit for the garbage heap (even a decent "hell" is too good for them), and others which remain meaningful for hundreds of years, because only God could perfect them, so they must remain fragments–I'm thinking, for example, of the *Art of Fugue*. If our life is only the most remote reflection of such a fragment, in which, even for a short time, the various themes gradually accumulate and harmonize with one another and in which the great counterpoint is sustained from beginning to end–so that finally, when they cease, all one can do is sing the chorale "Vor Deinem Thron tret' ich allhier"—then it is not for us, either, to complain about this fragmentary life of ours, but rather even to be glad of it. I can't get Jer 45 out of my mind anymore. Do you remember that Saturday night in Finkenwalde when I expounded it? Here too, necessarily, a fragment of life: "but I will give you your life as a prize of war."[95]

In the somewhat peculiar conclusion to the *Art of Fugue* (whereby an absent ending has been replaced by a strange-sounding chorale), and the contrast this creates, Bonhoeffer finds a pertinent theological illustration. The final chorale sits uneasily alongside the complex free play of contrapuntal forms in the polyphony that has preceded it. The result is dissonant. As the preface to the piano adaptation of the *Art of Fugue* used by Bonhoeffer and Bethge has it: "Without any external connection with the 'Art of Fugue', even in a different tune, a voice is heard, expressing humbly what should have been pronounced in metaphysical greatness by the final harmony of this work or rather the life's work: 'I come before thy

94. "The Art of Fugue as indication of the progress of the resistance movement, or the plot as performance of the Art of Fugue—the comparison gives a lot to think about." Pangritz, 40. He also points out that Bach's final composition originated through a process of resistance to the crisis of culture caused by the Reformation, in which the "scientific" approach of Bach's composition was itself a kind of "resistance" to the betrayal of the Reformation under the rule of Frederick II who executed both Jesuit and Protestant priests, alike. See: Pangritz, *The Polyphony of Life: Bonhoeffer's Theology of Music*, 32.

95. Bonhoeffer, *Letters and Papers from Prison*, 8:306.

throne."[96] In this distorted and uncomfortable finale there lies a metaphor for Bonhoeffer and his friends.

As Bonhoeffer's life ebbs away in prison and his co-conspirators on the frontline face the possibility of their untimely deaths, so, too, the contrapuntal themes of the *Art of Fugue* are cut short. For the resistance movement, the fragmentariness of their lives is multilayered: in addition to the ordinary suffering of everyone experiencing the war, they stand in solidarity with the Jews against the national majority; superadded to this is the ethical burden of their actions, as they operate against the grain of what is considered normal Christian behavior. In prison, facing the possibility of execution at the hands of an evil regime, Bonhoeffer grapples with whether God has called him to do what is illegal and abhorrent, in a teleological suspension of the ethical à la Kierkegaard; and, if God has called him to such action, will he save his life "as a prize for war"?

These are the kinds of questions Bonhoeffer is clearly grappling with, almost a year into his imprisonment. Two days before this letter on the *Art of Fugue*, he gestures to the idea of fate by finding the "thou" (God) in the "it" (present circumstances).[97] He writes: "Only on the *other side* of this twofold process can we speak of 'being led' … So my question is basically how 'fate' really becomes 'the state of being led.'"[98] In our passage Bonhoeffer is clinging to the verse from Jeremiah 45 like a prophetic word, one which has preoccupied him since the days of Finkenwalde: that God would give him his "life as a prize of war."[99] Is hope for his "life as a prize of war" hope that God approves of his action or is it hope of divine intervention that will turn his situation around now? Surely both are at stake and in these life-and-death matters there are no easy resolutions for Bonhoeffer. Once more, the dissonance of the chorale is especially congruent with the situation he finds himself in, an unwanted and confusing detour from the previous course his life had taken.

But the contrast offers an even deeper resonance with his situation. Despite the uneasy conclusion the chorale creates, the words being sung in it offer a promissory note: "Before your throne I now stand."[100] The promise contained therein is one of eschatological hope: a note of surrender and trust in the

96. As recalled in Pangritz, *The Polyphony of Life: Bonhoeffer's Theology of Music*, 33.

97. Bonhoeffer, 8:304.

98. Bonhoeffer, *Letters and Papers from Prison*, 8:304. Italics original.

99. Bonhoeffer, *Letters and Papers from Prison*, 8:150; 306; 361; 387. Reflecting on this verse in his message to Renate and Bethge's son on his Baptism, Bonhoeffer writes in May 1944: "If we come through the wreckage of a lifetime's acquired goods with our living souls intact, let us be satisfied with that … It will be the task of our generation not to 'seek great things,' but to save and preserve our souls out of the chaos, and to realize that this is the only thing we can carry as 'booty' out of the burning house." Bonhoeffer, 8:387.

100. The final chorale is entitled "*Vor deinen Thron tret ich hiermit*" ("Before your throne I now appear") but Bonhoeffer exchanges "*hiermet*" ("appear") for "*allhier*" ("stand").

mercy of God, who alone makes sense of the fragmentariness of life. As the chorale intones these words, a posture of acceptance and relinquishment can be imagined. It is God who "perfects" the meaningful fragments in "themes which harmonize" and God who decides what will be burned up. In this we see Bonhoeffer's commitment to the Lutheran *simul iustus et peccator*, and his acceptance that he may be sinning in the actions he has taken as part of the coup. As he goes on to write in *Letters*, in stark contrast with *Discipleship*, he is no longer trying to make something of himself as "a saint or a converted sinner or a church leader (a so-called priestly figure!), a just or an unjust person, a sick or a healthy person"; on the contrary, he is "living fully in the midst of life's tasks, questions, successes and failures, experiences, and perplexities."[101] In the midst of these he refuses to be placated by a false hope. Even as he grapples with the ultimate question of his eternal salvation, Bonhoeffer resists the comfort of cheap grace.[102]

Having examined this third musico-theological letter, we have seen that the words of the chorale of the *Art of Fugue* express the human longing for redemption and the eschatological hope of a divine word from beyond. The dynamic created between this and the main composition provides Bonhoeffer with a means of exploring the hinterland in which he resides. This musical example helps Bonhoeffer convey the complexity and even potential conflict of his situation and that of the resistance: the fragmentariness of life for Bonhoeffer and his friends, in which their once youthful luster is fading to an inglorious and unwanted ending; the hope that their coup will be successful; alongside the more ultimate hope of coming before the throne of God, and the refusal to let that hope predetermine what God's judgment will be.

This passage sits, thematically, close to the earlier letter exploring recapitulation through the music of Schütz, as Bonhoeffer focuses on making sense of intense

101. Bonhoeffer, *Letters and Papers from Prison*, 8:486. See also: "Being a Christian does not mean being religious in a certain way, making oneself into something or other (a sinner, a penitent, or saint) according to some method or other. Instead, it means being human, not a certain type of human being, but the human being Christ creates in us. It is not a religious act that makes someone a Christian, but rather sharing in God's suffering in the worldly life." Bonhoeffer, 8:480.

102. His choice of Bach's music is a careful one for conveying the starkness of reality, seen in a comparison he makes between Bach and Handel several months later: "I … was astonished once again, in the slow movement (like the largo), by his ability to offer comfort so broadly and directly, in a way we would never dare to do anymore. I think Handel is much more concerned about his listeners and the effect of his music on them than Bach. That must be why he sometimes comes across as something of a façade. Handel intends something with his music; Bach doesn't." Bonhoeffer, *Letters and Papers from Prison*, 8:473–4.

suffering and possible death. But unlike the second musico-theological discussion on Heinrich Schütz and recapitulation, this letter is not so intent on preserving every thread or pleasure or experience lost to the war.

Conclusion

Bonhoeffer's musical imagination flows out of a lifelong engagement with music which, at various points, both forms his Christian convictions and is informed by them. This relationship between music and Christian formation occurs reflexively for Bonhoeffer in the 1930s. It is not until *Letters*, when he comes to directly integrate music and theology to some extent formally (though not systematically), that we see his musical imagination serving his theology: a musico-theology. This, we saw, began to emerge in his treatment of "aesthetic existence" in which music, together with other aesthetic forms, is aligned with Christianity. This is an alignment we can see in retrospect in his engagement with African American spirituals which inspires his anti-racist action, and his public rejection of music exploited by the Nazis. In each case Bonhoeffer's prioritization of the Christian gospel is influenced by and finds expression in his decision to either engage with or reject certain forms of music against the grain of the dominant culture.

Bonhoeffer's musico-theology is also evident in his exploration of the Irenaean concept of recapitulation (which leads him to comment briefly on "restoration" by the Holy Spirit) via the music of Heinrich Schütz and Paul Gerhardt, and in his extended reflection on the fragmentariness of life and eschatological hope in relation to Bach's *Art of Fugue*. In these cases, he is able to articulate simultaneously ideas that would otherwise be mutually exclusive by appealing to the combination of music and texts. In the next chapter we turn to examine his appeal to the polyphony of life as a metaphor for seemingly contradictory ideas and behaviors.

Chapter 2

A MUSICO-THEOLOGICAL INVENTION

Introduction

In this chapter I continue my examination of Bonhoeffer's musico-theology by focusing on his most developed musical metaphor, polyphony. Through his appeal to polyphony, which he calls his "little invention" (*Fündlein*), we see Bonhoeffer's musical imagination of theological themes emerging most fully as an explicit musico-theology. I begin by providing a working definition of polyphony which offers valuable insights into how Bonhoeffer would have understood the term musically. With this definition in mind, I focus on Bonhoeffer's particular understanding of the term by locating the uses of polyphony in three of the prison letters. Following this, I provide an analysis of Bonhoeffer's appeal to the concept as it is applied to the following two areas: "polyphony of love," in which the metaphor is an instructive aid for the personal use of Eberhard Bethge to help him order his priorities between loving God and his family; and "polyphony of life," a broader construct relating to Bonhoeffer's late theology. With regard to the first, we see that polyphony helps Bonhoeffer overcome a conceptual block by providing a means of describing the love of God and "earthly love" as non-competitive. With respect to the second, I situate polyphony alongside other theological formulae ("religionless Christianity," "world come of age," and the "arcane discipline") which Bonhoeffer develops in the prison letters, and observe the brief and undeveloped associations which have been made (by Eberhard Bethge and Michael Welker) with a pneumatology. I conclude that polyphony is a potent metaphor for Bonhoeffer in his late writings, both with respect to the personal formation of a Christian friend and his account of Christianity more generally. It helps him imaginatively describe how God and the world are integrated in Christ without relying on religious terminology. The Christological importance of the metaphor is strongly implied in this arrangement and will be further explored in the next chapter.

Polyphony: A Musical Term

Between the poetry, liturgy and sermons; profound statements about faith, society, marriage, friendship and family; domestic trivialities and a secret conspiratorial code, the prison letters are populated with choice phrases brimming with theological potency. In addition to the musico-theology which I began to outline in the previous chapter, phrases such as "religionless Christianity," "a world come of age," and "the nonreligious interpretation of the Bible" have been interpreted by many scholars as evidence of a new development in Bonhoeffer's late theology. These highly suggestive "enigmatic utterances" cannot, in Karl Barth's view, possibly disclose a clear and settled theological position, impressionistic and undefined as they are.[1] Nevertheless, despite Barth's assessment, these imaginative expressions have provoked a profusion of insights, not only for Bonhoeffer studies but also for theological aesthetics and ecclesial practice in contemporary culture.[2] One of the most tantalizing of these expressions is "polyphony of life," which marries Bonhoeffer's musico-theology to his so-called "new theology."[3]

Before we can hope to appreciate the theological significance of this phrase for Bonhoeffer, we must be clearer about the musical phenomenon itself, especially with respect to what Bonhoeffer would have taken for granted in his application of the term. What follows is a typical example of a definition of polyphony which David Moseley provides when exploring Bonhoeffer's use of the metaphor:

> Polyphony is a musical texture consisting of *two or more independent melodic voices*. Polyphonic music is often expressed through "counterpoint" or "contrapuntal" music, a broad organizational category involving the simultaneous sounding of separate musical voices.[4]

1. See: Bonhoeffer, 8:591.

2. With respect to "polyphony of life" as an example of these imaginative expressions, we see that it has been freighted with meaning. For instance, Andreas Pangritz calls "polyphony of life" an interpretative key for understanding "revolutionary 'new formulas'" in Bonhoeffer's theology in relation to a theological turn taken near the end of his life. Pangritz, "Point and Counterpoint—Resistance and Submission: Dietrich Bonhoeffer on Theology and Music in Times of War and Social Crisis," 29. John W. de Gruchy suggests a latent aesthetic theology is being developed through the metaphor which, together with other references to music in the letters, affords possible new insights for theological aesthetics in general. De Gruchy, "Restoring Broken Themes of Praise," 145. More recently, Barry Harvey has identified it as "an image for construing the church's multifaceted relationship to a world come of age as it seeks in communion with the triune God to cultivate a profound this-worldliness." Harvey, *Taking Hold of the Real: Dietrich Bonhoeffer and the Profound Worldliness of Christianity*, 236. All three associate it with other formulae in the Letters, as we will explore in this chapter.

3. This is the term ascribed to the theology of the prison letters from April 1944 onwards by Eberhard Bethge and it is for this reason that Bethge sought to publish the letters. See: Bethge, *Dietrich Bonhoeffer: Theologian, Christian, Contemporary*, 757–95. See also, below, where the focus of this "new theology" is discussed with respect to the formulae Bonhoeffer developed in keeping with it, namely, "religionless Christianity" and "world come of age."

4. Moseley, "'Parables' and 'Polyphony': The Resonance of Music as Witness in the Theology of Karl Barth and Dietrich Bonhoeffer," in *Resonant Witness: Conversations between Music and Theology*, ed. Jeremy Begbie and Steven Guthrie, 2011, 256. Italics original.

This is a concise and accurate definition of the musical term. However, the use of the explanatory words "independent" and "separate" has the potential to be rather misleading. Left unqualified in a definition of Bonhoeffer's appeal to polyphony, such terms risk subverting the theological meaning of the metaphor at the outset. For instance, Bonhoeffer applies the metaphor to the Chalcedonian definition but he is assuredly not affirming the "independence" or "separation" of Christ's two natures.[5] A musical understanding of polyphony, therefore, is highly valuable for elucidating Bonhoeffer's use of the term, not least because Bonhoeffer himself employs the word "independence" [*selbständigkeit*] in his appeal to the metaphor.

When applied to music, such terms have a different meaning compared to their use in non-musical settings. To say that a melody is "independent" is to say that it can be classified *as* a melody; it is "independent" or "separate" insofar as its coherence as a melody is not reliant on the other music that is simultaneously played or sung. What "independent" should not be read to suggest is a melody within polyphony that has nothing to do with other melodies. In case this appears to be stating the obvious, it is worth noting that even when music-theorists define polyphony they tend to qualify the term "independent."[6] This is because there is a point at which the degree of independence (i.e., the degree to which a melody is distinct from another melody) can become such that the resulting musical style could no longer be described as polyphony.

Therefore, within polyphony musical voices termed "independent" are, in fact, *inseparably related* to other musical voices. They are also notably "particular," or "distinctive," to the extent that we can speak of them retaining their own particular or distinct integrities. Yet, not forgetting that they are played or sung simultaneously, these voices also enhance one another. This phenomenon, known as "musical resonance," occurs to some extent in all music involving more than one part or voice, and is therefore not usually mentioned in a music theorist's definition of polyphony; it is just assumed. These implicit or assumed dimensions to the term polyphony carry enormous theological potential when employed metaphorically, as this book attempts to show.

5. For more on polyphony as a Chalcedonian definition, see Chapter 3 which focuses on Bonhoeffer's Christology.

6. So, Frobenius describes the several musical voices in polyphony as moving "*to some extent* independently" and Bellermann, in his 1862 study *Der Kontrapunkt*, points out: "in every song for more than one voice the parts are to be developed melodically, and therefore independently, and because of the different rhythmic movement of individual parts there will be an enormous number of pieces in which the separate parts appear *too independent for the style to be reckoned homophonic, or even, polyphonic*." Wolf Frobenius, "Polyphony," *Grove Music Online*, Oxford Music Online (Oxford University Press), accessed August 4, 2017, http://www.oxfordmusiconline.com/subscriber/article/grove/music/42927. My emphasis.

With the foregoing discussion in mind, an alternative, working definition of polyphony which avoids the use of "independence" or "separate" and still adheres to the aspects of the term familiar to Bonhoeffer could be as follows:

> Polyphony is a form of music in which two or more distinct melodies or voices sound simultaneously, each melody or voice retaining its distinctiveness while enhancing and being enhanced by the others. Polyphony is sometimes constructed around a "cantus firmus", a pre-existing melody around which the other(s) are composed.

Polyphony originated out of the practice of singing a preexisting chant (*cantus firmus*) which formed the primary voice and the basis for additional voices.[7] The *cantus firmus* could be taken from plainchant, preexisting liturgical texts or hymns, and in the early twelfth century often became the lower foundational voice in a composition. While not all polyphonic music is composed around a *cantus firmus*, Bonhoeffer's understanding of polyphony relies upon the presence of this feature.

One final point with respect to the musical background to polyphony is to simply observe its relation to "counterpoint." While, as Moseley suggests, counterpoint is often used interchangeably with polyphony, it can also take on more specific senses: for example, the compositional technique used in combining the voices of polyphony, or the very strict forms of polyphony developed by J. S. Bach in, say, his *Art of Fugue*.[8]

Taking care to understand the musical definition of polyphony in this way provides us with some background to Bonhoeffer's specific use of the term. In particular, when he describes polyphony in terms of "independence" [*selbständigkeit*] of musical voices without further qualifying this, he is taking for granted the musical understanding of the term. We are to understand that he means the particularity and full development of melodic voices, not that the voices are separate from, or do not interact with one another (which would not, after all, be polyphony). Bearing in mind this background, we can now turn to the specific occasions when Bonhoeffer uses the term "polyphony" in his writings.

Polyphony in the Prison Letters

Bonhoeffer uses the term three times in letters of May 1944. These letters are part of the "theological letters"—so-called because in them Bonhoeffer appears to reform aspects of his theology in order to compose a compelling vision of

7. The first written descriptions of polyphony are from the ninth century, but the practice predates this. It is also noteworthy that the original practice was a theological one, in the deepest sense, growing out of sung liturgy in Monastic communities in which extempore singing was added to the cantus.

8. Frobenius, "Polyphony." Here the relationship between polyphony and, on the one hand, harmony, on the other, counterpoint, is discussed in two distinct categories.

Christianity for the future.[9] Indeed, the ideas in them were deemed sufficiently valuable to Bonhoeffer that he requested they be preserved and this led to the publication of *Letters and Papers from Prison* by his close friend and confidant, Eberhard Bethge.[10]

First Use of Polyphony, May 20, 1944

Bonhoeffer's first uses of polyphony occur in a letter to Bethge in which he responds to his newly married friend's struggles with fighting on the frontline in Italy in a war he doesn't support, and in wanting to survive and be reunited with his family. Bonhoeffer's advice to Bethge is that, rather than downplaying his affections for his wife, he must maintain his love for God. He writes:

> However, there is a danger, in any passionate erotic love, that through it you may lose what I'd like to call the polyphony of life. What I mean is that God, the Eternal, wants to be loved with our whole heart, not to the detriment of earthly love or to diminish it, but as a sort of cantus firmus to which the other voices of life resound in counterpoint. One of these contrapuntal themes, which keep their *full independence* but are still related to the cantus firmus, is earthly love. Even in the Bible there is the Song of Solomon, and you really can't imagine a hotter, more sensual and glowing love than the one spoken of here (cf. 7:6!). It's really good that this is in the Bible, contradicting all those who think being Christian is about tempering one's passions (where is there any such tempering in the Old Testament?). Where the cantus firmus is clear and distinct, a counterpoint can develop as mightily as it wants. The two are "undivided and yet distinct," as the Definition of Chalcedon says, like the divine and human natures in Christ. Is that perhaps why we are so at home with polyphony in music, why it is important to us, because it is the musical image of this Christological fact and thus also our *vita christiana*? This idea came to me only after your visit yesterday. Do you understand what I mean? I wanted to ask you to let the cantus firmus be heard clearly in your being together; only then will it sound complete and full, and the counterpoint will always know that it is being carried and can't get out of tune or be cut adrift, while remaining itself and complete in itself. Only this polyphony gives your life wholeness, and you know that no disaster can befall you as long as the cantus firmus continues.[11]

9. Of these letters de Gruchy writes: "These 'theological letters' remain central to the prison writings, and many readers will regard them as the core of its content." Bonhoeffer, *Letters and Papers from Prison*, 8:2.

10. Bonhoeffer wrote to Bethge on July 8: "By the way, it would be very nice if you didn't throw away my theological letters but, since they are surely a burden for you to keep there, send them off to Renate from time to time. I might perhaps like to read them again later for my work." Bonhoeffer, 8:458. See also: Bethge, *Dietrich Bonhoeffer: Theologian, Christian, Contemporary*, 764.

11. Bonhoeffer, *Letters and Papers from Prison*, 8:394.

Here Bonhoeffer's use of polyphony evokes the particularity of voices and the resonance between them. On the one hand earthly love retains its distinct integrity and importance, "remaining itself and complete in itself." On the other, loving God gives life wholeness; the *cantus firmus* must be kept "clear and distinct" so that other loves can "resound in counterpoint." While imaginatively describing how Bethge should conduct his relationship with his wife as a Christian, Bonhoeffer enriches his idea of the polyphony of life with Christological terms: the relationship between *cantus firmus* and counterpoint is "undivided and yet distinct … like the divine and human natures in Christ." In addition to this, he even reverses this sentiment and wonders if "the Christological fact" is, itself, imaged by polyphony, and whether this analogy accounts for his and Bethge's enjoyment of the musical phenomenon. Bonhoeffer's creative thinking exudes a kind of playfulness in the rapidly cascading development of ideas surrounding the musical metaphor; an enthusiasm which persists in the next letter.

Second Use of Polyphony, May 21, 1944

The day after he first mentions it, before Bethge has even received the letter of May 20, Bonhoeffer returns to the polyphony of life. On the day of his nephew, and godson's, baptism, at which Bethge will read Bonhoeffer's sermon, he writes:

> The image of polyphony is still following me around. In feeling some sorrow today at not being able to be with you, I couldn't help thinking that sorrow and joy, too, belong to the polyphony of the whole of life and can exist independently side by side.[12]

Bonhoeffer proceeds by comparing his situation in prison to that of Bethge who faces the prospect of having to join the frontline, conceding "I am in much less danger than you are." Nevertheless, he laments his loss of freedom, as he also entreats Bethge to enjoy his freedom, "which is truly the polyphony of life (forgive me for riding my newfound hobbyhorse!)."[13]

This second appeal to polyphony actually involves two brief uses of the term in the same letter. Through it, Bonhoeffer continues to articulate the importance of simultaneously sounding ("independent") parts, in such ways that each retains its full integrity while being undiminished by the other.[14] But now polyphony is used

12. Bonhoeffer, 8:397.

13. Bonhoeffer, 8:397.

14. *DBWE* translates the term *Selbständigkeit* as "independent/independence," though it can also be translated "self-action" or "self-activity." As we have already discussed, "particularity" and "distinct integrity" retain Bonhoeffer's description of the counterpoint's distinctiveness while also allowing for its essential relationship to, and dependence on, the *cantus firmus*.

to speak of distinct, coexisting emotions (of joy and sorrow) or experiences. While this is nowhere near the lengthy exploration of polyphony we find in the previous letter, here Bonhoeffer calls it his "little hobbyhorse" (*Fündlein*), a term which is better translated "little invention" since it is almost certainly intended to allude to Bach's well-known contrapuntal pieces.[15] Evidently, the metaphor continues to captivate Bonhoeffer.

Third Use of Polyphony, May 29, 1944

Nine days after his first use of polyphony, Bonhoeffer appeals to the metaphor a third time to explore the role of Christianity in enabling "how" one should live. Reflecting on his fellow inmates he finds that their capacity to experience life is restricted: they cannot "harbour many different things at the same time."[16] This is revealed in their responses to threat during the air-raids ("they are nothing but fear itself") or greed at the prospect of food or desperation when they fail to get what they want, so that "[E]verything, whether objective or subjective, disintegrates into fragments." He contrasts this position with Christianity:

> Christianity, on the other hand, puts us into many different dimensions of life at the same time; in a way we accommodate God and the whole world within us. We weep with those who weep at the same time as we rejoice with those who rejoice. We fear … for our lives, but at the same time we must think thoughts that are much more important to us than our lives. During an air raid, for example, as soon as we are turned in a direction other than worrying about our own safety, for example, by the task of spreading calm around us, the situation becomes completely different. Life isn't pushed back into a single dimension, but is kept multidimensional, polyphonic. What a liberation it is to be able to *think* and to hold on to these many dimensions of life in our thoughts.[17]

In this letter Bonhoeffer's use of "polyphonic" feels almost incidental. His main focus is on the multidimensionality of life for the Christian, and polyphony is being used to support his description of the Christian life in which he argues that

15. The German term *Fündlein* translated in *DBWE* as "hobbyhorse" is famously difficult to translate. John Morris argues, convincingly to my mind, that if the translation "my little invention" is accepted Bonhoeffer is probably making a deliberate allusion to Bach's Two- and Three-Part Inventions. See: Morris, "Bonhoeffer's Little Invention." My thanks to John de Gruchy for drawing my attention to this.

16. Bonhoeffer, 8:404.

17. Bonhoeffer, *Letters and Papers from Prison*, 8:405. The ellipsis near the beginning of the third sentence of this passage is where Bonhoeffer was interrupted by sirens, showing the fragmentariness of his immediate context.

no single experience (being in prison, experiencing air raids or other effects of war) should take precedent. Instead, Christianity means experiencing these many dimensions simultaneously.

Our brief account of Bonhoeffer's allusion to polyphony in these three letters reveals that its most developed use comes in the first letter, as an extended metaphor to formulate his response to Eberhard Bethge. I will first analyze the metaphor in the context of this personal correspondence as a means of speaking about ordering love. In the second part of my analysis, I will look at the potential for the term to be understood as a broader construct together with other formulations in the theological letters.

A Musico-Theological Invention for Love

In Bonhoeffer's first appeal to polyphony in his correspondence with Eberhard Bethge (concerning Bethge's marriage to Renate, Bonhoeffer's sister) he attempts to order what he regards as the proper arrangement love of God and earthly loves should take; both in Bethge's case and, it seems, for the Christian in general. According to Barry Harvey, Bonhoeffer's use of polyphony here suggests an implicit ontology.[18] This "leaves no room for the erroneous conception of God as *a* being among beings,"[19] and it would be mistaken, Harvey points out, to imagine that love of God and earthly loves are in competition: "According to this misconception, when we give our love to other creatures, we must take it from our love for God."[20] Harvey grounds this in his interpretation of Bonhoeffer's view of "reality," in which God is the "first and final reality" though in such a way that the world is not "sublimated."[21] So, says Harvey, "[I]n the representation that Bonhoeffer puts forward, which is the more rare and difficult conception, God does not stand alongside other creatures, for God's 'space' is not ours."[22]

18. "Implicit in Bonhoeffer's comments about the polyphony of life is an ontological surmise regarding the relationship between God and the world that is central to the basic grammar of theology." Harvey, *Taking Hold of the Real: Dietrich Bonhoeffer and the Profound Worldliness of Christianity*, 240.

19. Harvey writes: "Implicit in Bonhoeffer's comments about the polyphony of life is an ontological surmise regarding the relationship between God and the world that is central to his understanding of the basic grammar of theology." Harvey, *Taking Hold of the Real: Dietrich Bonhoeffer and the Profound Worldliness of Christianity*, 240.

20. Harvey, *Taking Hold of the Real: Dietrich Bonhoeffer and the Profound Worldliness of Christianity*, 240.

21. Harvey, *Taking Hold of the Real: Dietrich Bonhoeffer and the Profound Worldliness of Christianity*, 240. Bonhoeffer's understanding of "reality," with respect to *Ethics*, is examined in some detail in Chapter 5.

22. Harvey, *Taking Hold of the Real: Dietrich Bonhoeffer and the Profound Worldliness of Christianity*, 240.

Harvey's interpretation of polyphony well expresses the complexity faced by the Christian in navigating a commitment to love God and love others (and how the two relate) because, as Harvey seems to recognize, the practice of loving God is often felt to be in competition with other loves in the Christian's experience. Further, the Christian's love of God and God's love cannot always be easily distinguished because orthodox Christian theology recognizes that God's love is the source of all love.[23] However, Bonhoeffer's appeal to polyphony in the first letter is more obviously directed toward the human activity of loving God in relation to loving created things. On the face of it, it is more accurate to consider polyphony in Bonhoeffer's use of it as a heuristic device (intended to help a friend navigate his behavior).

Nevertheless, Harvey's reading exposes the inadequate theology which undergirds the view that loving others might detract from loving God, highlighting that the two are not in competition in a zero-sum game. He is surely accurate that *part* of the impulse behind Bonhoeffer's appeal to polyphony is the capacity for the metaphor to articulate both God and creation without competition.[24] For this reason, the statement "God's 'space' is not ours" is slightly misleading in a discussion of polyphony. I take it that Harvey does not want to convey a sense that God is separate from creation (in the sense of being uninvolved), but is, rather, intending to highlight how polyphony can convey an ontological commitment to the incommensurability of God and creation, on the one hand, and the ability to love God "through" the creation, on the other. Yet, it seems to me that it is the emphasis on God's involvement with creation which Bonhoeffer is after when he appeals to an acoustic-spatial metaphor; that is, he deliberately associates God's space with ours in order to emphasize the relatedness of God and creation. (In Chapter 5 we will see more closely how Bonhoeffer's concept of "reality," in *Ethics*, also emphasizes a kind of "shared space" between God and creation.)

Finally, with respect to Harvey's interpretation of Bonhoeffer's first use of polyphony, we must ask: Is Harvey accurate in his assessment that with polyphony Bonhoeffer intends to convey that love of God occurs through creatures?

23. The intractability of the relationship between love of God and God's love is implied in Harvey's discussion when he draws on Friedrich von Hügel. He quotes von Hügel as saying that love of God is "the form, principle and harmony" and our natural affections are "the matter, harmonized and set in order"; love of God is "the soul" and our natural affections are "the body" of the one Divine love "whose adequate object is God in, and not apart from, His creatures." See: Harvey, *Taking Hold of the Real: Dietrich Bonhoeffer and the Profound Worldliness of Christianity*, 240.

24. This we will see further in Chapter 3 with respect to Bonhoeffer's appeal to polyphony for the Chalcedonian definition.

Elsewhere, such an emphasis is apparent in one of his letters.[25] However, it is my contention that with polyphony Bonhoeffer is making a slightly more nuanced claim regarding love of God and creatures. As opposed to arguing that love of God occurs through creatures, I think Bonhoeffer is placing an emphasis elsewhere: by refocusing our love onto God (maintaining our *cantus firmus*) our other loves are subsequently kept in their rightful place, and are even enhanced.

It is possible to further understand this emphasis by briefly contrasting what Bonhoeffer is saying with Augustine of Hippo's proposed order of love, as outlined by Carol Harrison.[26] In Book 6 of *De Musica* Augustine writes about an "order of love," affirming the Christian's responsibility to order his affections for creation appropriately in relation to God, as well as his capacity to do so. Carefully distinguishing between *uti* ("use") and *frui* ("enjoyment"), Augustine proposes that love of oneself and one's neighbor occurs "on behalf of" (*propter*) or "in reference to" (*referre ad*) God (6.13.43–14.46) and we can "enjoy [someone] in God" (*frui in Deo*). We see that love of created things should be used to the end of enjoying the eternal and immutable God; not as ends in themselves but "like a plank in the waves, not by throwing them away as a burden, nor by embracing them as something well anchored, but by using them well" (6.14.45; cf. 6.11.29).

Augustine here addresses a similar issue to that faced by Bonhoeffer (and Bethge): how we can love created things in such a way that love of God is not displaced. By contrast, Bonhoeffer's reference to the *cantus firmus* emphasizes a focus on loving God but, crucially, *without* diminishing or undermining the value of earthly loves. Unlike Augustine, who manages this order of love by resisting an overattachment to earthly things so that they are used properly to the end of loving God, Bonhoeffer advocates for an increased attachment to God. God is the anchor which keeps earthly loves from being cut adrift, says Bonhoeffer. But how is this to be achieved? One of the ways that we will see Bonhoeffer try to achieve this is through the arcane discipline (*Arkandisziplin*), discussed further below. For

25. On December 18, 1943, Bonhoeffer also discusses this order of love but without the benefit of the metaphor polyphony. In this letter he also counsels Bethge regarding his impending military duty and separation from his wife. Writing about the difficulty of living with unfulfilled longings, which he relates to his own experience of prison and separation from his fiancée, he emphasizes the irreplaceability of those we love, for whom we long, and for whom there can be no substitutes. He goes on to argue that, while the final fulfillment of Christian life is being at home with God, this does not displace the significance of our life on earth; though "it is indeed something important but is nevertheless only the very last thing." Here he proposes that it is through the things we love on earth that we love God, as he writes: "I believe we are so to love God in our *life* and in the good things God gives us and to lay hold of such trust in God that, when the time comes and is here—but truly only then!—we also go to God with love, trust, and joy." Bonhoeffer, 8:228. Italics original.

26. See: Harrison, "Augustine and the Art of Music," 27–45.

now, we can simply acknowledge that Bonhoeffer's concern is to maintain both a commitment to loving God and a commitment to created loves without either diminishing the other.

In this analysis of Bonhoeffer's first and most extended use of polyphony we have seen that Bonhoeffer contours his description of the order of love so that God is superordinate and created loves are subordinate; yet, created loves are not diminished in this arrangement. Instead, by focusing on loving God, as *cantus firmus*, all other loves will resound. This is possible, as we saw in our definition of the term, because polyphony depends on the full integrity of distinct voices which are preserved while occurring simultaneously.

We have not yet investigated an important aspect of the metaphor conveyed in his first letter mentioning polyphony: the allusion to the Chalcedonian definition. This will be examined at length in the next chapter, as it requires a much deeper analysis of Bonhoeffer's Christology than can be carried out here. I will turn now to my analysis of Bonhoeffer's second and third uses of polyphony, which pertains to his late theology more broadly.

A Musico-Theological Invention for Life

We saw in the second letter in which it appears that Bonhoeffer calls polyphony his *Fündlein*, "little invention" (in what may be a deliberate allusion to Bach's contrapuntal Two- and Three-Part Inventions); a term which suggests that he thought he had alighted on a discovery of sorts. However, we also saw in the opening of the first section of this chapter that such "enigmatic utterances" are not difficult to come by in the prison letters and this *Fündlein* is by no means the only creative term to occur in the more directly theological letters. A preponderance of evocative phrases appears in these letters which, some have argued, gives the impression that Bonhoeffer's theology was undergoing a development of sorts. In conforming to the view that these "new formulae" signal a "late stage" in Bonhoeffer's theological development, I am adopting what is, these days, a relatively moderate position with respect to the many ways that Bonhoeffer's ideas in the letters have been interpreted. I neither hold to the extreme views that these terms reflect a loss of faith or promotion of secularism, nor do I see them as insignificant musings. Rather, they seem to me to be a part of a deliberate effort to reformulate biblical language about Jesus Christ for the present age in which religion has both despoiled Christianity and set itself at odds with the world.[27]

Two major formulations which indicate a shift in Bonhoeffer's late theological thought are "religionless Christianity" (*religionslose Christentum*) and "a world come

27. This view will become clearer, below. Details of the more extreme readings of Bonhoeffer's *Letters* are given in the Editor's Afterword. See: Bonhoeffer, *Letters and Papers from Prison*, 8:590–4. See also: Selby, "Christianity in a World Come of Age," 228.

of age" (*die mündig gerwordenen Welt*).[28] By exploring these major formulations, together with the comparatively minor "arcane discipline" (*Arkandisziplin*), we will see how polyphony connects with this theological development, which has been dubbed a "new theology";[29] how it is that Andreas Pangritz can call Bonhoeffer's polyphony of life "the essence of nonreligious Christianity" and John W. de Gruchy speak of it, together with the arcane discipline, as "essential to a genuine Christian 'worldliness' as Bonhoeffer began to articulate it in prison."[30]

Religionless Christianity

On April 30, 1944, Bonhoeffer writes to Bethge concerning the significance of Christianity in their age, in the first of the letters which he himself called "theological" and which inspired Bethge to publish the prison correspondence.[31] The nature and tone of his inquiry, Bonhoeffer concedes, might cause consternation.[32] In the letter many of the ideas which have sparked interest in Bonhoeffer's late theology abound through a series of pertinent questions, all proceeding from his most pressing concern: "What is Christianity … who is Jesus Christ for us today?"[33] This is followed by the first use of the expression "religionless Christianity" as Bonhoeffer asks, in deliberate allusion to Adolf von Harnack's metaphor of the kernel and husk (content and form) of Christianity: "If religion is only the garb in

28. The outline for a short book which he includes in a letter to Bethge evinces the importance of these ideas for Bonhoeffer. In just three chapters ("1. Taking stock of Christianity; 2. What is Christian faith, really? 3. Conclusions") Bonhoeffer proposes to cover such themes as "the religionlessness of the human being come of age," the relationship between worldliness and God and the nonreligious interpretation of biblical concepts" and the Church as a living example. Bonhoeffer, *Letters and Papers from Prison*, 8:499–504.

29. Eberhard Bethge identifies a "new impulse" in Bonhoeffer's letters from April 1944 onward, which, he suggests, results from a number of factors (including a "truce period" in which his legal hearing could not take place and an acceptance of his own guilt in joining the conspiracy). He writes: "Even before the political task had been completed it had made a new theological theme possible, opening the eye of the lonely man to the conditions and the possible form of Christian belief in the future." Bethge, *Dietrich Bonhoeffer: Theologian, Christian, Contemporary*, 758–9.

30. Pangritz, "Point and Counterpoint—Resistance and Submission: Dietrich Bonhoeffer on Theology and Music in Times of War and Social Crisis," 29. De Gruchy, "Restoring Broken Themes of Praise," 167.

31. Bonhoeffer, *Letters and Papers from Prison*, 8:458.

32. "What might surprise or perhaps even worry you would be my theological thoughts and where they are leading," he writes to Bethge, Bonhoeffer, 8:362. They were instead met with much enthusiasm and interest. See Bethge's response: Bonhoeffer, 8:367.

33. Bethge is not alone in asserting that this question with which Bonhoeffer leads the inquiry is the main issue at stake. It concerns not so much the religious forms of Christianity as the form Christ takes in the world. See: Bethge, *Dietrich Bonhoeffer: Theologian, Christian, Contemporary*, 767.

which Christianity is clothed—and this garb has looked very different in different ages—what then is religionless Christianity?" He goes on to ask, placing "religion" in unmistakably negative terms: "How do we talk about God—without religion, that is, without the temporally conditioned presuppositions of metaphysics, the inner life, and so on?"[34]

Bonhoeffer continues to contrast the idea of "religionlessness" with a negative view of religion in a number of ways in the theological letters.[35] Under the influence of Wilhelm Dilthey (1833–1911) whose "philosophy of life" preoccupies him in prison, Bonhoeffer affirms human autonomy and "life come of age" which have succeeded the age of religion.[36] From Dilthey he derives an historical approach to his critique of religion, identifying a loss of theological metaphysics in the Middle Ages which was subsequently replaced with a religious piety in modernity.[37]

34. Bonhoeffer, 8:362. April 30, 1944.

35. Religion has long been treated in critical terms in Bonhoeffer's work, and this continues in the letters. In his survey of the term "religion" in Bonhoeffer's writings, Ralf Wüstenberg finds that it is used in three ways: to describe religion in positive terms; in a critical way, following Barth and the dialectical method; and "in a way that suggests that the 'age of religion' has simply come to an end." Ralf K. Wüstenberg, "Religion and Secularity," in *The Oxford Handbook of Dietrich Bonhoeffer*, ed. Philip G. Ziegler and Michael Mawson, 2019, 322. However, Eberhard Bethge locates Bonhoeffer's idea of religion primarily in Barth's use of the term as diametrically opposed to faith (Wüstenberg's second category). See: Bethge, *Dietrich Bonhoeffer: Theologian, Christian, Contemporary*, 775. This influence is evident even in Bonhoeffer's early criticisms of religion as a merely human means of finding God in his lecture on "Jesus Christ and the essence of Christianity" in Barcelona in 1928. Likening Christianity to Buddhism, he insists that "Christ is not the bringer of a new religion, but the bringer of God." Bonhoeffer, Dietrich, *Barcelona, Berlin, New York: 1928–1931*, 10:358. Similarly, in *Ethics* Bonhoeffer distinguishes the Church from religion when he writes: "The church's concern is not religion, but the form of Christ and its taking form among a band of people." From "Ethics as Formation," an important manuscript for our purposes. Bonhoeffer, *Ethics*, 6:97.

36. The influence of Dilthey on Bonhoeffer's Prison Theology was first established in 1969 in essays by Ernst Feil and Christian Gremmels, Clifford Green reminds us. See: Green, *Bonhoeffer: A Theology of Sociality*, 260. But Ralf Wüstenberg has provided the fullest treatment of Bonhoeffer's connection to Dilthey's philosophy of life, to date. See: Wüstenberg, *A Theology of Life: Dietrich Bonhoeffer's Religionless Christianity*, 104ff; 112–46; Wüstenberg, "Religion and Secularity."

37. Ralf Wüstenberg calls it a "religious-moral inwardness." See: Wüstenberg, "Religion and Secularity," 323. Though Bonhoeffer seems to conceive of the "religious" in modernity in a number of distinct ways; at various points he uses it to refer to liberal theology, Christian apologists, methodists (meaning those following a religious method). The importance of the historical approach of Dilthey's "philosophy of life" to Bonhoeffer is also attested to by de Gruchy, who remarks that Bonhoeffer prefers the work of Dilthey to the writings of Kierkegaard or Nietzsche "because it located life within an objective historical framework rather than reducing it to the subjective alone." De Gruchy, "Restoring Broken Themes of Praise," 151.

However, quite unlike Dilthey (who continued to attach positive connotations to "religion"), Bonhoeffer, writing some sixty years later, is more straightforward: human progress has brought an end to the religious age, and it is no longer accurate to resort to "God" as the explanation for existence.[38]

The religious are those who cling onto this untenable worldview. Bonhoeffer attacks those who rely on God as a "deus ex machina" to be the solution when human strength fails. This he regards, disdainfully, as intellectual dishonesty. He also criticizes those who affirm a "religious a priori" because it undermines the contingency of God's revelation.[39] He even goes so far as to protest that forms of religious piety, which he relates to a kind of methodism, prey on human weakness to inveigle people into assenting to Christian principles and are akin to committing "religious rape"![40] The term "religion" in *Letters*, therefore, refers to a range of views which share in common the desire to recover a bygone era (which can summarily be called Christendom), and which present themselves as Christian but, in actuality, espouse human laws and values. Religion, by Bonhoeffer's account, is anthropocentric rather than Christocentric.[41]

By contrast, the religion*less* Christian neither elides scientific progress by pretending that God is still the answer to all questions pertaining to human nature and experience, nor panics that there is an apparently diminishing space for God

38. So Bonhoeffer can write: "human beings have learned to manage all important issues by themselves, without recourse to 'Working hypothesis: God.'" Bonhoeffer, *Letters and Papers from Prison*, 8:425–6.

39. In the same letter of April 30, 1944, he puts it this way with respect to the ever-decreasing space for God in contemporary life: "Religious people speak of God at a point when human knowledge is at an end (or sometimes when they're too lazy to think further), or when human strength fails. Actually, it's a deus ex machina that they're always bringing on the scene … Inevitably that lasts only until human beings become powerful enough to push the boundaries a bit further and God is no longer needed as deus ex machina." Bonhoeffer, 8:366. The "religious a priori" is also treated critically by Bonhoeffer in *Act and Being* where he attributes the term to his doctoral supervisor Reinhold Seeberg and likens it to natural revelation and the human ability to receive revelation. See: Bonhoeffer, Dietrich, *Act and Being*, 2:58. De Gruchy, in the editor's introduction to *Letters*, summarizes it as "the religious longing and sense of weakness in human beings that could be appealed to in preaching the gospel with that in mind as the point of contact." Bonhoeffer, *Letters and Papers from Prison*, 8:24.

40. Bonhoeffer, *Letters and Papers from Prison*, 8:363.

41. "What matters is not the beyond but this world, how it is created and preserved, is given laws, reconciled, and renewed. What is beyond this world is meant, in the gospel, to be there for this world—not in the anthropocentric sense of liberal, mystical, pietistic, ethical theology, but in the biblical sense of the creation and the incarnation, crucifixion, and resurrection of Jesus Christ." Bonhoeffer, 8:373.

in various intellectual discourses.[42] Instead, the religionless Christian lives "etsi deus non daretur."[43] On the face of it this statement suggests a radical reappraisal of Bonhoeffer's theology is required, but it soon becomes apparent that Bonhoeffer actually intends to reaffirm the priority he has long given to Christology. We are called to live in the world as though God did not exist because of what God has done in Christ.[44]

On July 16, 1944, Bonhoeffer writes to Bethge that God makes us live in the world without God as a working hypothesis. This same God "consents to be pushed out of the world and onto the cross; God is weak and powerless in the world and in precisely this way, and only so, is at our side and helps us."[45] He proceeds:

> This is the crucial distinction between Christianity and all religions. Human religiosity directs people in need to the power of God in the world, God as deus ex machina. The bible directs people toward the powerlessness and suffering of God; only the suffering God can help.[46]

In this way Bonhoeffer qualifies his concept of religionless Christianity with the *suffering* God. The one who was marginalized when he was crucified on the cross continues to be pushed out of the world today. It is the willingness to share in this powerlessness which characterizes the religionless, Bonhoeffer suggests.[47]

It is difficult to say much more about religionless Christianity without also addressing the world come of age. But before we come to this, it is noteworthy that Dilthey's influence may have also touched on Bonhoeffer's appeal to polyphony as a metaphor. In prison Bonhoeffer requests a copy of Dilthey's *Von deutscher Dichtung und Musik* (published posthumously in 1933) in which the latter uses

42. In the letter dated July 16, 1944, he lists the areas which have relegated God to the fringes as: morality, politics, natural sciences, philosophy, and even religion itself, with respect to Feuerbach. Bonhoeffer, 8:478.

43. "And we cannot be honest unless we recognise that we have to live in the world 'etsi deus non daretur.' And this is precisely what we do recognise—before God! God himself compels us to recognise it." Bonhoeffer, 8:478. "Etsi deus non daretur" is a contraction of the maxim used by Hugo Grotius (1583–1645) in his work on the law of war and peace.

44. In his discussion on living before God, and with God, as though we are without God, Bonhoeffer cites Mark 15:34 ("And at the ninth hour Jesus cried with a loud voice," "Eloi, Eloi, lema sabachthani?" which means, "My God, my God, why have you forsaken me?"). He, therefore, suggests that to live "etsi deus non daretur" is to live like Christ. See: Bonhoeffer, 8:478–9.

45. Bonhoeffer, 8:478.

46. Bonhoeffer, 8:478.

47. The next day Bonhoeffer will write about those in the New Testament who were faithful without following any religious method or making any explicit or obvious confession. "The one thing they all have in common is their sharing in the suffering of God in Christ. That is their 'faith.'" Bonhoeffer, 8:481.

polyphony as a concept for articulating the human need for redemption, inter alia, and a feeling for the divine.[48] It is striking, nonetheless, that Dilthey's philosophy of life should have so influenced Bonhoeffer's emphasis on life in his idea of religionless Christianity and may also have been part of the inspiration for the expression "polyphony of life."

In summary, the formulation "religionless Christianity" is not a rejection of Christianity or an indication that Bonhoeffer has lost faith in God, despite some startling and provocative statements, but is in actuality a reaction to religion. In particular, it is Bonhoeffer's response to a counterfeit presentation of God as the answer or solution to an ever-narrowing set of problems; a false notion which operates hand in hand with a refusal to acknowledge and accept the process of secularization.[49] Put in more positive terms, through the concept of religionlessness Bonhoeffer affirms Jesus Christ as the source of life through whom God is both intimately involved in the world and, paradoxically, goes unrecognized as the suffering God. Religionless Christians are those who live fully in the world, which includes suffering, and do not use their faith in God to try and escape this.

The World Come of Age

Bonhoeffer's notion of "the world come of age" (*die mündig gerwordenen Welt*) is the other side of the coin to religionless Christianity. *Die mündige Welt* is a description of the present post-religious age. As Clifford Green observes, it is best understood in anthropological, rather than theological, terms, as an accurate title for the development of the Western world, particularly following the Renaissance and Enlightenment periods.[50]

The expression first appears in a letter on June 8, 1944, in which Bonhoeffer criticizes Christian apologetics for attacking the world come of age. He writes:

> I consider the attack by Christian apologetics on the world's coming of age as, first of all, pointless, second, ignoble, and third, unchristian. Pointless—because it appears to me like trying to put a person who has become an adult back into puberty, that is, to make people depend, to shove them into problems that are in fact no longer problems for them. Ignoble—because an attempt is being made here to exploit people's weaknesses for alien purposes to which they have not

48. See: Dilthey, *Von deutscher Dichtung und Musik*, 197–8. As Andreas Pangritz has it, Dilthey's theological reflection on polyphony is reminiscent of Schleiermacher's religious consciousness. See: Pangritz, *The Polyphony of Life: Bonhoeffer's Theology of Music*, 56.

49. As Bonhoeffer puts it, and as we will shortly see, the development of the world come of age has actually cleared the way "by eliminating a false notion of God" and freeing "us to see the God of the Bible." Bonhoeffer, *Letters and Papers from Prison*, 8:478.

50. Green, *Bonhoeffer: A Theology of Sociality*, 253. According to Green this formulation is the one really new ingredient in Bonhoeffer's prison writings. Green, 248.

> consented freely. Unchristian—because it confuses Christ with a particular stage of human religiousness, namely, with a human law.[51]

Here Bonhoeffer identifies the religious ("Christian apologists") with a denial of the world come of age which is tantamount to propagating delusion or, worse still, exploiting the vulnerable. By implication his own view, as that of a religionless Christian, is quite different. Contrary to the beliefs of those who attack it, the world come of age does not oppose Christianity. It *has* replaced the religious age which, for a while, predominated, but it is simply a neutral category pertaining to the present situation.

However, in addition to being a neutral descriptor for the present age, Bonhoeffer writes, approvingly, that the world come of age may be closer to Christianity than the religious age was.[52] In a post-Christendom world, he suggests that the illusion that religious conformity once provided is no longer possible and, with the veil removed, that the world may even be closer to God than it was when it thought it had understood God. Following his account of religionless Christianity, we can understand Bonhoeffer here as referring to the relative benefit of living without God over living with a false notion of God, which is the greater deception.

This more positive view of the expression "world come of age" needs to be read in light of two further, contrasting presentations of worldliness as "banal," on the one hand, and "profound," on the other. These are expressed in what Bethge describes as his favorite letter:[53]

> In the last few years I have come to know and understand more and more the profound this-worldliness of Christianity … I do not mean the shallow and banal this-worldliness of the enlightened, the bustling, the comfortable, or the lascivious, but the profound this-worldliness that shows discipline and includes the ever-present knowledge of death and resurrection.[54]

In this passage we see that Bonhoeffer's idea of the world come of age is further inflected in a negative sense by a "shallow and banal this-worldliness" which is content to accept the present religionless age without faith in God. While Bonhoeffer approves of worldliness as part of his vision of religionless Christianity, he recognizes the potential hubris of the present age when it relies on its enlightened understanding instead of depending on God. Therefore, although he does not perceive the world come of age as a threat, the situation nevertheless presents a challenge: How can one be Christian and shape Christianity for such a world? In

51. Bonhoeffer, *Letters and Papers from Prison*, 8:427.

52. "The world come of age is more god-less and perhaps just because of that closer to God than the world not yet come of age." Bonhoeffer, 8:482.

53. Bonhoeffer, *Letters and Papers from Prison*, 8:485n1.

54. Bonhoeffer, 8:485.

this respect, the world come of age should not be read as a fulfillment, according to the modern idea of progress. He is not advocating for unreserved worldly independence, nor is he espousing universalism by saying that those people who reject God are, in actuality, Christians. On this understanding, the "profound this-worldliness" of Christianity presents a counter-challenge to the world come of age to live with the awareness that God in Christ is present in this world. As Barry Harvey puts it: "Bonhoeffer leaves little doubt that the church's profound this-worldliness is distinct from, and stands in permanent tension with, the way worldliness is understood and performed in and by a world come of age."[55]

In summary, the world come of age is Bonhoeffer's formulation for his historical context. The "enlightened" world can no longer be called religious because advances in the natural sciences, as well as politics and morality have led to a process of secularization. In this respect, *die mündig gerwordenen Welt* is a neutral category which simply describes how things are. Although it is viewed negatively by the religious because it threatens their form of Christianity, the religionless Christian can accept the world come of age for what it is and even enjoys worldliness as something to be validated over the deception of the false claims of religion. However, there is a deeper and more profound kind of worldliness which, Bonhoeffer says, is characterized by faith in Jesus Christ.

Arcane Discipline

The final formulation we need to examine from *Letters* at this stage is "the discipline of the arcane" (*Arkandisziplin*). Although a comparatively minor concept, it further enlarges our understanding of Bonhoeffer's accounts of religionless Christianity and world come of age. The *Arkandisziplin* has its origins in the early Church practice of prohibiting uninitiated catechumens from fully participating in aspects of the worship service (in particular communion, but also confessing the Nicene Creed) until their training was completed.[56] Bonhoeffer mentions the practice on just two occasions in *Letters*.[57] Yet, the context in which these references appear signals its importance to Bonhoeffer, as in both letters it is part of his proposed solution to preserving Christian faith without religion.[58]

55. Harvey, *Taking Hold of the Real: Dietrich Bonhoeffer and the Profound Worldliness of Christianity*, 237.

56. David Ford calls it the "climactic act of worship" and "locus of identity" in the Church. Ford, "Polyphonic Living: Dietrich Bonhoeffer," 263.

57. See: Bonhoeffer, *Letters and Papers from Prison* 365; 373. Bethge points out that he tried to revive the practice in Finkenwalde. See: Bethge, *Dietrich Bonhoeffer: Theologian, Christian, Contemporary*, 784.

58. It is first used at the end of the first theological letter from April 30, 1944, which we have already discussed at some length, where Bonhoeffer writes: "In a religionless situation, what do ritual [Kultus] and prayer mean? Is this where the 'arcane discipline' [Arkandisziplin], or the difference (which you've heard about from me before) between

With the *Arkandisziplin* Bonhoeffer seems to be homing in on his understanding of what the core of Christianity is which should be maintained in a religionless world come of age. As Bethge understands it, the religionless Christianity which expresses itself in the *Arkandisziplin* results from the preached word and the Spirit, as he writes:

> What he [Bonhoeffer] means is clearly that when the Gospel is preached the relationship between God's word and his world is not an obvious thing and cannot be established artificially or by a trick ... This relationship is something Pentecostal.[59]

Here Bethge points to the difficulty in describing the core of Christianity. By calling it "something Pentecostal," he indicates the spiritual aspects of the faith which resist definition. In this respect the arcane discipline, which preserves religionless Christianity and prevents it from regressing into religion, should perhaps not be too narrowly defined, but held together with other Church practices like preaching, as well as the work of the Spirit.[60] Above all, we can see that Bonhoeffer's interest in the *Arkandisziplin* discloses his continued commitment to Christ and Christian praxis, in contradiction to those who read in his last writings an antithetical attitude to Christianity itself.

Polyphony of Life as a New Theological Term

We have seen that Bonhoeffer's ideas of religionless Christianity, the world come of age, and the arcane discipline demonstrate his commitment to Christianity and, at the same time, his commitment to the world in its maturity. We can now relate polyphony to these other important formulations, interpreting how it encapsulates some of their essential features.[61]

As a formulation for religionless Christianity, the metaphor "polyphony of life" is not a means of endorsing worldliness or engagement with the world without exercising Christian discipline or restraint. As we saw in our examination of the

the ultimate and penultimate have new significance?" Bonhoeffer, *Letters and Papers from Prison*, 8:365. It appears again less than a week later (May 5, 1944), once again with religionlessness as the primary subject and in the context of criticizing Barth's "positivism of revelation." There Bonhoeffer writes: "There are degrees of cognition and degrees of significance. That means an 'arcane discipline' must be reestablished, through which the mysteries of the Christian faith are sheltered against profanation." Bonhoeffer, 8:373.

59. Bethge, *Dietrich Bonhoeffer: Theologian, Christian, Contemporary*, 786.

60. See: Bethge, 786.

61. Pangritz, "Point and Counterpoint—Resistance and Submission: Dietrich Bonhoeffer on Theology and Music in Times of War and Social Crisis," 29. De Gruchy, "Restoring Broken Themes of Praise," 167.

polyphony of love, Bonhoeffer's design is to help Bethge prioritize Christ without denying his love for his wife; so, likewise, polyphony of life is not a concept which shears Christianity of Christ but rather articulates Christ's central involvement in a world which, increasingly, denies such involvement. Indeed, it is the capacity of the metaphor to convey nuance in the relationship between Christ and the world which makes it so potent for navigating this tensile relationship. As the *cantus firmus* and counterpoint retain their complete integrity while simultaneously enhancing one another, so knowing Jesus Christ and participating in the world both occur without either threatening the integrity of the other. Crucially, these are not independent activities; they are intimately connected. As we have seen, it is Bonhoeffer's quest to find Christ *in the world*, by asking, "who is Jesus Christ, for us, today?" that generates the rest of his first theological letter.

Polyphony of life as a figure for a worldly Christianity, or a Christian worldliness, articulates how Christ and the world are integrated in the Christian's experience. Indeed, the "profound this-worldliness of Christianity" is well summed up in Bonhoeffer's use of polyphony of life in his third letter (dated May 29, 1944), in which he states that, for the Christian, "Life isn't pushed back into a single dimension, but is kept multidimensional, polyphonic."[62] In this Bonhoeffer describes the polyphony of Christian life as being in the world without being dominated by any single emotion or experience because of faith in God. It is this that enables Bonhoeffer to mark the occasion of Pentecost during his imprisonment on the same day that he endures air raids; we may recall, too, his reflections on the "strange mix of reserved melancholy and eruptive joy" of the sorrow songs of African Americans.[63] The multidimensionality of Christian experience which Bonhoeffer calls polyphony of life describes how the Christian relates to Christ in and through the world.[64] The multidimensionality of life which the metaphor articulates by integrating Christian faith with worldly reality leads Michael Welker to associate Bonhoeffer's use of polyphony with pneumatology. He writes: "Bonhoeffer could and, it seems,

62. Bonhoeffer, 8:405.

63. See: Bonhoeffer, Dietrich, *Barcelona, Berlin, New York: 1928–1931*, 10:315. See previous chapter, p. 17.

64. It is as a metaphor for the life of the church's witness to the world that Barry Harvey finds polyphony so potent. Harvey suggests it can be a measure for engaging the world as a Christian, for instance stating: "The figure of the polyphony of life, its contrapuntal voices interacting with each other at multiple levels, beautifully represents the dynamic interactions on the part of the members of Christ's body with the same good that the technological organizations of modernity use, and therefore with those whose performance is orchestrated within these technologies. At times the result is stridently dissonant; at others it harmonizes more readily with the form of Jesus Christ." Harvey, *Taking Hold of the Real: Dietrich Bonhoeffer and the Profound Worldliness of Christianity*, 237. See also: Gardiner, *Melodies of a New Monasticism: Bonhoeffer's Vision, Iona's Witness.*

should have mentioned the doctrine of the Holy Spirit in this context."[65] Precisely what Welker means by this he does not explain.

With respect to the *Arkandisziplin*, the correlation between this formulation and polyphony is, to my mind, less secure than some have made out. Indeed, most scholars who discuss polyphony in Bonhoeffer interpret the arcane discipline as the means by which the *cantus firmus* is kept clear and distinct; by which they mean it is through the discipline of the arcane (in taking Eucharist and confessing Christ) that Christians can strengthen their love of God.[66] On the one hand, this interpretation is convincing because it necessitates the sacrament as the primary means by which one's love of God is strengthened. But on the other hand, we must ask why the arcane discipline needs to be associated so strongly with the *cantus firmus*, when Bonhoeffer himself does not make that connection.

Part of the reason for drawing such a strong connection between the *Arkandisziplin* and *cantus firmus*, it seems to me, is the result of an interpretative tradition in which Bethge's reading of Bonhoeffer is often privileged. In his biography, Bethge loosely relates the *Arkandisziplin* to polyphony, stating: "There is no doubt that Bonhoeffer regarded an arcane discipline as the essential *counterpoint* of non-religious interpretation."[67] In this way, he indirectly connects polyphony ("counterpoint"), the *Arkandisziplin*, and religionlessness. Even though this connection is not made by Bonhoeffer, those who provide more developed accounts of Bonhoeffer's use of polyphony accept Bethge's reading almost as though Bonhoeffer himself established it.[68] This association is all the more remarkable given that Bethge does not discuss polyphony as a theological metaphor himself.

Nevertheless, in spite of this unfortunate tendency to overplay what is only the merest association in Bethge's comment and thereby inadequately defend the connection between the *Arkandisziplin* and polyphony, it remains my contention that polyphony of life *is* an important concept for Bonhoeffer that corresponds to other theological formulations in the letters, though it is far less developed than these. There are two main reasons for this.

65. Welker, *God the Revealed: Christology*, 170n4.

66. de Gruchy, "Restoring Broken Themes of Praise," 166–7; Pangritz, *The Polyphony of Life: Bonhoeffer's Theology of Music*, 59; Ford, "Polyphonic Living: Dietrich Bonhoeffer," 262–3.

67. Bethge, *Dietrich Bonhoeffer: Theologian, Christian, Contemporary*, 785. Italics mine.

68. For instance, Andreas Pangritz echoes Bethge's view of the arcane discipline as a means of knowing Christ in the fullness of the world: "In order to avoid the danger of such revelational positivism, Bonhoeffer wants to practice an 'arcane discipline' … In that way the cantus firmus of love for God could emerge from the arcane, within the multiple counterpoints of earthly love." See: Pangritz, *The Polyphony of Life: Bonhoeffer's Theology of Music*, 59–60. De Gruchy, likewise, calls the arcane discipline the means by which Christian worldliness is anchored in the *cantus firmus*, Christ. See: de Gruchy, "Restoring Broken Themes of Praise," 166.

First, Bonhoeffer himself ascribes importance to the term. He is somewhat preoccupied with the metaphor, albeit only for a brief time. He elaborates on the term as an extended metaphor in the first letter in which he uses it and then returns to it in a subsequent letter, calling it his "*Fündlein*." He returns to it again in a third letter in which, as we have argued in agreement with other interpreters, the concept closely relates to his idea of profound this-worldliness. Moreover, he alights on the term in the theological letters, just when he is grappling with issues surrounding Christian identity in a world come of age. Thus, polyphony of life seems to be very closely connected to the theological ideas which occupy him in prison.

Arguably, with more encouragement Bonhoeffer might have further developed his thinking about polyphony. Unfortunately, the circumstances of his imprisonment and Bethge's military service mean that the letters in which polyphony is discussed are not immediately answered by Bethge, though Bonhoeffer is evidently interested in what Bethge thinks about the expression. On May 27, Bonhoeffer asks, "Did you get the thing about the cantus firmus and my questions and the meditations for Pentecost?" It is not until June 3 that we have a letter of response from Bethge which does not address this question.[69] This is particularly frustrating because Bonhoeffer so often develops his theology in prison through a dialogue with Bethge whose voice continues to interpret Bonhoeffer. We are left to imagine how Bonhoeffer might have developed the concept had it generated more immediate interest.

Second, we have seen that the metaphor is a salutary one for Bonhoeffer's own theology, as a means of conceptualizing the Christian's engagement with Christ in and through her engagement with the world. Even though Bonhoeffer does not himself relate polyphony to the formulations he mentions more frequently (particularly religionlessness and the world come of age), the kind of multidimensional experience of life that it conveys, incorporating earthly experience and commitment to Christ, is highly consonant with these other formulations.

While polyphony may not be a diagnostic term for Bonhoeffer in the same way as religionlessness or the world come of age, it does seem to provide an essentially dynamic solution to the problem of how the Christian can live before God and the world and relate to both. While it is possible that too much has been made of Bethge's view of the *Arkandisziplin*, another aspect of his interpretation which has generated comparatively little attention is his description of a Pentecostal interpretation of Bonhoeffer's late theological formulations. Bethge's reading of religionlessness echoes in Welker's view of multidimensionality in suggesting a pneumatology: both hint at the idea that, for Bonhoeffer, knowing God in a world come of age, without religion, is a work of the Holy Spirit. And while Welker claims Bonhoeffer does not develop

69. The letters mentioning polyphony are couched either side with a visit by Bethge, the content of which we are not privy to. Bonhoeffer, *Letters and Papers from Prison*, 8:404.

a pneumatology, Bethge takes some interpretative license in claiming that what Bonhoeffer actually means by religionless Christianity is "Pentecostal." Examining a nascent pneumatology in Bonhoeffer in future chapters (especially Chapters 4 and 5) will show that while neither Welker nor Bethge substantiates their claims, both intuit accurately.

Conclusion

In conclusion, in this chapter we have examined the most advanced form Bonhoeffer's musico-theology takes, his "little invention," the metaphor of polyphony. With polyphony Bonhoeffer imaginatively shapes and articulates a relationship between our love of God and earthly love in which both maintain their distinct identities while also interrelating in the same space. In view of other imaginative theological formulations reflective of a "new theology" in *Letters*, polyphony of life is a compelling term for Christianity in the world come of age; shorn of "religion," the phrase describes the world *and* God as unified in Christ while each retains its distinctiveness. We have seen that some commentators recognize pneumatological possibilities in this stage of Bonhoeffer's theology, as well as in the phrase itself. Although they do not elucidate these, this is an important observation with respect to the development of this study.

We have yet to account for how this metaphor also corresponds to a Chalcedonian Christology, a vital component in Bonhoeffer's appeal to polyphony. This will be the subject of Part II.

Part II

THE POLYPHONIC SHAPE OF CHRISTIAN FORMATION

In Part I, I made the case that Bonhoeffer's musical imagination profoundly contributes to his theological development; that musical patterns of thought and musical language help to shape and articulate his theological ideas in striking ways. This is particularly evident in the prison writings where musical patterns of thought and language most fully emerge as theologically significant, especially in the metaphor of polyphony; a "little invention" which I situated in the context of Bonhoeffer's more explicit theological formulations. Polyphony helps Bonhoeffer to describe the deep integration between God and the world with granularity, successfully conveying a sense of difference as well as relationality. The *cantus firmus* corresponds to the love of God which interacts with the contrapuntal melodies of "earthly loves," anchoring them and even expanding them while also, crucially, remaining distinct from them.

In my explication of polyphony as a metaphor for Christian formation, the Person of Christ has, unsurprisingly, been an important point of reference, if at times only indirectly. For instance, as we saw in the last chapter, in answer to his question in *Letters*, "Who is Jesus Christ, for us, today?" Bonhoeffer avers that Christ is available in and through the world today, as part of the polyphony of life, the multidimensional experience of Christian existence. It remains to be seen *how* Christ is available in the world today. That is, while it is clear that Bonhoeffer's understanding of Christ is a vital element of his appeal to polyphony, it is not yet clear how polyphony corresponds to Bonhoeffer's Christology. This will be the subject of Part II, as I investigate how polyphony relates to Bonhoeffer's Christology, which, in turn, contours his account of Christian formation.

In Chapter 3, starting with his Christology lectures we will begin to see how Bonhoeffer's Christology relies upon the Lutheran idea of promeity as it is inflected by the Kierkegaardian view of the incognito; an account of Christ's mode of being which carries implications for an ontology of Christ, as well as for ethics and ecclesiology. Thus, we will see, the metaphor of polyphony gives imaginative and dynamic expression both to Christology and to the Christian life which proceeds from it. Further examining the pattern of Christian formation which emerges from Christology, for Bonhoeffer, in Chapter 4, we will see that Christology and ecclesiology are so closely associated that the distinction between Christ and the Church is not always clearly maintained. Nevertheless, in *Sanctorum Communio* Bonhoeffer mitigates against the possibility of overidentifying Christ and the Church by means of a pneumatology.

Chapter 3

THE POLYPHONY OF CHRIST

Introduction

This chapter investigates how Bonhoeffer understands polyphony to be a metaphor for a Chalcedonian Christology. I analyze Bonhoeffer's claim that Christ himself is polyphonic in his first appeal to the metaphor, in light of his Christology as it is expressed in his lectures of 1933. This chapter is foundational to my analysis of Bonhoeffer's theology of Christian formation. Not only does it further clarify how he is using the term polyphony to articulate a Chalcedonian Christology, it also begins to unearth how that Christology corresponds to his idea of Christian formation which unfolds from Bonhoeffer's claim that Christ's presence and promeity directly shapes the Church.

First, I will examine the main interpretations of Bonhoeffer's idea of the polyphony of Christ. This will show that the terms of the metaphor are, at times, assigned a Christological significance without sufficient explanation. Of these interpretations of Bonhoeffer's description of the polyphony of Christ, the most compelling and clearly argued suggests that it generates a correlative economy of polyphony in the Church. Second, turning to Bonhoeffer's Christology lectures, I probe this line of inquiry further by examining the interrelation of Christ and the Christian. This will show the extent to which his Christology is characterized by an essential relatedness between Christ and the Christian, in which the Christian takes on a new mode of existence enabled by Christ. I argue that this description of the composite Christ's mode of being in the Christology lectures, with its emphasis on the Lutheran *pro me*, *Christus Praesens*, and two states of Christ, informs an understanding of the hypostatic union in which the finite human nature is enabled by the infinite divine Son. Drawing upon Rowan Williams's interpretation of this Christology, we will see that Bonhoeffer's account of the composite Christ carries direct implications for an ontology of Christ. In this way his Christology corresponds to a form of kenosis which I call existential: Christ's existence through his mode of being, as Bonhoeffer describes it, discloses the disposition of the divine toward creation.

With Bonhoeffer's Christology more clearly in view, I will reexamine and reinterpret polyphony as a Christological metaphor which conceptualizes the interrelationship of the divine and human natures. I will argue that Bonhoeffer's appeal to the metaphor for distinct areas of theology (the hypostatic union, the person of Christ in relation to the Christian, and the relation between God and the world) is salutary because the shapes of each of these relationships are, themselves, interrelated in his theological method. However, I conclude that ultimately for Bonhoeffer it is the polyphony of Christ which determines the polyphonic character of Christian formation (the polyphony of life).

A Christological Construct

In addition to describing the relationship between love of God and the world in terms of *cantus firmus* and counterpoint, Bonhoeffer also identifies Christ himself as polyphonic. Recall his first extended use of the metaphor on May 20, 1944, in which he remarks:

> The two are 'undivided and yet distinct,' as the Definition of Chalcedon says, like the divine and human natures in Christ. Is that perhaps why we are so at home with polyphony in music, why it is important to us, because it is the musical image of this Christological fact and thus also our *vita christiana*?[1]

He wonders whether the enjoyment he and Bethge derive from the musical phenomenon is itself grounded in the Christological pattern of the divine and human natures as they are united in Christ and also in the pattern of Christian life itself. This allusion to the Chalcedonian definition has elicited a number of responses from Bonhoeffer scholars who address his use of musical metaphors, which I will now briefly summarize.

John de Gruchy

Acknowledging that Bonhoeffer makes two observations about polyphony, the first with respect to earthly love and the second with respect to the Christological definition, de Gruchy connects the two via a reference to the *Song of Songs* which also occurs in the key passage concerning polyphony. In his description of polyphony of love, Bonhoeffer mentions the *Song of Songs* as an example of a biblical approbation of earthly love.[2] This, de Gruchy points out, discloses something of his views on Christology because he rejects the traditional allegorical interpretation of the text as a love song between Christ and the Church, writing in another letter to Bethge: "I would in fact read it as a song about earthly love,

1. Bonhoeffer, 8:394.

2. "Even in the Bible there is the Song of Solomon, and you really can't imagine a hotter, more sensual and glowing love than the one spoken of here (cf. 7:6!). It's really good that this is in the Bible, contradicting all those who think being Christian is about tempering one's passions (where is there any such tempering in the Old Testament?)."

and that is probably the best 'christological' interpretation."[3] This interpretation of *Song of Songs* further supports de Gruchy's argument that Bonhoeffer develops an interest in the aesthetic dimension of life in prison; *Song of Songs* reveals Yahweh as a hidden God who is life-affirming, he argues. Just as, in Bonhoeffer's view, *Song of Songs* and the Old Testament[4] are "Christological" without directly focusing on Christ, so, too, are earthly love and aesthetic existence, de Gruchy is saying.

The importance of Christology is such, in de Gruchy's reading, that he proceeds to interpret the *cantus firmus* as referring to Christ himself. With respect to Bonhoeffer's arrangement in the polyphony of life which likens love of God to the *cantus firmus* and earthly loves to counterpoint, de Gruchy views the former element, the *cantus firmus*, as God's revelation in Christ and the means by which the counterpoint can be developed to its limits. This Christological interpretation is by no means of secondary importance, according to de Gruchy, but is absolutely crucial to the primary meaning of the metaphor. He underscores this by stating:

> The Christological *cantus firmus* is not a fulcrum on which everything else balances in systematic equivalence irrespective of context, but rather the centre within which everything finds coherence in the midst of life without losing its distinctive character and quality.[5]

However, de Gruchy only briefly justifies this Christological interpretation. He states that Bonhoeffer's Christology "since 1932" has been characterized by a *theologia crucis*, in which Jesus as the one who is truly human and a man for others reveals "the 'hidden' way of God."[6] This obviously alludes to the Chalcedonian definition, but de Gruchy does not explore in any detail how polyphony relates to it.

Barry Harvey

In a similar vein, Barry Harvey accords great importance to the Christological aspect of the metaphor. Like de Gruchy, he associates the *cantus firmus* with Christ.[7] Of the first passage in Bonhoeffer's letters on polyphony, Harvey remarks that the connection between love of God and our earthly loves to the Chalcedonian

3. Bonhoeffer, *Letters and Papers from Prison*, 8:410.

4. Of the relationship between Old and New Testaments he wrote to Bethge: "Only when one knows that the name of God may not be uttered may one sometimes speak the name of Jesus Christ." Bonhoeffer, 8:213.

5. de Gruchy, "Restoring Broken Themes of Praise," 166.

6. de Gruchy, 165.

7. "Only a polyphonic counterpoint in concert with Christ is able to give life its wholeness." Harvey, *Taking Hold of the Real: Dietrich Bonhoeffer and the Profound Worldliness of Christianity*, 239.

formula should come as no surprise because of Bonhoeffer's "Christological focus."[8] He proceeds by quoting an extract from *Ethics*: "Human beings are not called to realize ethical ideas, but are called into a life that is lived in God's love, and that means lived in reality."[9] But as this makes no mention of Christology, it does not clearly account for the link between polyphony and the Chalcedonian definition. That is, Harvey admits there is a Christological aspect to the metaphor and suggests this is important but he does not explain this in any detail with respect to the Chalcedonian definition.[10]

Andreas Pangritz

Andreas Pangritz and Craig Gardiner provide more detailed explications of polyphony as a metaphor for the Chalcedonian definition. Pangritz offers an array of mutually inclusive possibilities concerning the allusion to Chalcedon. As with de Gruchy and Harvey, he sees the *cantus firmus* as corresponding to Christ and the counterpoint to the world, making polyphony a metaphor for expressing the Christian's commitment to "true worldliness" because of Christ.[11] He also wonders whether the analogy of contrapuntal music to Chalcedon suggests a "secret affinity" between the Word of God and music of the sort many would say lies at the heart of Luther's theology of music.[12]

But the most captivating of the possibilities Pangritz presents is that of polyphony as a positive expression for the four negative statements of Chalcedon. The contrapuntal melodies of polyphony as "an image of the Christological fact" are said to conceptualize the divine and human natures communicating with each other, "undivided and yet distinct."[13] Pangritz suggests that interpreting polyphony theologically allows Bonhoeffer to turn the Chalcedonian formula "into virtual musical movements" and "make analogical musical statements" about

8. See: Harvey, 239.

9. Harvey, 239; Bonhoeffer, Dietrich, *Ethics*, 232. We will see in Chapter 5 how Bonhoeffer's description of reality results from his Christological focus.

10. Elsewhere, he does discuss the significance of the incarnation for defining reality and uniting God and the world, with reference to Bonhoeffer's Christology lectures, but not with respect to the metaphor of polyphony. See: Harvey, *Taking Hold of the Real: Dietrich Bonhoeffer and the Profound Worldliness of Christianity*, 28. Harvey's bricolage treatment of Bonhoeffer is appropriate given that his overall objective is not exegetical but a constructive effort to develop the application of polyphony to theology.

11. "In contrapuntal music it is the cantus firmus that corresponds to the arcane (the mystery) of Christ; within the 'polyphony of life' it is the thematic love of God and eternity." Pangritz, *The Polyphony of Life: Bonhoeffer's Theology of Music*, 59–60.

12. Here Pangritz cites: Söhngen, *Theologie der Musik*.

13. "a lively expression of the four negative definitions of the Chalcedonian confession of Christ," which Bonhoeffer's supervisor, Adolf von Harnack, had denounced as "barren." Pangritz, *The Polyphony of Life: Bonhoeffer's Theology of Music*, 55.

Christology.[14] Pangritz describes it as follows: "Polyphony in music as adoration, but at the same time also as an image of the 'Christological fact,' that in Christ God and humanity communicate with each other."[15] In this, we are to understand, the multivalence of the metaphor is beneficial, as it describes both a Chalcedonian Christology and the Christian life itself: the polyphonic Christ in whom divine and human natures are united is the means by which the polyphony of life is known.

Craig Gardiner

For Craig Gardiner the value and purpose of polyphony in respect to the Christological definition lie primarily in its implications for Church practice, but he grounds this in Bonhoeffer's Christological application of the term.[16] To my mind Gardiner offers the clearest and most convincing interpretation of the Chalcedonian dimension of the metaphor; it is worth quoting fully:

> Bonhoeffer argues that the attraction and importance of polyphony in music might consist particularly in its being a reflection of the divine and human natures bisociated in the one person of Christ. His polyphony of heavenly *logos* and earthly incarnation was the music that Christ alone could sing. Music was a "vestige" of Christ left remaining in the world: an eternal echo of the divine epiphany.[17]

Gardiner is saying that the echoes of divinity in the world which are the result of the union of the divine and human natures in Christ (which Gardiner elsewhere calls the 'Supreme Bisociation')[18] are heard in polyphonic music, which is, then, an analogue of the deeper reality of the polyphony of Christ. This helps make sense of what Bonhoeffer means by relating his enjoyment of polyphony to the Chalcedonian definition and also to the "*vita christiana*."[19] But Gardiner's interpretation further deepens the meaning of the polyphonic identity of Christ, beyond what Bonhoeffer writes, by positioning it within a

14. He proceeds, in colorful and rather abstract terms, to speak of "an almost-musical liquefication, a dissolving of the dogmatic structure" of the bare claims of Chalcedon and of "reason liberated to maturity." Pangritz, *The Polyphony of Life: Bonhoeffer's Theology of Music*, 59.

15. Pangritz, *The Polyphony of Life: Bonhoeffer's Theology of Music*, 59.

16. Thus, he writes: "The purpose of the polyphony of Christ is to call humanity into participative performance with the melodies of divine being made known in the world. It is called discipleship." Gardiner, *Melodies of a New Monasticism: Bonhoeffer's Vision, Iona's Witness*, 55.

17. Gardiner, 56. On the idea of "bisociation," which Gardiner derives from Arthur Koestler, see: Gardiner, 2.

18. Gardiner, *Melodies of a New Monasticism: Bonhoeffer's Vision, Iona's Witness*, 54.

19. Bonhoeffer, *Letters and Papers from Prison*, 8:394.

Trinitarian theology. Drawing on David Cunningham and Robert Jenson, both of whom liken polyphonic music or fugue to the perichoresis of the Trinitarian persons, he argues that the person of Christ is polyphonic only as a result of these interrelations.[20]

A final observation of particular note with respect to Gardiner's reading is that he views the correspondence between the polyphony of Christ and the polyphony of the Church as interrelated on the basis of Bonhoeffer's Christology, especially in the emphasis Bonhoeffer puts on the Lutheran *pro me* which means that Christ cannot be conceived of without the Church.[21] Participating in the music of Christ, says Gardiner, means awareness that Christ's belonging to heaven does not restrict his belonging to earth and, vice versa. Christ's divinity does not restrict his humanity, but God chooses to bind himself to creation in Christ.[22]

In summary of the foregoing survey: each of these interpretations demonstrates the importance of a Chalcedonian Christology in Bonhoeffer's appeal to polyphony. For de Gruchy and Harvey the Christological meaning is of central importance in their interpretations of Bonhoeffer's use of polyphony, but the union of the natures which Bonhoeffer explicitly refers to is not directly discussed in connection with this. Pangritz is more precise in explaining how polyphony can image the union of the natures as a lively alternative to the negative strictures of Chalcedon. Craig Gardiner goes further still, providing an explanation for the interrelationship of Christology and ecclesiology grounded in a Trinitarian framework, which moves beyond Bonhoeffer's explicit application of the metaphor but is, I find, highly compelling. Through a careful account of the polyphony of Christ himself Gardiner manages to draw the two main uses of the term into the closest correspondence; the polyphony of Christ properly conceived makes the church's participation in the work of Christ inevitable, Gardiner seems to be saying.

The relevance of Christology to the musico-theological invention polyphony is, then, beyond doubt. Christology is intimately related to Bonhoeffer's view of the polyphony of Christian life. But how the two interrelate has not been made entirely clear in the foregoing. In what follows I will examine Bonhoeffer's Christology more closely in order to better understand this correlation between Christology and ecclesiology in his appeal to the metaphor. In so doing, we will further clarify how Bonhoeffer's musico-theological invention shapes both his Christology and his theology of Christian formation.

20. "If the one God found in the community of Trinity is by nature polyphonic, then each One of the Three is polyphonic too: the person of Christ, insofar as Christ may be isolated from the others, is then also polyphonic." Gardiner, *Melodies of a New Monasticism: Bonhoeffer's Vision, Iona's Witness*, 54.

21. "Christ was never Christ in himself but always in his relation to the world and in his standing *pro me*," Gardiner writes with reference to the Christology lectures. Gardiner, *Melodies of a New Monasticism: Bonhoeffer's Vision, Iona's Witness*, 55.

22. Gardiner, *Melodies of a New Monasticism: Bonhoeffer's Vision, Iona's Witness*, 57.

The Christology Lectures

Bonhoeffer delivered his Christology lectures at Berlin University in the summer semester of 1933 and they are seen by Bethge as marking the apex of his academic career.[23] Their published form in *DBW* and *DBWE* comprises the notes of Bonhoeffer's student Gerhard Riemer, cross-referenced with other students' notes where relevant.[24] As such, care should be exercised to interpret Bonhoeffer's meaning without expecting theological precision from every sentence. Nevertheless, Bonhoeffer's approach to Christology is sufficiently distinctive and the lectures are consistent enough with his thought elsewhere, that we can identify his leading ideas with a certain degree of confidence.

A brief outline of the course will assist this examination. The lectures open with "The Development of the Christological Question" and "The Person and Work of Christ." Part One addresses "The Present Christ—The Pro-Me" which examines: (1) "The Form of Christ" as i. Word; ii. Sacrament; and iii. church-community; and (2) "The Place of Christ" as (i) the Centre of Our Existence; (ii) the Centre of History; and (iii) the Centre of Nature. Part Two, on "The Historical Christ," addresses, first, the question of "access to the historical Christ"; and, second, a history of "critical or negative Christology," which especially looks at various heresies in Christology. Finally, tacked on to the end of Part Two, but appearing as if it should form a distinct third part, Bonhoeffer discusses positive Christology in two sections: "The One who became humiliated"; and the two states of Christ, humiliated and exalted.

In what follows, I will focus my analysis of the lectures, initially at least, on Bonhoeffer's point of departure ("The Development of the Christological Question") for its modulating effect on the remainder of the lectures and, indeed, on his subsequent approach to Christology beyond the lectures. After this I will address "The Person and Work of Christ" in which he describes the presence and promeity of Christ. Bonhoeffer's highly distinctive Christology is evident in his insistence on the composite Christ and, at the same time, a decisive Lutheranism is also strongly indicated by his emphasis on the presence and promeity of Christ. Upon further examination, we will see that the composite Christ's mode of being as characterized by his promeity and presence carries significant implications not only for Bonhoeffer's ecclesiology but also, as I will argue, for an ontology of Christ. At this juncture Rowan Williams's recent reading of Bonhoeffer's Christology, which makes a strong case for its kenotic character, is highly relevant to our interpretation.

23. According to Bethge. Bethge, *Dietrich Bonhoeffer: Theologian, Christian, Contemporary*, 164.

24. By contrast to the first publication of the lectures in English, *Christ the Center* (1966) which was a composite recreation based on the notes of several students, *DBW* and *DBWE* rely solely on the notes of Gerhard Riemer, transcribed in 1960 from the shorthand original of 1933. His original long-hand notes having been destroyed. See: FN [1], Bonhoeffer, "Lectures on Christology," 299.

Who Is Jesus Christ?

The lectures are highly distinctive from the outset, as Bonhoeffer argues that the task of all theology is Christological and this Christology must be approached via the question, "Who is Jesus Christ?" as opposed to asking "*How* is Jesus Christ?"[25] What may initially appear to be an overtly simplistic observation, even a superficial device to capture students' attention, holds considerable weight in Bonhoeffer's theology. The question recurs and orientates his theology until the very end, as we have seen with respect to its updated form in *Letters*: "Who is Jesus Christ, for us, today?" According to Rowan Williams the question "carries doctrinal implications" which Bonhoeffer clarifies as his Christology develops.[26] Ernst Feil concurs, suggesting that it is this point of departure that allows Bonhoeffer to develop his Christology in the way he does and that this even carries potential value for the Christology in and of itself.[27]

A more conventional approach to Christology asks, "How is Jesus Christ God and man?" with a view to accounting for how Christ is one person in two natures. This commits a myriad of ills, Bonhoeffer argues. To demonstrate, he delineates a selection of the major treatments of Christology (in modernity, the Reformation and post-Reformation period, and early Church)[28] and, in this way,

25. Identifying theology as the scholarly discipline par excellence, Bonhoeffer says that Christology "as logology becomes that which makes all knowledge possible." Bonhoeffer, "Lectures on Christology," 305.

26. Williams puts it thus: "They are more than a ground-clearing exercise; the very fact of identifying—as Bonhoeffer does—a fresh starting point carries doctrinal implications, to be spelled out in his later writing." Williams, *Christ the Heart of Creation*, 184.

27. "The theological point of departure that shows itself quite clearly in these lectures allowed Bonhoeffer to pursue a certain direction in christology within which he could bring the problem of the historical Jesus and the biblical Christ closer to a solution." Feil, *The Theology of Dietrich Bonhoeffer*, 19.

28. With respect to the modern period, he is critical of Ritschl, Hermann, and Schleiermacher (for positioning Christology in soteriology in such a way that overlooks the person of Christ for his benefits). Bonhoeffer, "Lectures on Christology," 311. He also challenges "transcendental philosophy" and the metaphysical claims of Roman Catholicism which seek, respectively, the mere idea of the transcendent Logos by asking "how" or to understand the being of Christ without being confronted with his person; both subjects which he has already addressed critically at length in his *habilitationsschrift, Act and Being*. Of the Reformation and post-Reformation periods, he criticizes the way in which Reformed and Lutheran traditions sought answers to the "how" question via the *extra calvinisticum* and *genus maiestaticum*, especially. See: Bonhoeffer, "Lectures on Christology," 343–50. With regard to the early Church, he outlines the many approaches to Christology which deviate into heresy, interspersed with their modern equivalents, including Docetism and Ebionitism, Monophysitism and Nestorianism, Modalist and Subordinationist heresies. See: Bonhoeffer, "Lectures on Christology," 332–50.

indirectly delivers a more traditional course which sketches various standard approaches to Christology. But this is only as part of a subtext of his primary concern, the *whole* person of Christ.[29] Framing this overview in critical terms, he emphasizes that the problematic tendency of traditional Christology lies in its attempt to describe *how* Christ is, thereby circumnavigating what is most important about him.

What matters most about Christology is who Christ is for me, for us, says Bonhoeffer. With shades of Martin Buber's *I and Thou*, he describes Christology as the place of personal encounter with the other.[30] The question of "who" entails a commitment to Christology as personal communication which is not only *about* Jesus Christ, but also occurs *in* and *through* the person of Christ. Christ is not only the subject being disclosed; he also discloses the identity of the one asking the question and, moreover, creates the condition of faith which makes this knowledge possible. This is boldly expressed through the dialectic of the logos and Counter-logos in which the question asked of Jesus is reflected back onto the one making the inquiry, interrogating her identity in the process and, ultimately, defining it.[31]

Describing the confrontation elicited by questioning who Jesus is, Bonhoeffer's provocative and demanding language is evident, even as it comes to us through his students:

> This is the question asked by horrified, dethroned human reason, and also the question of faith: Who are you? Are you God's very self? This is the question with which Christology alone is concerned. Every possibility of classification must fall short, because the existence of the Logos means the end of my logos. He *is* the Logos. He *is* the counter Word.[32]

The encounter with Jesus Christ is high-stakes ("the existence of the Logos means the end of my logos") because the identity of Jesus as God-man simultaneously

29. "The personal ontological structure of the whole, historical Christ is the subject matter of Christology." Bonhoeffer, "Lectures on Christology," 310.

30. As Charles Marsh points out, Bonhoeffer makes no explicit reference to Buber in the lectures, although he had recently read, and praised, Buber's *I and Thou*. The influence here is unmistakable. Marsh, *Strange Glory: A Life of Dietrich Bonhoeffer*, 171.

31. "Where does he stand? For me, he stands in my place, where I should be standing. He stands there because I cannot, that is, he stands at the boundary of my existence and nevertheless in my place. This is an expression of the fact that I am separated, by a boundary that I cannot cross, from the self that I ought to be. The boundary lies between my old self and my new self, that is, in the center between myself and me. As the limit, Christ is at the same time the center that I have regained. As boundary, the boundary can only be seen from its other side, outside the limit. Thus, it is important that we human beings, in recognizing that our limit is in Christ, at the same time see that in this limit we have found our new center." Bonhoeffer, "Lectures on Christology," 324.

32. Bonhoeffer, "Lectures on Christology," 302.

challenges, and seemingly assails, the one who asks, "Who are you?" Bonhoeffer proceeds to speak of the death of either logos or Counter-logos as a result of the other.[33] This takes some explanation because it reads, on the face of it, as if the presence of the one eliminates the other. On the contrary, when Bonhoeffer writes, "the human being must either die or kill Jesus"[34] the death that he refers to is an existential one that actually results in life for the human logos.[35] Rowan Williams puts it this way:

> The *logos* of my self-affirmation, refusing to live in the presence of and for the sake of the other, is a poisonous fiction, an unreality, and as such it cannot be affirmed or undergirded by God: it is simply not *there* to be affirmed, since it exists only in the fearful imagination of a human self threatened by the incursion of God's truth. In other words, what must die in the encounter with Christ is precisely *not* finitude or createdness but the delusion that we can live in denial of our finitude, our dependence on infinite agency.[36]

What is being put to death, therefore, is not the human logos or creatureliness, per se, but rather a deception. The Counter-logos counteracts the particular lie humans believe, namely that we can live without divine agency. The independent or individual logos does not die because it never existed independently of divine sustenance in the first place. As Charles Marsh observes, with respect to the influence of Heidegger on Bonhoeffer's approach to Christology, "the authentic question is not primarily an address to particular beings in their ontic character (entities) but is the decisive way of turning to the original source of human being (of being attuned to the voice of the call)."[37] In the divine other the self finds its meaning.

There is a further dimension to Bonhoeffer's description of the meeting of logos and Counter-logos, a more overtly theological element underpinning the philosophical shades, which lies in the concrete historical death of Jesus of Nazareth. When Bonhoeffer discusses the particular historical event in which

33. "The logos cannot bear the presence of the counter-Logos because it knows that one of them must die," and "[T]here are only two possibilities when a human being confronts Jesus: the human being must either die or kill Jesus." Bonhoeffer, "Lectures on Christology," 305; 307.

34. Bonhoeffer, 307.

35. The use of the term "logos" also evinces the continued influence of his engagement with transcendental philosophy which predominates in *Act and Being*, published just three years prior to the lectures. For a close analysis of the sustained influence of that text, especially through the distinction between *actus reflectus* and *actus directus*, see: Feil, *The Theology of Dietrich Bonhoeffer*, 29.

36. Williams, *Christ the Heart of Creation*, 190–1.

37. Marsh, *Reclaiming Dietrich Bonhoeffer: The Promise of His Theology*, 120.

Jesus of Nazareth was put to death through the decisive actions of various specific humans, and the resurrection which followed, he describes the present, existential significance of this. As Christiane Tietz makes clear, the self can only transcend "the circle of the I" by the one who is *extra me*, making the reality of the other known; only through Christ's death is the *cor curvum in se* turned upward and outward to God in Christ.[38] As Tietz affirms, the resurrection is where the human logos was finally overcome:

> Bonhoeffer unfolds the life of Jesus Christ as a struggle between Jesus as the Logos of God and the human logos. He stresses that the crucifixion and death of Jesus Christ, the Logos of God, were caused by the human logos, because the human logos was provoked by the existence of the Logos of God, the Counter-Logos, which limited the human logos. The resurrection of Christ showed that the human logos finally is powerless.[39]

This conveys in stark terms the profound reality of conversion; the death and resurrection of the Counter-logos bring about the rebirth of the logos, who is re-formed in Christ's image.[40]

Jesus Christ, pro me

The question of who Jesus Christ is in the lectures is further answered by the Lutheran idea of promeity, which goes hand in hand with the conviction that Christ is present. Bonhoeffer relates the presence of Christ to his incarnate form as follows:

> The presence of Jesus Christ compels the statement that Jesus is wholly human, as well as the other statement that Jesus is wholly God—otherwise he would not be present. Thus, from the presence of Christ arises the twofold certainty that he is both human and God.[41]

Central to Bonhoeffer's understanding of the identity of Christ, the presence and promeity of Christ is not only the subject of Part One of the lectures but permeates

38. Bonhoeffer himself sees thinking according to the "how" question as a product of the *cor curvum in se*: "That we are asking the 'how' question shows how we are chained to our own authority. It is the *cor curvum in se* (Luther)." Bonhoeffer, "Lectures on Christology," 303.

39. Tietz, "The Role of Jesus Christ for Christian Theology," 17.

40. The soteriological importance of Christology to Bonhoeffer is underscored as he says: "But on our confrontation with Jesus depend life and death, salvation and damnation." Bonhoeffer, "Lectures on Christology," 306.

41. Bonhoeffer, "Lectures on Christology," 312.

his account of Christology.[42] The commitment to Christ's promeity is the closest Bonhoeffer comes to formulating an ontology of Christ; indeed, he calls the *pro me* the "very core" of Christ's person, in what he calls an "ontological statement" about Christ. He does so, he says, because it is not possible to consider the being of Christ "in and of itself" but only in relation to me, as "being-for-me."[43] He, thereby, insists that Christ is *essentially* related to me.[44] It is this characterization of Christ as "for me" which makes better sense of Williams's interpretation of the confrontation between Counter-logos and logos: encounter with the Counter-logos does not annihilate or overpower my human logos because he is *pro me*. Bonhoeffer's understanding of the promeity of Christ is the pivot of his Christology; it imbues it with a strong emphasis on a deeply personal and intimate connection between the individual Christian and Christ.[45]

The promeity of Christ has a particular form, as Jesus Christ is present in sermon, sacrament, and church community.[46] Michael DeJonge credits the undialectical "is" language in the lectures (as Bonhoeffer unreservedly states that Christ *is* the Logos, Christ *is* the preached word, Christ *is* the sacrament, and Christ *is* the church community) with an appeal to Luther's stock phrase, "This man is God."[47] Emphasizing the Lutheran core of the lectures, DeJonge

42. That is, Bonhoeffer's discussions of the person of Christ as Word, Sacrament and church community and the place of Christ at the center of our existence, history and nature are modified by the Lutheran commitment to Christ's presence and promeity.

43. It "is not a historical, factual or ontic statement, but rather an ontological one: that is, I can never think of Jesus in his being-in-himself, but only in his relatedness to me." Bonhoeffer, "Lectures on Christology," 314.

44. As the students' notes record it, he says: "The being of Christ's person is essentially relatedness to me. His being-Christ is his being-for-me." Bonhoeffer, "Lectures on Christology," 314.

45. A point echoed in Philip Ziegler's observation that Bonhoeffer's Christology, especially with respect to the idea of promeity, connects his ontology and his theology of sociality, when he writes: "If there is a dialectical relation between the ontological and the personal-existential aspects in Bonhoeffer's theology, it is one set in motion and decisively controlled by the fact that the being of God in Christ is itself ever concrete, personal and so personalizing by virtue of its gracious promeity." Ziegler, "Christ For Us Today—Promeity in the Christologies of Bonhoeffer and Kierkegaard," 34–5.

46. "To be present means to be in the same place at the same time (presence). We are talking about Christ's ability to be simultaneously present to us all." Bonhoeffer, "Lectures on Christology," 312.

47. An example of an occasion when Bonhoeffer makes the connection to Luther explicit is when he states with respect to the form of Christ: "This is why Luther says, "This is the human being to whom you should point and say, this is God! We say, this is the human word to which you should point and say, this is God!" Bonhoeffer, "Lectures on Christology," 318.

argues, convincingly, that in Bonhoeffer's Christology the words of institution are analogous to the creative Word of God spoken at creation, "Let there be light."[48] In both instances the Word of God qualifies what occurs. The orientating factor for Bonhoeffer, as with Luther, is the identity of the "divine word."[49]

The promeity by which Bonhoeffer characterizes Christ applies also to his understanding of God: for it speaks of God's commitment to his creatures.[50] It is God who binds himself to us in the Word, writes Bonhoeffer in the lectures.[51] In short, the promeity of Christ reveals a God who is for us; echoing Luther, Bonhoeffer writes: "It is one thing if God is present, and another if he is present for you."[52]

Crucially, while Bonhoeffer is clear that Christ is *pro me*, which he expands in terms of Christ being present in the preached word, sacrament, and church community, he is careful to avoid subjectivism. The potential for exaggerating the *pro me* by overlooking the objective reality of Christ and focusing primarily on the church's self-knowledge, for instance, is blocked by his insistence that Christ can only be *pro me* by also being *extra me*.[53] The *pro me* is not "an effect" but is the person of Christ

48. DeJonge proceeds: "Christ's presence in the sacrament rests on the words of institution and rests on nothing other than this word. Christ, who is the divine word, speaks the creative word that enacts his presence. To ask whether Christ really is present in the sacrament (the 'that' question) or to question the possibility of Christ's presence (the 'how' question) is to fall back into faithless forms of thinking that implicitly challenge Christ's claim to be the divine word who accomplishes what he speaks." DeJonge, *Bonhoeffer's Reception of Luther*, 70.

49. DeJonge, *Bonhoeffer's Reception of Luther*, 70.

50. As Ziegler argues: "Importantly, Christ's promeity displays God's sovereign *self*-disposal for the sake of his creatures." Ziegler, "Christ For Us Today—Promeity in the Christologies of Bonhoeffer and Kierkegaard," 31.

51. "God wanted to reveal himself in the Word … God has bound himself. And God's Word never changes—that is not God's way." Bonhoeffer, "Lectures on Christology," 316. This, as Ziegler points, echoes his earlier views articulated in Act and Being in which he writes, memorably, that God is present "not in eternal non-objectivity but … 'haveable,' graspable in the Word within the church." Ziegler, "Christ For Us Today—Promeity in the Christologies of Bonhoeffer and Kierkegaard," 31. Bonhoeffer, Dietrich, *Act and Being*, 2:90.

52. See "Word and Sacrament III," *Luther's Works*, 37:68.

53. For a closer analysis of this possibility see: Ziegler, "Christ For Us Today—Promeity in the Christologies of Bonhoeffer and Kierkegaard," 34. Ziegler argues that the promeity of Christ, firmly understood in the context of the theology of the Living Word, grounds "the concreteness of revelation and redemption" in Christ's own person "rather than in any subjective capacity we might have to appropriate his value in and from our personal and communal contexts." Ziegler, "Christ For Us Today—Promeity in the Christologies of Bonhoeffer and Kierkegaard," 34.

himself,[54] who can only be present to us because Christ is both human and divine.[55] By insisting that Christ comes to us *extra me*, Bonhoeffer relies on the prevenience of God. In this we see that Bonhoeffer's commitment to the promeity of Christ goes hand in hand with his commitment to Christ's presence.

In the foregoing analysis, which has focused on the first part of the lectures, we have seen that Bonhoeffer's Christology unfolds from a Lutheran core. Presenting Christology through the model of a personal encounter with Christ with priority given to the question, "who is Jesus Christ?" orientates Bonhoeffer's Christology. This encounter between Christ and the Christian, presented as a seemingly antithetical confrontation between the Counter-logos and logos, is modified by Bonhoeffer's appeal to promeity. Bonhoeffer describes how a self can come to understand herself or another only through the single human Self who is also divine; and this relies, moreover, on the divine and transcendent one also being *pro me*. The promeity of Christ is possible, therefore, not only because it relies on the Incarnate One, who as both human and divine is truly beyond me and able to be present to me, but also because it rests on the prevenience of God who is *pro me*. In what follows I turn to Bonhoeffer's explicit discussions in the lectures of Chalcedon as a negative theology, before analyzing, in light of this, his appeal to the two states theory by which he further specifies Christ's mode of being.

Chalcedon Christology

It is in Part Two of the lectures, among a description of various Christological heresies, that we find Bonhoeffer's explicit discussions of a Chalcedonian Christology which he will later describe using the metaphor of polyphony in the letters.[56] Bonhoeffer overwhelmingly affirms the results of the conciliar debates at Chalcedon in the lectures by stating: "Everything is encompassed in its very clear yet paradoxical agility [*Lebendigkeiten*]."[57]

Although the terms of Chalcedon were necessarily interpreted and clarified in the years that followed the Council, and continued to be the subject of much

54. Bonhoeffer explains: "[T]his pro-me is not to be understood as an effect that issues from Christ or as a form that he assumes incidentally, but is to be understood as the being of his very person." Bonhoeffer, "Lectures on Christology," 314.

55. "Even as the Risen One, Jesus remains the human Jesus. Only because he is human can he be present to us. But that he is eternally with us here, eternally with us in the now—that is his presence as God. Only because Jesus is God can he be present to us." Bonhoeffer, "Lectures on Christology," 312.

56. This covers Docetism, Ebionitism, Monophysitism, and Nestorianism, Modalism and Subordinationism and Bonhoeffer interweaves their origins in the early Church with examples from the Reformation period and modernity.

57. Bonhoeffer, "Lectures on Christology," 343.

debate between Lutheran and Reformed theologians (as Bonhoeffer explores in the lectures), it is worth briefly recounting them. The council of 451 AD affirmed that the Lord Jesus Christ, the Son of God,

> is complete in his deity and complete—the very same—in his humanity, truly God and truly a human being, this very same one being composed of a rational soul and a body, coessential with the Father as to his deity and coessential with us—the very same one—as to his humanity, being like us in every respect apart from sin.

Furthermore, the council pronounced that in his divine nature Jesus was born of God "before the ages" and in his human nature born of Mary. With specific respect to the union of the natures, it affirmed an inseparable and undivided union, on the one hand, and the unalterable preservation of each nature, on the other, "since the difference of the natures is not destroyed because of the union, but on the contrary, the character of each nature is preserved." Moreover, the natures are said to be united in "one person and one hypostasis, not divided or torn into two persons but one and the same Son and only-begotten God, Logos, Lord Jesus Christ."[58] The natures are said to be united: "without confusion or change, without division or separation."[59]

For Bonhoeffer Chalcedon is particularly valuable for what it resists: he praises it for providing a bulwark against various heresies which betray its tenets. He insists that no "positive assertion" regarding "what happens in Jesus Christ" can be made, and proceeds:

> In the Chalcedonian formula, the doctrine of the two natures has itself been surmounted. We must carry on in this Chalcedonian sense. This can only happen when we have overcome our way of thinking about the divinity and humanity of Christ as objects that are before us, when our thinking does not begin with the two natures in isolation, but rather with the fact that Jesus Christ is God. The is may not be interpreted any further.[60]

In this way, Bonhoeffer endorses a negative Christology, arguing that it is not possible to speak positively about the relationship between Christ's divine and

58. See the entry "Council of Chalcedon" in Denzinger and Hünermann, *Compendium of Creeds, Definitions, and Declarations on Matters of Faith and Morals.*

59. See the entry "Council of Chalcedon" in Denzinger and Hünermann, *Compendium of Creeds, Definitions, and Declarations on Matters of Faith and Morals.*

60. Bonhoeffer, "Lectures on Christology," 342. Likewise, he says: "What is being said with the Chalcedonian formula is this: that all options for thinking of all this together and in juxtaposition are represented as impossible and forbidden options." Bonhoeffer, "Lectures on Christology," 342.

human natures in the light of Chalcedon.[61] And, yet, the Christology lectures conclude with a section entitled "Positive Christology"; an apparent U-turn which is quickly clarified. Bonhoeffer is not now asking the "how question" by addressing the two natures in Christ, as the doctrine was originally employed, but is rather further developing his description of who Jesus Christ is in his promeity. He achieves this by appeal to the doctrine of two states in Christ, humiliated and exalted (the *status exinanitionis* and the *status exaltationis*). I offer a brief description of the original intention of the doctrine before showing how Bonhoeffer differs in his use of it.

Jesus Christ, Humiliated and Exalted

The two-states doctrine was developed in the late sixteenth and early seventeenth centuries in response to the *communicatio idiomatum*, which posits that the attributes of the divine and human natures are communicated to the one incarnate Son while the natures themselves remain distinct.[62] Commonly, the different states were understood to correlate to the different natures, the humiliated with the human nature and exalted with the divine nature, and they are in operation at distinct times: Jesus Christ is in the humiliated state throughout his earthly lifetime until the point of his death, and only enters the exalted state following the resurrection.[63] This goes hand in hand with the doctrine of kenosis which has its basis in the ancient hymn of the early Church recorded in Paul's letter to the Philippians.[64] As Bruce McCormack observes: "The building-blocks of all later theories of kenosis are found in the words ἐκένωσεν ('emptied' in v.7) and ἐταπείνωσεν ('humbled' in v.8)."[65] Kenotic theories posit the "self-emptying" as

61. He underscores this by asserting: "Thus the matter itself is left as a mystery, for we cannot enter into it within the parameters of positive thinking." Bonhoeffer, "Lectures on Christology," 342.

62. The *communicatio idiomatum* was itself a development in response to debates about the Eucharist in the post-Reformation period, and while it originated in order to resolve a sacramental dispute, it has "its technical extension in christology." DeJonge, *Bonhoeffer's Reception of Luther*, 48. For a detailed account of Lutheran debates concerning the two-states doctrine and how the doctrine also developed in the Reformed tradition, see: Hoogland, "Calvin's Perspective on the Exaltation of Christ in Comparison with the Post-Reformation Doctrine of the Two States," 11–44. Hoogland concludes this chapter by observing that it was the Giessen pattern of thought concerning the two states which became decisive for Lutheran orthodoxy. Hoogland, "Calvin's Perspective on the Exaltation of Christ in Comparison with the Post-Reformation Doctrine of the Two States," 44.

63. Hoogland makes clear that the Lutheran position was not that Jesus only became exalted with the resurrection (as though he received something new at this time). Rather, the exalted state only becomes manifest with the resurrection and ascension. Ibid.

64. Phil. 2:6-11.

65. McCormack, "Kenoticism in Modern Christology," 445.

occurring in one of two ways: prior to the incarnation or as an ongoing activity in the life of Jesus.[66] The Lutheran doctrine of the two states related to the latter, the ongoing process of how the natures relate.[67] In particular, the state of humiliation is said to be the result of "*a willed non-use* of divine attributes" by contrast to the state of exaltation in which "the full effects of the union and the communication it makes possible were realized."[68]

In the lectures' finale, Bonhoeffer creatively recasts the Lutheran two-states doctrine to promote a Christology in which Christ comes to us in humility as a result of being exalted. In his appeal to the doctrine of two states, he refuses to disassemble Christ in his two natures but discusses the two states as simultaneous, insisting that Christ always comes to us humiliated *and* exalted. He says, clearly alluding to Kierkegaard's incognito (on which, more below): "The Humiliated One is *pro nobis* only as the Exalted One. Only in seeing him as the Risen One, the Exalted One, do we know this incognito God-human."[69] In this way, he does not use the doctrine of the two states for its intended purpose, to address how the natures communicate without change; indeed, he is unambiguously critical of the doctrine of kenosis for the way it attempts to go beyond the terms of Chalcedon, indicating his willingness to depart from Lutheran tradition.[70] Unlike the doctrine of kenosis, traditionally construed, Christ's humiliation is not aligned with his humanity alone and his exaltation with his divinity alone, according to Bonhoeffer.[71] Therefore, while existing alongside each other, the two states are not in competition.

66. McCormack calls these the "two basic options where the question of the 'subject' is concerned—all others consisting in modifications of one or the other." McCormack, "Kenoticism in Modern Christology," 445.

67. McCormack's account of the introduction of a third *genera* of the communication of attributes by Martin Chemnitz in the Formula of Concord in 1577 (revised and expanded in 1578)—the majestic genus—demonstrates how the two states were virtually necessary as a result of the introduction of volition ("a local and physical presence of Christ wherever he wills"). While the focus of this was on the bodily presence of Christ in the sacrament, Chemnitz also applied it to the life of Jesus of Nazareth in his willed non-use of divine attributes. See: McCormack, "Kenoticism in Modern Christology," 446–8.

68. McCormack, "Kenoticism in Modern Christology," 448. Italics original. He writes this with regard to Martin Chemnitz's argument that the Logos could suffer human infirmities as a result of withholding his majesty and displays of power.

69. Bonhoeffer, "Lectures on Christology," 359.

70. "This amounts straightaway to a rejection of the doctrine of the two natures altogether, since it goes beyond the negative definitions at which the Chalcedonian formula had arrived. Here we have a construction of the affirmation of Christ, and not the unvarnished assertion of the 'who.' Here the question is the 'how.'" Bonhoeffer, "Lectures on Christology," 350.

71. "To be humiliated does not mean to be more human and less God, and to be exalted does not mean to be more God and less human." Bonhoeffer, "Lectures on Christology," 355.

There is a quiet echo of kenosis in Bonhoeffer's description of Christ concealing his divinity unless he reveals himself. For instance, when he writes: "If he had done signs and wonders, people would have believed him. But when it comes down to cases, he withdraws. That creates a stumbling block."[72] Yet, his refusal to align Jesus' divine nature with miraculous displays of power runs completely counter to that doctrine. Likewise, he does not align the state of humiliation with human nature, in and of itself. Rather the particular events of Christ's life, in being misapprehended as a sinner and outcast and in his death as a criminal on a cross, *are* his humiliation.[73] As Rowan Williams puts it:

> In other words, it is not that *humanity* as such conceals God—not even that *finitude* as such conceals God. It is the suffering and failure and ambiguity of *this* particular human being that is the issue, the fact that God exists in and as this specific human identity.[74]

In his particular emphasis on Christ's humiliation Bonhoeffer leans heavily on Kierkegaard's idea of the incognito, most thoroughly developed through the pseudonym Anti-Climacus in *Practice in Christianity*.[75] There Kierkegaard defines the incognito as "unrecognizability" like a policeman in plain clothes; Christ is unrecognizable and is a sign of contradiction because he does not appear as we think he ought to; that is, as God.[76] In *Practice in Christianity* the incognito conveys the hiddenness of Christ and his abasement (Dan. *Fornedrelse*) in a number of ways, but at the most fundamental level, it expresses how Christ's very existence in two natures is a paradox, a seeming contradiction, "the profoundest incognito." The God-man, says Anti-Climacus, "is the most profound incognito or the most impenetrable unrecognizability that is possible, because the contradiction between being God and being an individual human being is the greatest possible, the infinite qualitative contradiction."[77]

72. Bonhoeffer, 358. The phrasing here is admittedly rather awkward, but it is clear enough that Bonhoeffer is referring to the Gospel accounts of Jesus withdrawing from the public eye when attention is drawn to his miraculous acts. For instance, what is described with reference to Mark's Gospel as the messianic secret, in which Jesus conceals his identity as the Son of God.

73. "In people's eyes, he must have looked like a sinner. So he entered in, to the extent of his being unrecognizable." Bonhoeffer, 357.

74. Williams, *Christ the Heart of Creation*, 189.

75. The extent to which the pseudonymous author Anti-Climacus reflects Kierkegaard's own views is, itself, the subject of much discussion. Although this falls outside the purview of this work, we can observe that in one place in the pseudonymous authorship Kierkegaard designated *Practice in Christianity* the most accurate portrayal of his own views. Kierkegaard, *Journals and Papers*, 6:227.

76. Kierkegaard, *Practice in Christianity*, 127.

77. Kierkegaard, *Practice in Christianity*, 131.

But this has a further implication beyond the union of the natures in Christ, for Kierkegaard. Christ is a profound incognito in another sense, in that he does not communicate the truth about himself directly, but always remains hidden. Beyond the logical possibility of the incarnation, Christ is further humiliated because he cannot be known in a direct manifestation of his identity as God. As M. Jamie Ferreira points out, this is a kenotic Christology since it describes the emptying of God in Christ, locating the kenosis of God "in the physical conditions of Christ's poverty and suffering" as a human being.[78] We see this inflection in Bonhoeffer when he says: "He comes among us humans … incognito, as a beggar among beggars, an outcast among outcasts; he comes among sinners as the one without sin, but also as a sinner among sinners."[79]

There is a further parallel between Kierkegaard's *Practice in Christianity* and Bonhoeffer's Christology lectures, and that is with respect to the idea of promeity, already discussed. In *Practice* Kierkegaard creatively employs the Lutheran idea of promeity in his account of Christ's contemporaneity.[80] Much like Bonhoeffer's construal in the lectures, for Kierkegaard Christ is *pro me* by being present himself and this is only possible because of who he is, as God.[81] As Philip Ziegler puts it: "Both theologians conceive of promeity in ways which stress the prevenient agency of God, and locate it firmly in the *fides quae creditur*."[82]

In the foregoing we have seen that Bonhoeffer praises Chalcedon for its *Lebendigkeiten* and argues that the four adverbs of the definition restrict Christological studies and should not be further interpreted. He is clearly resistant to the approach taken in the post-Reformation debates which attempted to explain the relationship between the natures. Nevertheless, he modifies and recasts the

78. Ferreira, *Kierkegaard*, 173.

79. Bonhoeffer, "Lectures on Christology," 356.

80. Philip Ziegler observes the irony that Kierkegaard, renowned for his emphasis on subjectivity, employs the concept of promeity in his emphasis on the contemporaneity of Christ: "Unexpectedly perhaps, at the heart of a modern defence of Christian faith infamous for its radical commitment to the subjectivity of truth, we find determined assertion of the seminal importance of the objective, paradoxical presence of Christ for us." Ziegler, "Christ For Us Today—Promeity in the Christologies of Bonhoeffer and Kierkegaard," 28.

81. So, Kierkegaard seems to say that Christ is not bound by history but is present to us today as he writes: "The past is not actuality—for me. Only the contemporary is actuality for me … Thus every human being is able to become contemporary only with the time in which he is living—and then with one more, with Christ's life upon earth, for Christ's life upon earth, the sacred history, stands alone by itself, outside history." Kierkegaard, *Practice in Christianity*, 64.

82. Ziegler, "Christ For Us Today—Promeity in the Christologies of Bonhoeffer and Kierkegaard," 39. Ziegler proceeds: "Theological concern for the necessary and proper subjectivity of faith—*fides qua creditur*—arises precisely and inescapably therefrom and not otherwise." Ziegler, "Christ For Us Today—Promeity in the Christologies of Bonhoeffer and Kierkegaard," 39.

theory of the two states of Christ in a way that resists limiting the humiliation to the incarnate life of Jesus of Nazareth before the resurrection or to the human nature. And under the influence of Kierkegaard's concept of the incognito, Bonhoeffer indirectly supports a form of kenosis. In both Kierkegaard and Bonhoeffer, Christ's promeity is further modified by the incognito. The one who is present to us (contemporaneous, according to Kierkegaard) is also a stumbling block, because the way in which Christ comes to us is as exalted *and* humiliated, in such a way that in his self-revelation he always remains at the same time hidden.

Existential Kenosis

Largely on the basis of such striking similarities with Kierkegaard, Rowan Williams identifies in Bonhoeffer's Christology a form of kenosis.[83] Williams positions this in the mode of being of the whole person of Christ. In order to distinguish this from the classical kenosis which Bonhoeffer explicitly rejects, let us call this aspect of Bonhoeffer's Christology an "existential kenosis" because it concerns the existence of the composite Christ's mode of being. This expression reflects the evident influence of Kierkegaard, whose kenotic Christology locates self-emptying in the composite Christ's very mode of being; his whole existence as opposed to the relationship between his natures.[84]

In the two-natures paradigm, Bonhoeffer's presentation of Christ's humiliation is a description of Christ's basic "solidarity" with vulnerable, marginalized

83. Although Williams overlooks the works of Geffrey B. Kelly and Matthew Kirkpatrick in comparing Kierkegaard with Bonhoeffer, and Philip Ziegler and Jennifer McBride in their specific attention to Kierkegaard's possible influence on Bonhoeffer's Christology lectures (he states, mistakenly, that "[A] detailed examination of Bonhoeffer's relation to Kierkegaard still needs to be done"), he is surely accurate in saying that the extent to which *Philosophical Fragments* echoes in Bonhoeffer's Christology lectures is greater than many have recognized; that is, the similarities between the two thinkers lie not only in references to the "incognito" or idea of promeity but also in the Counter-logos/logos confrontation. As he puts it: "As, for Kierkegaard, the passion of reason is to seek out its limit, so for Bonhoeffer human logos recognizes its true destiny only when confronted with what demands its death." Williams, *Christ the Heart of Creation*, 187. See also: Kelly, "Kierkegaard as 'Antidote' and as Impact on Dietrich Bonhoeffer's Concept of Christian Discipleship"; Kirkpatrick, *Attacks on Christendom in a World Come of Age: Kierkegaard, Bonhoeffer, and the Question of "Religionlessness Christianity"*; McBride, *The Church for the World: A Theology of Public Witness* especially Chapter 3: "Christ's Public Presence"; Ziegler, "Christ For Us Today—Promeity in the Christologies of Bonhoeffer and Kierkegaard."

84. Although Williams does not use the modifier "existential" when he writes about this kind of kenosis, the expression seemed to me to be an obvious choice for distinguishing this type of kenosis. I have since discovered David Law's use of the term in relation to Kierkegaard's kenotic Christology. See: Law, *Kierkegaard's Kenotic Christology*, 288. Law uses the term to describe Kierkegaard's emphasis on the individual's relation to Christ. Here I use it to refer to Christ himself.

humanity, in Williams view.[85] *Contra* usual portrayals of power, it is Christ's vulnerability which has the power to transform humanity, Williams insists, and this he identifies in Bonhoeffer's employment of the two states.[86] "If Christ for a moment sought to coerce my response," Williams writes, "that would mean that he ceased to be 'for me' in this radical sense; he would be seeking to implement his will as a rival to mine, and this is precisely what he has forgone in becoming human."[87]

Moreover, this mode of being is shaped by the divine life itself and is, also, reflective of it. Williams puts it this way:

> [T]he significance of what is (following Phil. 2.7) regularly called the *kenosis*, the self-emptying, of Christ is not that it involves a sort of collision between divine action and human action, such that one or the other element must be denied, qualified or diminished, but that a certain *mode* of finite life (self-sacrifice, other-directed love) is so attuned to the eternal mode of divine action that it becomes the occasion and vehicle of that infinite agency within the finite world.[88]

Williams's account of kenosis suggests that Bonhoeffer's view of Christ's mode of being discloses the posture of the divine life itself, as it has revealed itself in Christ. Here Williams suggests that in Bonhoeffer's account of Christology, Christ's mode of being relies on God ("the eternal mode of divine action") to be present in the world and insofar as he is "the occasion and vehicle of that infinite agency within the finite world," he also displays God to the world. This parallels Ziegler's assessment of Christ's promeity in Bonhoeffer's Christology which stresses "the prevenient dynamism of God's self-giving in Christ."[89]

This understanding of divine agency through Christ's mode of being, Williams argues, has implications for the union of the natures themselves. He writes of the lectures:

> The Lutheran emphasis on refusing to seek ways to go behind the actuality of the God-human is clear and unambiguous in his writing; but equally Bonhoeffer echoes a characteristically Reformed concern to the extent that he refuses to see

85. "If the kenosis of incarnation is seen not as the taking on of human nature but as the living-out of a humiliated and vulnerable life, the scandal, the 'stumbling-block' is not humanity but this kind of humanity, a humanity that entails solidarity not simply with humanity in general but with the most powerless and apparently distant from God." Williams, *Christ the Heart of Creation*, 189.

86. "The divine revealed as overwhelming power or unconstrained agency as we understand those things will not recreate us, re-beget us; it will not require the death of our logos." Williams, *Christ the Heart of Creation*, 187.

87. Williams, *Christ the Heart of Creation*, 190.

88. Williams, *Christ the Heart of Creation*, 56.

89. Ziegler, "Christ For Us Today—Promeity in the Christologies of Bonhoeffer and Kierkegaard," 29.

> the integrity of the finite somehow disrupted or diminished by the infinite: the union of natures is a union that allows the finite to be supremely what it is.[90]

The implications of this for Bonhoeffer's understanding of the two natures suggest a tension in his Christology in which he both upholds a Lutheran center and is also willing to depart from it; Williams goes so far as to express this in terms of Bonhoeffer's sympathies with a Reformed theology. Leaning toward different sides of the Chalcedonian tightrope, Luther's Christology stresses the union of the natures ("undividedly" and "inseparably"), while Calvin's emphasizes their distinction ("unconfusedly" and "unalterably").[91] The result is that Reformed Christology is persistently accused of presenting an awkward union between natures, alike to two boards glued together,[92] while Lutheran Christology insists on God's full presence in the incarnate Christ, but risks eliding the distinction between the natures. Thus, Williams attests, while Bonhoeffer's insistence on the whole person of Christ is thoroughly Lutheran, his concern for the integrity of the natures, supposedly, reveals a Reformed sympathy.[93]

Debates concerning the extent to which Bonhoeffer aligns with Reformed and Lutheran positions in his Christology aside,[94] what is most highly instructive

90. Williams, *Christ the Heart of Creation*, 194. Here, Williams observes in a footnote that Bonhoeffer: "echoes the concerns of the Byzantine theologians he has criticized. And, as we shall see at more length in the next chapter, his way of expressing it has some significant parallels with the Christology of Barth's Roman Catholic interlocutor, Erich Przywara."

91. This observation is widely accepted. See, for example: Wendel, *Calvin: Origins and Development of His Religious Thought*, 222–3; Habets, "Putting the 'Extra' Back into Calvinism," 448.

92. "However, this personal union is not to be understood, as some incorrectly explain it, as though the two natures, the divine and the human, were united with one another, as two boards are glued together, so that they realiter, that is, in deed and truth, have no communion whatever with one another." "The Solid Declaration of the Formula of Concord: VIII. The Person of Christ."

93. Expressed in the lectures by his apparent agreement with the statement: "Finitum capax infiniti non per sed per infinitum" (the finite is capable of the infinite not by itself but by virtue of the infinite). Bonhoeffer, "Lectures on Christology," 346.

94. Attention to Bonhoeffer's apparent agreement with Reformed Christology has tended to concentrate on his relationship with Barth, distilled into his application of a phrase in the lectures (*Finitum capax infiniti non per sed per infinitum*) which appears to support the Reformed view that the "finite cannot bear the infinite." Andreas Pangritz, for instance, asserts that Bonhoeffer makes "a Reformed proviso" and situates him with Barth. Opposing this, Michael DeJonge emphasizes the Lutheran character of Bonhoeffer's thought by pointing to the context in which he employs this phrase. A fresh approach is taken by Javier Garcia who rejects "facile categorization" of Bonhoeffer as Lutheran or Reformed but nonetheless draws particular attention to similarities with Calvin. He finds points

about Williams's analysis are the consequences for an ontology of Christ, and the corresponding implications of this for ecclesiology and ethics (as we shall see in the next chapter). By Williams's reading, what Bonhoeffer's Christology specifies about Christ—that he is *pro nobis* by being a humble presence which resists dramatic displays of overwhelming power—reveals Bonhoeffer's understanding of the divine life itself and, further, suggests the manner in which the natures are united. Or, alternatively put: although Bonhoeffer's Christology focuses on the composite Christ, it has a technical extension in the doctrine of the two natures.

That Williams perceives implications of this Christology for an understanding of the hypostatic union, despite its focus on the composite Christ, is further evidenced by his employment of the terms "finite" and "infinite" with respect to Bonhoeffer's Christology. Williams appears to use these as placeholder terms so that what is said about Christology is also applied to the hypostatic union.[95] For instance, when Williams writes that in his Christology Bonhoeffer "refuses to see the integrity of the finite somehow disrupted or diminished by the infinite" and "the union of natures is a union that allows the finite to be supremely what it is,"[96] he is clearly extrapolating from Bonhoeffer's understanding of Christ's mode of being and applying it to the relationship between the natures. In this way Bonhoeffer's Christology, as Williams reads it, has its technical extension in the doctrine of the two natures and conveys that the divine nature is *pro* the human nature.[97]

We have seen that Bonhoeffer grounds Christology in a personal encounter with Christ which establishes an essential relatedness between Christ and the Christian; Christ is identified only in his being-for-me. I have argued, in agreement with Rowan Williams, that Bonhoeffer's account of the whole Person of Christ's mode of being toward humanity, characterized as it is by promeity and

of agreement in their respective ecclesiologies and views of sanctification. See: DeJonge, *Bonhoeffer's Reception of Luther*; Pangritz, "Dietrich Bonhoeffer: 'Within, Not Outside, the Barthian Movement,'"; Pangritz, Andreas, *Karl Barth in the Theology of Dietrich Bonhoeffer*; Garcia, "Bonhoeffer and Reformation Ecclesiology."

95. In this respect he is guilty of a criticism Michael DeJonge makes concerning the use of placeholder terms with respect to Bonhoeffer's Christology. With considerable acuity DeJonge argues that those who have identified in Bonhoeffer indirect support of the Reformed position regarding the *extra Calvinisticum* have mistakenly applied "finite" and "infinite" as placeholder terms without specifying their content or the theological locus under discussion. For instance, he writes: "To specify, as we must, the content of 'finite' and 'infinite' is to guide the conversation into one dogmatic locus rather than another"; and: "The phrases assert a relationship about the finite and the infinite but, absent context, do not specify what the finite thing or infinite thing in question is. The terms finite and infinite are in this sense placeholders to be filled in with specific content." DeJonge, *Bonhoeffer's Reception of Luther*, 44.

96. Williams, *Christ the Heart of Creation*, 194.

97. Williams, *Christ the Heart of Creation*, 56.

the incognito, specifies how the divine and infinite is postured toward the human and finite; which is in solidarity and hospitality. This, I have suggested, indicates that Bonhoeffer's Christology has a technical extension in the union of the natures.

In view of this examination of the Christology lectures, I return to polyphony in order to clarify our understanding of what Bonhoeffer means by employing it as a metaphor for Christology.

The Polyphonic Christ

In view of all of this, we can see that polyphony articulates the kind of union of divine and human natures which Bonhoeffer's Christology, according to our reading above, requires: a union in which neither nature is restricted nor threatened by the presence of the other, nor loses "their essential and habitual reality."[98] Rather, the inseparability of the natures is maintained as well as the complete integrity of each. In this way, it is "a union that allows the finite to be supremely what it is."[99] The polyphony of Christ describes the very being of Christ in which finite and infinite natures are held together because the infinite is "for" the finite, just as the *cantus firmus* grounds the counterpoint without overpowering it or causing it to lose its distinct melodic voice.

We can now better understand what Andreas Pangritz means by calling polyphony "a lively expression of the four negative definitions of the Chalcedonian confession of Christ."[100] Through the above discussion we can perceive how polyphony can give expression to Christology in positive terms by conveying the capaciousness of the two natures interacting, attuning, and resonating with one another. Therefore, in employing it as a metaphor for Christology Bonhoeffer overlooks his earlier convictions that the negative terms of Chalcedon form a bulwark against positive Christological claims. Nevertheless, he does not depart from Chalcedonian Christology—as the metaphor articulates the complete integrity of each nature interrelating—but rather manages to uphold it while also effectively expressing the positive implications of the union.

Indeed, the metaphor is particularly advantageous for expressing Bonhoeffer's Christology, characterized as it is by an existential kenosis, over alternative metaphors which rely on visually determined concepts of space to describe kenosis. For instance, imagining the self-emptying of the Son of God into a physical vessel, as classical kenosis often does, constrains Christological thought so that an antithesis between finite and infinite can hardly be avoided.[101]

98. Williams, *Christ the Heart of Creation*, 173.

99. Williams, *Christ the Heart of Creation*, 194.

100. Pangritz, *The Polyphony of Life: Bonhoeffer's Theology of Music*, 55.

101. T. F. Torrance effectively elucidates the damage of receptacle or container theories of space to our Christological thinking in both of the following texts: Torrance, *Space, Time, and Incarnation*; Torrance, *Space, Time and Resurrection*.

Polyphony, on the other hand, articulates how the natures interrelate. In this respect, it is similar to the idea of perichoresis reimagined as a kind of dance, but goes further than that metaphor by conveying the *interpenetration* of distinct natures which nevertheless maintain their distinction. This interpenetration is further nuanced by the capacity, inherent to the metaphor as an acoustic construct, to conceptualize the resonance that results from this union and the possibility of attunement. The union of the natures is a relationship in which the natures communicate a depth of reality by virtue of their presence to each other; they resound.

Conclusion

In this chapter, I have argued that Bonhoeffer's Christology focuses on the composite Christ's mode of being toward humanity; a mode of being which is strongly inflected by an emphasis on the Lutheran understanding of promeity which, in turn, is modified by a Kierkegaardian view of the incognito. For Bonhoeffer, God is demonstrably for us in Christ not, primarily, as through miraculous expressions of divine power but in the vulnerability of Jesus of Nazareth whose existence manifests suffering as he shares in the human condition. This Christology seemingly depends on and discloses a union of the natures in which the divine supremely enables and is *for* the human. This, I have contended, is expressed with accuracy and vitality in the metaphor polyphony which maintains the distinction between the natures as well as capturing the fullness of their union. In and through Christ's polyphonic being, finite reality is attuned to God. In the next chapter I will examine the ethics and ecclesiology entailed by this Christology and how this is supported, at times, by a theology of the Holy Spirit.

Chapter 4

THE CONTRAPUNTAL CHRISTIAN

Introduction

This chapter focuses on the formation of the Christian whose life forms the contrapuntal melody to Christ, the *cantus firmus*. I begin by examining Bonhoeffer's most explicit discussion of Christian formation in *Ethics* in which he describes Christ forming the Christian in personal and direct ways, interlacing this with events in the life of Christ. This confirms what we discovered in the previous chapter, that Bonhoeffer's Christology is characterized by an integral ontological relation between Jesus Christ and the Christian. In this chapter I analyze the implications of this Christology for Bonhoeffer's ethics and ecclesiology.

Drawing on Rowan Williams's careful interpretation of Bonhoeffer's Christological pattern of formation will illumine how Christ's mode of being, which we saw in the previous chapter, is modified by his notion of promeity and the incognito translates into human relationships which, in turn, manifest Christ to the world. Therefore, we will see that for Bonhoeffer, Christology not only entails an encounter between Christ and the Christian (because Christ can only be known as *pro me*) but it also necessitates an ecclesiology, what I call a "participative ecclesiology." This reading, nevertheless, raises a difficulty: the extent to which Christ can be convincingly distinguished from the Church.

To address this dilemma, I examine Bonhoeffer's pneumatology with respect to his ecclesiology in *Sanctorum Communio*, where the close association between Christ and the Church is clearly described in the phrase "Christ existing as church-community." Bonhoeffer's pneumatology in this text, I argue, ameliorates his participative ecclesiology by specifying that it is the Spirit who "actualizes" in the Church what Christ has "established." In view of this, I will reexamine our earlier discussion of Bonhoeffer's participative ecclesiology, demonstrating how this account is subtly improved by a pneumatology; an ecclesiology which depends on a carefully related Christology and pneumatology. I will contend that without a pneumatology Bonhoeffer's Christological ethics is in danger of not sufficiently differentiating between Christ and the Church.

This chapter is unusual for its lack of discussion of musical metaphors, yet it is crucial to my wider argument. Having shown in Part I that polyphony helps Bonhoeffer imaginatively describe the Christian's relationship with God and the world, and having looked more attentively in the previous chapter at Bonhoeffer's

Christological views which the metaphor also articulates, we now focus on the ethics and ecclesiology which correspond to this Christology. In other words, the pneumatology which emerges in this chapter will be vitally important for understanding the significance of polyphony as a theological metaphor for Bonhoeffer.

Christian Formation

Having explicated Bonhoeffer's Christology lectures in the previous chapter, we are now well placed to examine how they inform his understanding of Christian formation. Here, the term "formation" refers most broadly to Bonhoeffer's ethical and ecclesiological commitments; his theological anthropology. The term *Gestaltung* is used by Bonhoeffer in the explicit discussion of formation which occurs in the manuscript "Ethics as formation," which he wrote for his magnum opus, *Ethics*.[1]

"Ethics as Formation"

Bonhoeffer began working on *Ethics* in 1940, the same year that he joined the *Abwehr*, and he continued to work on it until his arrest in 1943. His struggle against the groundswell of support for Nazism in his country, which brought upheaval to every aspect of life in Germany—political, military, social, economic, and ecclesial—meant that his duties were divided between writing *Ethics*, his ongoing pastoral role for the Old Prussian Council of Brethren, and traveling as a member of the Resistance aiding the Allies. The events which led to his imprisonment prevented him from completing his *Ethics*, which remained an unfinished set of manuscripts upon his death.[2]

Ethics cannot be treated in a strictly systematic way because the intended order of the manuscripts and, therefore, the narrative arc of the argument is unknown.[3] This point notwithstanding, the editor of the English translation of

1. As described in the introduction to this book.

2. Despite his evident desire to finish it. He wrote to Eberhard Bethge on December 15, 1943: "[I] sometimes think my life is more or less behind me and all I have to do is to complete my *Ethics*." Bonhoeffer, *Letters and Papers from Prison*, 8:222.

3. Since it was first published in German in 1949 the structure of the material has changed significantly. Without a finalized table of contents and with only first drafts of all but one manuscript, attempts to assemble Bonhoeffer's intended chapter order have had to be laid aside. In *DBW* and *DBWE* the manuscripts are arranged in the order in which they were believed to have been written (resisting the more heavy-handed approach of previous editions which aimed for overall cohesion). This has the advantage of focusing the reader on the content of each manuscript rather than a supposed progression of argument. For an account of the editorial process, see: Bonhoeffer, *Ethics*, 6:33.

Ethics, Clifford Green, has identified two major themes threading through the text: Bonhoeffer's own specific context and humanity's future.[4] Regarding the first, Bonhoeffer negotiates the tyranny of Nazism in his present situation, attempting to understand and qualify the kind of conditions in which the normal ethical course of action might be overturned—for instance, the *ultima ratio* in which a consideration of tyrannicide may be permissible.[5] The second has a forward-looking focus, imagining how life beyond the war should be approached for the next generation. *Ethics*, therefore, goes beyond Bonhoeffer's concentration on the Church struggle in *Discipleship* by looking at the church's role in reforming society.[6]

Infusing both of these themes are Bonhoeffer's Christological views. In particular, for our purposes, we find in *Ethics* the necessary conclusion to the Christology of the 1933 lectures; a kind of logical outworking of his view that Christ, who is ontologically *pro nobis*, personally encounters us and exposes our dependence on God; a dependence which entails our own interdependence as creatures. This link to his Christology is so strong that Rowan Williams can claim of *Ethics* that "the Christological pattern moulds the argument at every point".[7] In apparent agreement with Williams, Green calls the centrality of Christ the core

4. In this respect Bonhoeffer addresses not only the church's struggle to resist Nazism but also the church's responsibility to rebuild life following its destructive force, which distinguishes *Ethics* from the Finkenwalde project. As Clifford Green comments: "*Ethics* differs from *Discipleship*, however, in looking beyond the church struggle and beyond the war to the tasks of peace and reconstruction; it focuses on society and history, and the responsibility of Christians and the church in that public world." Bonhoeffer, 6:5.

5. The extent to which Bonhoeffer was advocating for tyrannicide or simply looking at the ethical conditions in which it might be considered has been the cause of much debate in Bonhoeffer studies. For instance, Clifford Green leans slightly more toward the former position, pointing out that Bonhoeffer's indirectness results from the risk that his papers would be confiscated by the Gestapo. He remarks: "Put bluntly, a Nazi prosecutor who was familiar with Bonhoeffer's theology could find plenty of evidence through a careful reading of the ethics to charge him with treason—according to Nazi views of loyalty." Green, *Bonhoeffer: A Theology of Sociality*, 305. Rowan Williams, on the other hand, is more reserved when he writes: "He is not developing an apologia for tyrannicide, though he is certainly laying the groundwork for a theology of civil disobedience." Williams, *Christ the Heart of Creation*, 213.

6. Bonhoeffer, *Ethics*, 6:5. See above, 89n4.

7. Williams, *Christ the Heart of Creation*, 212. He continues "—a Christological pattern which is itself a refinement of the themes of the 1933 Christology lectures with their austere emphasis on the death of the ego in confrontation with Jesus, and the well-known injunctions of *The Cost of Discipleship*." Ibid.

of Bonhoeffer's ethics in general.[8] The Christological pattern in *Ethics* is arguably nowhere clearer than in his account of Christian formation.

The concept "formation" (*Gestaltung*) does not appear in Bonhoeffer's writings until *Ethics*. Indeed, so rare is the term in Bonhoeffer that the index to the English translation of his works entirely overlooks it.[9] Yet, it plainly appears as the subject of the manuscript "Ethics as Formation," in which it is treated at length. Here we also find an explanation of its absence elsewhere in Bonhoeffer's thought, in his demurral of practical theologians who promote formation. He writes:

> The word "formation" [*Gestaltung*] arouses our suspicions. We are tired of Christian agendas. We are tired of the thoughtless, superficial slogan of a so-called practical Christianity to replace a so-called dogmatic Christianity. We have seen that forces which form the world come from entirely other sources than Christianity, and that so-called practical Christianity has failed in the world just as much as so-called dogmatic Christianity. Hence, we must understand by "formation" something quite different from what we are accustomed to mean.[10]

In this passage Bonhoeffer illuminates what Christian formation is by establishing what it is not. He explicitly rejects "practical Christianity" which has promised results and failed to deliver. This is preceded by a critique of a series of forms of Christian living, the result of wearisome "Christian agendas," so that the conscientious reader has already endured a penetrating analysis of her own way of life. He lists various ethical modes of being (the failure of "reasonable people"; the bankruptcy of ethical "fanaticism"; isolated "men of conscience"; the responsibility-avoiding "way of duty"; the hedonistic actions of those following their "very own freedom"; the public-fearing person of "private virtuousness") which all fail because they are insufficient to the task of the Church struggle in tackling the tyrannical despiser of humanity.[11] This acts as a diagnostic of the present situation, and the same list resurfaces in his letter to his fellow-conspirators in the Resistance movement, *After Ten Years*.[12]

This bleak indictment of "practical theology" and apparent rejection of ethical systems of behavior could, at first blush, appear to contravene his thinking in *Discipleship*, where he incites Christians to live costly lives, perhaps indicating a possible development in his thought between *Discipleship* and *Ethics*. Is he now

8. "This centrality of Christ is the core of Bonhoeffer's ethics of one reality constituted by the reconciliation of the God who became human in Jesus Christ." Bonhoeffer, *Ethics*, 6:5.

9. Although it does list the terms "form," "form of Christ," and "transform." The latter two, the index tells us, are discussed primarily in *Ethics* (*DBWE 6*) and *Discipleship* (*DBWE 4*), both of which are addressed in the discussion of "formation" in this chapter.

10. Bonhoeffer, *Ethics*, 6:92–3.

11. Bonhoeffer, 6:78–80.

12. Bonhoeffer, *Letters and Papers from Prison*, 8:4–5.

rejecting an explicitly Christian way of being, in a manner which might appear to conform to readings of his late theology as being synonymous with Christian secularism? By no means. Instead, by situating ethics in the presence of the person of Jesus Christ he places the emphasis on Christ's action in forming Christians. Soon after the above passage he continues as follows:

> Formation occurs only by being drawn into the form of Jesus Christ, by being conformed to the unique form of the one who became human, was crucified and is risen. This does not happen as we strive "to become like Jesus," as we customarily say, but as the form of Jesus Christ himself so works on us that it molds us, conforming our form to Christ's own (Gal. 4:9). Christ remains the only one who forms. Christian people do not form the world with their ideas.[13]

This draws our attention to a characteristic feature of *Ethics*: the tension between ethical systems of behavior in general and true Christian ethics as grounded only in Christ. This emphasis on the *a priori* of Christ in formation is entirely consistent with Bonhoeffer's thinking in *Discipleship*. He proceeds in "Ethics as Formation" to describe a pattern of Christian formation which has its precursor in the final chapter of *Discipleship*: conformation to Christ incarnate, crucified and risen;[14] a pattern which recurs throughout *Ethics* "like a litany."[15]

In what may be described as a "tri-formative" model of Christian formation, Bonhoeffer situates Christian formation in relation to particular historical events of Christ's life, interlacing them. The incarnation is the condition for humanity, as Bonhoeffer writes that being conformed to the one who became human "is what being really human means."[16] He proceeds by describing conformation to the crucified One as being judged by God, which involves suffering from "the wounds that sin inflicts on body and soul," submitting to God's will, and dying to one's own.[17] Finally, being conformed to the risen One means being a new human being living in the world who differs "very little from other people."[18] Though there are some identifiable characteristics, such as an absence of self-promotion, the

13. Bonhoeffer, *Ethics*, 6:93-4.

14. In the final chapter of *Discipleship* Bonhoeffer writes: "To be conformed to the image of Jesus Christ is not an ideal of realizing some kind of similarity with Christ which we are asked to attain. It is not we who change ourselves into the image of God. Rather it is the very image of God, the form of Christ, which seeks to take shape within us (Gal. 4:9). It is Christ's own form which seeks to manifest itself in us … Our goal is to be shaped into the entire form of the incarnate, the crucified, and the transfigured one." Bonhoeffer, 4:285.

15. "Repeated like a litany in Ethics are meditations on the incarnation, crucifixion, and resurrection of Christ." Bonhoeffer, *Ethics*, 6:7.

16. He adds: "God Loves the Real Human Being. God became a real Human Being." Bonhoeffer, 6:94.

17. Bonhoeffer, 6:95.

18. Bonhoeffer, Dietrich, *Ethics*, 95.

transformation lies for the most part in bearing the cross, as Bonhoeffer writes: "Transfigured into the form of the risen one, they [new human beings] bear here only the sign of the cross and judgment. In bearing them willingly, they show themselves as those who have received the Holy Spirit and are united with Jesus Christ in incomparable love and community."[19]

As in the Christology lectures, we see a clear emphasis on the past historical events of Christ (incarnation, death, and resurrection) as well as Christ's presence and, crucially, also on the "real" (Ger. *real*) Christian who receives the form of Christ. He goes on to write:

> Formation according to the form of Christ includes, therefore, two things: that the form of Christ remains one and the same, not as a general idea but as the one who Christ uniquely is, the God who became human, was crucified, and is risen; and that precisely because of the form of Christ the form of the real human being is preserved, so that the real human being receives the form of Christ.[20]

An especially important aspect of Christian formation, for Bonhoeffer, becomes evident here: prioritizing Christ should not override "the real human being" who receives Christ's form. So far, Bonhoeffer has spoken about the dynamic of Christian formation in terms of a personal encounter between the human and Christ. However, Christian formation is only partially realized in these terms. It is fully realized in the Church:

> Ethics as formation is possible only on the basis of the form of Jesus Christ present in Christ's church. The church is the place where Jesus Christ's taking form is proclaimed and where it happens. The Christian ethics stands in the service of this proclamation and this event.[21]

Bonhoeffer's recalcitrance with respect to *Gestaltung* is alleviated by what he identifies as the biblical understanding of Christian formation;[22] that is, formation as conformation to Christ. It is clear that this Christological pattern of ethics and

19. Bonhoeffer, *Ethics*, 6:95. This brief reference to the work of the Holy Spirit will be further discussed in the next chapter, following our examination of a pneumatology in *Sanctorum Communio* later in this chapter.

20. Bonhoeffer, 6:99.

21. Bonhoeffer, 6:102.

22. "Hence we must understand by 'formation' something quite different from what we are accustomed to mean, and in fact the Holy Scripture speaks of formation in a sense that at first sounds quite strange … This does not happen as we strive to 'become like Jesus,' as we customarily say, but as the form of Jesus himself so works on us that it molds us, conforming our form to Christ's own (Gal. 4:9)." Bonhoeffer, 6:93. As the editor observes, the correct scriptural reference which speaks of Christ being "formed" is actually Gal. 4:19 ("My dear children, for whom I am again in the pains of childbirth until Christ is formed in you").

ecclesiology is not another ethical program, something which he vehemently derides. For instance, there is no suggestion that the tri-formative pattern he outlines entails a progression in which the Christian advances along a series of stages. Rather than providing a static model of formation which relies on past historical events in the life of Christ as a blueprint for imitation, Bonhoeffer's pattern of formation is more dynamic; Christ is alive and actively engages in forming the Christian.

Nevertheless, there is a degree of opacity to this account of formation. While insisting on the real presence of Christ in forming the Christian, Bonhoeffer also insists on the present relevance of the incarnation, death, and resurrection, but he does not explain how the two relate. It is unclear how the historical actuality of the past events in the life of Jesus of Nazareth integrates with Christ's present relation to the Christian. Furthermore, while the pattern of being accepted as human, judged, and renewed is decidedly not a program in the sense of following a line of progression, it is less clear whether it describes the one-off moment of becoming a Christian or an ongoing process of sanctification. These issues are best addressed by inquiring as to how Bonhoeffer maintains the distinction between the integrity of the Christian, or the Church, and the integrity of Christ. We can frame this most directly in the form of a question: How do Christ's agency and the agency of the Christian interact in Bonhoeffer's account of ethics?

We will see that Bonhoeffer closely aligns the ongoing presence of Christ with the Church in such a way that they can appear to be undifferentiable; that is, the unbreakable ontological relation between Christ and the Christian which characterizes his Christology presents some problems within the locus of his ecclesiology. In what follows I will draw on Rowan Williams's explication of Bonhoeffer's Christological ethics and ecclesiology to further demonstrate the importance, and the difficulty, of distinguishing Christ from the Church in Bonhoeffer's Christologically infused ethics and ecclesiology. After this, I will further evaluate Bonhoeffer's Christological ecclesiology by examining his pneumatology in *Sanctorum Communio*.

Christological Ethics and Ecclesiology

As I have already stipulated, Williams emphasizes the continuity between Bonhoeffer's ethics and ecclesiology, especially as they are presented in *Ethics* and his Christology lectures. To use Williams's terms as discussed in the previous chapter, the shape of Bonhoeffer's Christology enables the integrity of finite existence (allowing "the finite to be supremely what it is"),[23] and this, in turn, determines that the content of that finite existence is shaped by radical other-directedness. That is to say, "the solidarity of Creator and creation" within Christ shapes all finite relationships. Thus, with respect to Bonhoeffer's Christologically

23. Williams, *Christ the Heart of Creation*, 194.

patterned *Ethics*, Williams interprets Bonhoeffer as saying that the human's dependence on God which is revealed by the personal encounter with Christ is evident in the interdependence of human relationships. Moreover, Williams argues, through these human relationships the "divine act" extends itself.[24] He puts it this way:

> where the interdependence of human life shows the radical quality of Christ's responsibility and representation … *it becomes a manifestation of Christ's underlying and ongoing agency.*[25]

In saying this he demonstrates that human relationships which express Christ's mode of being actually manifest Christ in creation.[26] In this way Christians cooperate with Christ by living out a pattern of connecting which is made possible by Christ. Christ's presence and promeity not only provide a pattern to live by, a mode of being that we can imitate, but effectively transform our relationships.[27]

To spell this out Williams elaborates on Bonhoeffer's description of the mandates and *Stellvertretung* ("vicarious representative action") which shape the "interdependence" of human life in order that it might maximally represent and manifest Christ's agency. Although, he concedes, the mandates are somewhat outdated (for instance, the conservatism of Bonhoeffer's description of the father's role in family life),[28] they describe the nexus of human relationships in which we are *necessarily* involved and thereby have unavoidable responsibility. These relationships, as we saw in Chapter 1, are: work and culture; family life and government. But it is the concept of *Stellvertretung* which characterizes these relationships above all and connects Christ's mode of being and that of the Church.

24. "It is *the solidarity of Creator and creation* … a free divine act of self-immersion into the networks of the created world. And this divine act seeks to extend itself as human agents are incorporated into Christ, and Christ's solidarity with the whole world is formed in them." Williams, *Christ the Heart of Creation*, 203. Italics original.

25. Williams, *Christ the Heart of Creation*, 204. Italics mine. He also writes, with respect to the passages we have examined in "Ethics as Formation": "[More specifically,] this means human agents taking on the representative and responsible role that Christ exercises." Williams, *Christ the Heart of Creation*, 203.

26. "The Christological transformation of humanity is the transformation of all our constitutive relationships as humans so that they are now able to move more freely towards this maximal for-otherness." Williams, *Christ the Heart of Creation*, 204.

27. "Bonhoeffer outlines a Christological ethic not primarily in terms of an 'external' imitation of Christ but as the outworking of a transformation of human agency into the kind of life that is uninterruptedly embodied in Jesus—the consistent refusal of a place to defend and the allied readiness to stand in the other's place for their good or their rescue." Williams, *Christ the Heart of Creation*, 215–16.

28. Williams, *Christ the Heart of Creation*, 203.

Williams defines *Stellvertretung* as "acting in or from the place of another, 'standing in' for the other, being actively there on behalf of the other, negotiating for the other."[29] Crucially this is located in Christ's own *Stellvertretung*, so that it is on the ground that Christ already stands with the other that I must stand with them.[30] Here Williams raises an extremely important question with respect to *Stellvertretung* as he writes: "If, as Bonhoeffer asserts, Christ's incarnate identity is nothing other than 'standing in' for us, and if this establishes that human life is in its essence a 'standing in' for one another, what is the content of this representative action?"[31]

Williams's answer is that *Stellvertretung* should neither look like an idealistic but impossible aim to save the world nor well-intentioned, but victimizing, attempts at neighborly love.[32] Rather than providing detailed particulars of what *Stellvertretung* will entail (an impossible task but also one that would contradict his clear critique of ethical programs) what Bonhoeffer instead gives us in his Christological topology is a means of developing ethical discernment. Williams puts it this way:

> The Christological "directedness" of our behaviour means that we must learn to ask how we may act so as to relinquish whatever fashions, conventions and securities prevent us from standing with another, whatever self-images protect us from seeing the reality of another, whatever generalities block our attention to the particularity of another. This is how ethical discernment embodies the death that the human ego undergoes in the presence of Christ.[33]

Ethical behavior, as Williams points out, is often hum-drum, boring, and repetitive,[34] yet it is through regular acts of obedience that a rhythm is established which will make any interruptions plain, providing a diagnostic "for clashes of duty, acute temptation or whatever."[35]

29. Williams, *Christ the Heart of Creation*, 203.

30. "The other person I encounter is already the one with whom Christ is in solidarity, and the death I must endure is the death of anything that stops me acknowledging that and acting accordingly." Williams, *Christ the Heart of Creation*, 209.

31. Williams, *Christ the Heart of Creation*, 207.

32. He rightly argues that "It must be more than just a way of underlining the imperative to give priority to the need of the other, and it is certainly not a sentimental injunction to search for objects of benevolence." Williams, *Christ the Heart of Creation*, 207.

33. Williams, *Christ the Heart of Creation*, 208.

34. He explains that the Lutheran "mandates" work, family, state, and Church which Bonhoeffer discusses in *Ethics*, as an alternative to the "orders of creation," are "routine ethical practice." The faithful completion of the mandates is habit-forming as it is the task of daily ethical obedience which conditions Christians to be able to respond appropriately when faced with more complicated ethical dilemmas.

35. Williams, *Christ the Heart of Creation*, 208.

In answer to the primary question we asked following our discussion of "Ethics as Formation" (how do Christ's agency and the agency of the Christian interact in Bonhoeffer's account of ethics?), there are three ways in which we can see Christ's agency and human agency interacting according to Williams. Examining these will not only demonstrate the perspicuity of Williams's reading of Bonhoeffer's Christological ethics but will also expose some of the challenges of Bonhoeffer's Christological ethics.

First, Williams carefully articulates how Christ and those who seek to follow him (Williams, unlike Bonhoeffer, rarely uses the terms "Christian" or "church") interact in such a way that through the agency of Christians Christ is actually manifest in the world. At the same time, Williams strongly affirms that, according to Bonhoeffer, Christlikeness is achieved through the transformative work of Christ himself; it is Christ who transforms those who are now "Christologically directed." This is consistent with what we saw in "Ethics as Formation": Bonhoeffer leaves no room for construing ethical behavior as a self-generated effort to imitate Christ.

The second clarification we can take from Williams's interpretation concerning the interrelation of Christ's agency and human agency in Bonhoeffer is that the two are not in competition. Williams, we have seen, draws particular attention to the relationship between finite and infinite (in which the integrity of the former is enabled by the latter), which he derives from Bonhoeffer's description of Christ; as seen, for instance, in his description of *Stellvertretung.* Consequently, human relationships as properly characterized by Christ are self-othering rather than self-defended. In the personal life of the Christian, the Christian "stands in" for others on the basis of the transformation of her ego in relation to Christ.[36] Williams also sheds light on the significance of this at an institutional level. The Church is not in competition with the world; it is not distinct from the world for the purpose of its own self-protection or self-aggrandizement but in order to benefit the world, as an expression of Christ's solidarity with the world.[37]

Third, Williams's interpretation of Bonhoeffer's Christological ethics with respect to the relation between Christ's agency and human agency underscores the importance of the distinct integrity and reality of humanity and the world.

36. As Williams puts it: "The other-directed life is what I now, as a believer, live by in every approach to every finite other." Williams, *Christ the Heart of Creation*, 210.

37. As Bonhoeffer says elsewhere in *Ethics*: "The space of the church is not there in order to fight with the world for a piece of its territory, but precisely to testify to the world that it is still the world, namely, the world that is loved and reconciled by God." Bonhoeffer, 6:63. We will discuss this further in the next chapter as we address Bonhoeffer's search for suitable metaphors to express this idea. Williams puts it this way: "The church inevitably appears as a visible social unit—and thus it occupies real space in the world; it jostles up against other social forms. But its fundamental challenge is to occupy that space *solely* for the sake of the world's eschatological solidarity." Williams, *Christ the Heart of Creation*, 202.

Williams's reading emphasizes the value of the world and humanity becoming *more fully* what it is through the incarnation.[38] As the divine and human natures maintain their integrity while also interacting, the world and the Church maintain their distinct identities while also interacting with God-in-Christ. Briefly appealing to our musical metaphor, we can say that the contrapuntal melodies of the world and the Church are discrete while also resounding with the *cantus firmus* of Christ who is heard through them.

In short, then, there is an ongoing relation between Christ's agency and the Christian's but there is also an emphasis on their distinctness. Williams's nuanced interpretation of Bonhoeffer's account of Christian formation describes how human agents *manifest* Christ's agency through their own patterns of relating. These patterns of relating, as grounded in Bonhoeffer's Christology, are further characterized by non-territorialism and the value of upholding and even enabling distinct integrities. Through Williams's account, we can see that Bonhoeffer's description of participating in Christ essentially creates an ecclesiological structure, a "participative ecclesiology," in which those who have been transformed by Christ are distinguishable by their service to others; ethical behaviors which are only possible because of Christ, and which themselves transform the world. This is a depiction of the church community as a people who are radically hospitable, standing with those who suffer and, in so doing, sharing in their suffering; taking a risk in being identified with the outcast;[39] a reading of Christ and the Church which ingeniously challenges the church's relation to power at an institutional level, while also expressing how a people who follow simply in the way of Christ subtly and even unwittingly transform the world.

But this reading of Bonhoeffer is not without some problems, in particular with respect to the way in which Williams, in his discussion of Bonhoeffer, negotiates Christ's ongoing relation to the Church. In this analysis, Christ's agency appears to retreat to the background, behind the human relationships which reflect Christ; it is these relationships that seem to be the primary, even exclusive way that Christ is present and active in the world today. We see this when Williams states: "The key point is that Christ has *no 'identity' that is not an embodying of unconditional solidarity with us and of acceptance of our vulnerable, guilty and desperate condition*."[40] Construing Christ's identity so narrowly in terms of solidarity with humanity raises a number of issues. I will draw out two main issues here: the first broadly Christological, and the second, its ethical corollary.

38. "the union of natures is a union that allows the finite to be supremely what it is." Williams, *Christ the Heart of Creation*, 194.

39. John Swinton's work, in particular, comes to mind, as he describes the church community as a place of hospitality among strangers; as Christ himself was a stranger on earth, evidenced throughout the Gospels, so too Christians are strangers who minister to the world through hospitality. See, for example: Swinton, *Dementia: Living in the Memories of God*. Chapter Ten specifically addresses the subject of hospitality among strangers.

40. Williams, *Christ the Heart of Creation*, 209. My emphasis.

First, Christologically, we must inquire as to the substantial identity of Christ and, related to this, the question of his actual presence. In his reading of Bonhoeffer, Williams insists on Christ's other-directed behavior, in which Christ "above all others has no territory to defend, nothing that impedes his solidarity." This comes dangerously close to suggesting that Christ lacks any identity to share with us; or, alternatively, it would seem by this interpretation that Bonhoeffer makes Christ merely a vehicle for the infinite's solidarity with the finite, or vice versa. Although Williams's interpretation of Bonhoeffer effectively corrects persistent and harmful suppositions about the dominance of divine power, if the content of Christ is nothing other than his solidarity with the finite (if he has "no 'identity' that is not an embodying of unconditional solidarity with us") and this also displays the Creator's solidarity with the creation, we are left wondering about other, perhaps more traditional construals of divine power (for instance, miracles or answered prayer) which suggest a more direct mode of divine involvement.

Moreover, how Christ is related to the world apart from the Church is not entirely clear in Williams's reading of Bonhoeffer. At this juncture, it seems that he might be guilty of underplaying Bonhoeffer's insistence that Christ is really present and active. Although Williams does recognize that, according to Bonhoeffer, Christ has really transformed humanity, the emphasis he places on human relationships as "representative" of Christ can sound, on the one hand, like human relationships are merely imitating Christ or, on the other, as though Christ's ongoing activity is entirely dependent upon these human interrelations.

Second, there are significant ethical consequences of this view of Christ, if Williams's interpretation of Bonhoeffer is correct, with respect to how it informs the Christian imagination. Focusing on Christ's "unconditional solidarity" with us in "our vulnerable, guilty and desperate condition"[41] without also discussing the possibility of divine help appears to leave humanity impeded by its brokenness. If Christ's identity is nothing other than solidarity with us in our vulnerability what, if any, can our expectations be of Christ's help? The ministry of Jesus of Nazareth, which reaches its climax with the resurrection, seems to invite us to hope in the merciful possibility of freedom from oppression, release from captivity; ultimately in life instead of death.

Further, Williams's insistence on our undefended attitude to the other based on Christ's solidarity with us seems to prioritize our patterns of connectedness over self-preservation. But what happens when these relationships genuinely threaten our lives? Is self-preservation entirely precluded in this account of Christian formation? A mode of being which is nothing other than vulnerable to the other leaves open significant possibilities of abuse.[42]

41. Williams, *Christ the Heart of Creation*, 209.

42. A possibility which Bonhoeffer's description of *Stellvertretung* does open the door to, as Lisa Dahill observes in her important study which takes into account the impact of such theology on female victims of domestic abuse. See: Dahill, *Reading from the Underside of Selfhood: Bonhoeffer and Spiritual Formation.*

Do these difficulties result from misconstruing Bonhoeffer's account or do they result from Bonhoeffer's Christologically centered ethics itself? In what follows, we will see how Bonhoeffer's participative ecclesiology does leave itself open to a loss of distinction between Christ and the Church, but that he ameliorates this with a theology of the Holy Spirit. To address the subject of Bonhoeffer's appeal to the agency of the Holy Spirit for his Christologically centered ecclesiology we turn to *Sanctorum Communio.*

The Church through Christ and the Spirit

Aspects of Bonhoeffer's first dissertation have been highly praised for their enduring merit,[43] but there has been a tendency to view the pneumatology in that text as either deficient or to overlook it altogether.[44] This is the result, in part, of a wider, prevailing inclination to ignore Bonhoeffer's discussions of the Holy Spirit, as exemplified by Rowan Williams bald statement: "Reference to the Holy Spirit in his entire corpus is slight—not absent, as a glance at his hermeneutics will confirm, but not strongly developed in relation to his Christology."[45] Not only

43. Karl Barth called *Sanctorum Communio* a "theological miracle" and seemingly implied that Bonhoeffer's theological thought reached its zenith in his first dissertation. He wrote: "If there is one thing that justifies Reinhold Seeberg, it may lie in the fact that there emerged from his school this man and this thesis which, with its broad and deep vision, not only rouses the deepest respect when one looks back at the situation at the time, but also is to this very day more instructive, more stimulating, more enlightening and more truly 'edifying' to read than a great deal of the better-known writing that has since been published on the problem of the church." Barth, *Church Dogmatics*, IV.2:641.

44. For instance, Clifford Green, whose appraisal of *Sanctorum Communio* remains invaluable, does not recognize a pneumatology in that text; despite acknowledging that the Spirit has a role in "actualizing," he apparently does not consider this to be developed enough to call it a pneumatology. Green, *Bonhoeffer: A Theology of Sociality*, 19–65. In response to D. S. Bachtell's observation (in an unpublished thesis) that reference to the Holy Spirit is entirely lacking in Bonhoeffer's works except in *Sanctorum Communio*, Ann Nickson remarks that, on the contrary, the "pneumatological inadequacies" are most conspicuous in that text. She writes: "in my view it is in that early work that the pneumatological inadequacies are most obvious, particularly in the concept of 'Christ existing as the church', where a greater role for the Spirit seems to be required." Nickson, *Bonhoeffer on Freedom: Courageously Grasping Reality*, 59. In what follows it is precisely this expression in which we will locate Bonhoeffer's pneumatology in *Sanctorum Communio*, *contra* Nickson.

45. Williams, *Christ the Heart of Creation*, 197. Williams is not alone in this assessment, as Michael Mawson observes: "It is noteworthy that Bonhoeffer's account of the work of the Holy Spirit in *Sanctorum Communio* has not received much attention, and indeed it has often been suggested that his wider theology lacks an adequate pneumatology." Mawson, "Christ, Spirit, and Church," 128.

does this overlook a number of other discussions of the Holy Spirit in Bonhoeffer's works themselves,[46] but this also fails to recognize a growing body of support for the central role the Spirit plays in Bonhoeffer's account of a Christologically conditioned ecclesiology.[47]

For instance, Christiane Tietz describes the role of the Holy Spirit in the close identification of Christ and the Church in *Sanctorum Communio* in terms of "actualizing" the effect of Christ in the Church, as follows: "Even if in Christ the church has become realized for eternity, the Church only becomes actualized in time through the Holy Spirit, as the Spirit leads concrete, empirical human beings into the church through the church's words about the crucified and risen Christ (cf. *DBWE* 1: 157f.)."[48]

In apparent agreement with Tietz, that for Bonhoeffer the Spirit is vital to understanding how the historical Church is concretely, visibly and empirically the body of Christ, Tom Greggs writes:

> To understand Bonhoeffer's ecclesiology through a singular focus on its relation to Christology would be to neglect the operation of God the Holy Spirit in Bonhoeffer's account of the saving divine economy. While the church-community is certainly the body of Christ, the efficient cause that brings about its existence in time is the action of the person of the Holy Spirit. The church is

46. In addition to *Sanctorum Communio*, Bonhoeffer produced two essays for his theological studies on the Holy Spirit (the first, to which Williams is probably referring, on the pneumatological interpretation of scripture and the second, a seminar paper on the Holy Spirit according to Luther), he writes inquiringly of the intractable problem of differentiating the Holy Spirit's agency from human agency in *Creation and Fall* and there are various references to the Spirit throughout *Ethics*, some of which are vital to his argument in that text and are discussed in the next chapter. Furthermore, the writings of the Finkenwalde period reflect Bonhoeffer's views on the Spirit's role in the life of the Church at some length. See, for instance, his description of Pentecost as "a one-time revelation of God in salvation-history—analogous to the event of the incarnation" and his extensive teaching on the Spirit's role in establishing the Church which we also discuss in Chapter 5. Bonhoeffer, *Theological Education at Finkenwalde: 1935–1937*, 14:488; 434–76. See: the entire second half of *Discipleship* in which he addresses baptism in the Spirit and in creating the church community. See also: Bonhoeffer, *Creation and Fall*, 3:64.

47. The most recent handbook of Dietrich Bonhoeffer contains a whole chapter on The Holy Spirit. See: Holmes, "The Holy Spirit." (See also below.) Compare this to another esteemed reference book for Bonhoeffer studies, *The Cambridge Companion to Dietrich Bonhoeffer* published two decades earlier, in which the Holy Spirit is not only absent as a chapter but is not mentioned in the entirety of that text (according to the index). This is just one example of Bonhoeffer scholarship embracing the subject of the Holy Spirit in Bonhoeffer's thought. Others are discussed in more detail in the chapter.

48. Tietz, "Christology," 156.

> the church only as it is realized and actualized by an act of God in Jesus Christ *through the agency of the Holy Spirit*.[49]

Following a similar trajectory, Javier Garcia views the Holy Spirit's activity as integral to Bonhoeffer's account of Christ's continued presence in the Church as Word and Sacrament. He views *Sanctorum Communio* together with *Life Together* as "adding a pneumatological dimension to Bonhoeffer's doctrine of ecclesial participation in Christ."[50] He proceeds: "On the level of theological anthropology, the Holy Spirit is the divine agent behind personhood, restoring the broken ontic and ethical basic relations, and creating persons in community, both in their relation to God and to each other."[51]

Add to this Christopher R. J. Holmes's comment on Bonhoeffer that "the new humanity whose ontological reality is Christ becomes socially and historically real in the community of the church by the work of the Holy Spirit".[52] In light of the foregoing opinions of a number of Bonhoeffer scholars we can say with some confidence that Bonhoeffer *does* have a theology of the Holy Spirit.[53] Moreover, we see something of a consensus of opinion concerning the importance of the role of the Holy Spirit in his theology. It will be incumbent upon me in what remains of this chapter to explain how this pneumatology functions for Bonhoeffer; how it plays a significant, even vital, role in Bonhoeffer's participative ecclesiology, in *Sanctorum Communio* at least. Before I can begin to address this question, however, I must briefly describe the kind of text *Sanctorum Communio* is and its importance in the Bonhoeffer corpus.

49. Greggs, "Ecclesiology," 232. Italics original. In agreement with my observation concerning the paucity of appreciators of Bonhoeffer's writing on the Holy Spirit, Greggs proceeds: "This latter point is much overlooked in the extant literature on Bonhoeffer, who (like many Lutherans) is often criticized (wrongly perhaps) for an underdeveloped pneumatology. But Bonhoeffer's account of the existence of the Church is one which does in fact account for both the person and work of Christ and the person and work of the Holy Spirit." Greggs, "Ecclesiology," 232.

50. Garcia, "Bonhoeffer and Reformation Ecclesiology," 174.

51. Garcia, "Bonhoeffer and Reformation Ecclesiology," 174.

52. Holmes, "The Holy Spirit," 169. Furthermore, Holmes views Bonhoeffer's descriptions of the Spirit as the agency who enables Christ to be both identified in the Church and also distinct from it, as risen and ascended. He writes with respect to Bonhoeffer's descriptions of the Spirit in *Discipleship*: "The Lord Jesus remains in heaven even as he exists as the church-community, and all this in and by his Spirit. Hence the theological distinction between Christ and his community is maintained, though perhaps not in the most robust of ways, through a creative deployment of ascension teaching." Holmes, "The Holy Spirit," 173.

53. In addition to these scholars who advocate for pneumatology in *Sanctorum Communio*, Michael Mawson's important treatment of this subject will be discussed more fully in this chapter. Mawson, "Christ, Spirit, and Church."

A cursory glance at the contents of Bonhoeffer's doctoral thesis on the communion of the saints will quickly reveal a combination of social-philosophical, sociological, and theological terms.[54] Turning to the first page of the preface we discover that basic sociological categories ("individual," "I-You" relation, and "community") are applied to the Church in *service* to theology.[55] What soon becomes clear upon further reading is that Bonhoeffer treats with all seriousness the historical reality of the Church as a people who exist in the world today (accounting for the sociological and social-philosophical elements) and also as a people characterized by faith (the theological aspects). And while the success of his attempt to bring such distinct disciplines together has been queried,[56] his resolute commitment to the social existence of the Church as the transformed body of Christ cannot be in any doubt.[57]

Further, while ecclesiology is the express focus of his thesis, the Christological heartbeat which characterizes the lectures and *Ethics* also pulses through his account of the structure of church community. Christ the Counter-logos who reveals our dependence on God, as we read in the lectures, brings us into community with God and with one another, we read in *Sanctorum Communio.*[58]

54. The subtitle notwithstanding ("A Theological Study of the Sociology of the Church"), these intertwining disciplines are evinced in the chapter headings, with the first three chapters defining social philosophy and sociology, addressing social basic-relations and the primal state and the problem of community, respectively, after which Bonhoeffer turns to the explicitly theological issue of sin and the broken community in Chapter Four. Chapter Five is the longest chapter, longer than the four chapters which precede it, and is the climax of the work, the titular 'Sanctorum Communio'.

55. "In this study social philosophy and sociology are employed in the service of theology." This is the very first line of Bonhoeffer's preface. A little further on, on the same page, he underscores the point: "If genuinely theological concepts can only be recognized as established and fulfilled in a special social context, then it becomes evident that a sociological study of the church has a specifically theological character." Bonhoeffer, Dietrich, *Sanctorum Communio*, 1:21.

56. Bonhoeffer's cousin, Hans-Chrisoph von Hase believed Bonhoeffer's dissertation was successful because the theologians did not understand the sociological aspects and the sociologists did not understand the theological aspects and neither would admit ignorance. See: Marsh, *Strange Glory: A Life of Dietrich Bonhoeffer*, 56. In a more admiring recollection of Bonhoeffer's thesis, Clifford Green observes that even his advisor Reinhold Seeberg "had difficulty with its sophisticated conceptuality and intricate argument." Yet, Green also observes more critically some weaknesses with the text, such as the lack of any empirical data on the actual social role of the Church. Green, "Human Sociality and Christian Community," 20; 27.

57. Bonhoeffer's decision to put thought to practice in Finkenwalde speaks for itself.

58. "in Christ … humanity has been brought once and for all—this is essential to real vicarious representative action—into community with God." Bonhoeffer, Dietrich, *Sanctorum Communio*, 1:146.

We are now the body of Christ which Bonhoeffer describes in no uncertain terms as "Christ existing as church-community."

Christ Existing as Church-Community

This formulation "Christ existing as church-community" (*Christus als Gemeinde existierend*) has provoked a number of critical comments which largely rest on the close approximation of the Church and Christ. Von Soosten points out, though, that it is precisely the close connection between Christ and the church community which Bonhoeffer is pursuing in his application and modification of the phrase "God existing as church-community" used by Hegel.[59] Yet, by apparently failing to differentiate adequately between Christ and the Church, the Church lacks accountability and is positioned beyond critical reflection (as Christ) or Christ has insufficient integrity apart from the Church.[60] This is the line of criticism followed by opponents of Bonhoeffer's Christology and ecclesiology in *Sanctorum Communio*; criticisms which, it might be observed, could also be directed toward Williams's interpretation of Bonhoeffer's Christological ecclesiology. But it is here that Bonhoeffer's pneumatology becomes relevant.

The Spirit Actualizes what Christ Establishes

The main way in which the Church and Christ are distinguished from one another by Bonhoeffer in *Sanctorum Communio*, as we have already read in the analyses of Tietz et al. is through the Holy Spirit. In Bonhoeffer's own words, we read in the final chapter (or second half) of *Sanctorum Communio*:

> In order to build the church as the community-of-God [*Gemeinde Gottes*] in time, God reveals God's own self as Holy Spirit. The Holy Spirit is the will of God that gathers individuals together to be the church-community, maintains

59. See the Afterword: Bonhoeffer, Dietrich, 1:295. Bonhoeffer's modification of this Hegelian phrase is important as it demonstrates his concern to differentiate his project from Hegel's; an effort that can be seen in blatant terms in his critique of idealism and the idealist philosophy of immanent *Geist*. Bonhoeffer, Dietrich, 1:43. See also: Bonhoeffer, Dietrich, 1:196; 198; 203. Although he shares Hegel's commitment to the importance of the church community as a place of revelation. See: Bonhoeffer, Dietrich, 1:130. Unlike Hegel, however, Bonhoeffer is adamant that the church does not complete a work only began in Christ. For more on Bonhoeffer's critical engagement with Hegel in *Sanctorum Communio*, see: Mawson, "Christ, Spirit, and Church," 130–41.

60. Mawson particularly points to Eberhard Bethge's assessment that ecclesiology overrode Christology at this point in Bonhoeffer's thinking, and Ernst Feil's concern that the church community was placed beyond critical reflection by the identification with Christ. Mawson, "Christ, Spirit, and Church," 121.

> it, and is at work only within it. We experience our election only in the church-community, which is already established in Christ, by personally appropriating it through the Holy Spirit, by standing in the *actualized* church.[61]

Here we discover the work of the Spirit is characterized as the actualization (*Aktualisierung*) of Christ within history. As Bonhoeffer also puts it: "The 'possibility' of the church not being actualized by the Holy Spirit simply no longer exists; the church that is established (*gesetzt*) in Christ and already completed in reality must necessarily be actualized."[62]

What does Bonhoeffer mean by distinguishing between the Holy Spirit "actualizing" and Christ "establishing" the Church? According to Michael Mawson in *Christ Existing as Community: Bonhoeffer's Ecclesiology*, in a chapter entitled "Christ, Spirit, and Church," it is this distinction which preserves the integrity of Christ and the Church.[63] In order to better understand Bonhoeffer's account of the Spirit in *Sanctorum Communio*, we will explicate Mawson's argument first with respect to what Christ establishes.

Christ establishes a new humanity, and this rests on a particular theological anthropology articulated in *Sanctorum Communio*. In identifying in Bonhoeffer's presentation of the church a fully human community and historical entity, Mawson also provides an important explication and defense of the first four chapters of *Sanctorum Communio* against those who overlook them in favor of the theologically luminescent fifth chapter.[64] Unearthing a theological framework

61. Bonhoeffer, Dietrich, *Sanctorum Communio*, 1:143. Italics mine. He continues: "we have to reflect on the work of the Holy Spirit as the will of God for the historical actualization of the church of Jesus Christ. But we must pay strict attention to the fact that here [in the church] the counterpart of *actualization by the Holy Spirit is not potentiality in Christ, but the reality of revelation in Christ*." Bonhoeffer, Dietrich, 1:144. Italics original.

62. Bonhoeffer, Dietrich, *Sanctorum Communio*, 1:144.

63. "Bonhoeffer organizes his account of the church around a claim that this community has been established by Christ and is built up in history through the work of the Holy Spirit." Mawson, "Christ, Spirit, and Church," 126.

64. He particularly addresses an early essay by American sociologist Peter Berger, one which has continued to be influential for how scholars perceive the sociological and social philosophy of *Sanctorum Communio*. See: Berger, "Sociology and Ecclesiology." Mawson shows that, *contra* Berger, Bonhoeffer's preference for formal sociology over historical-philosophy can be clearly defended on the grounds that it is easier to bring formal sociology into the service of theology because it makes fewer normative claims about human beings. He writes: "By remaining more systematic and phenomenological, they make fewer normative claims about what human beings are, and thus fewer claims that inherently conflict with a theological anthropology." Mawson, "Theology and Social Theory—Reevaluating Bonhoeffer's Approach," 74. By contrast, historical-philosophical approaches to sociology, or 'atomistic social philosophy', are more inherently at odds with a Christian sociology and social philosophy.

for social philosophy and sociology which emerges through the first four chapters, Mawson shows how this is ultimately distinct from sociology or social philosophy which is not Christian on the basis of *a priori* claims about humanity.[65] A Christian social philosophy and sociology understands humanity as being "in Christ," and this forms the basis of the social relationships of the community.[66] This means that the Church has its own inner history, which Bonhoeffer describes in terms of creation (or "primal state"), fall, and reconciliation.[67] Mawson explains:

> Primarily, this means that the Christian community, and any existence or identity therein, cannot be conceived of as a unified whole; it is only available to us as a ruptured and fragmented existence. Existing before God and in the church means existing simultaneously, and without resolution, as creatures, sinners, and those reconciled in Christ.[68]

To be clear, Mawson is saying that Bonhoeffer's theological anthropology specifies that humanity exists in a broken and fragmented state, a condition which continues to be the case in the Church. This is because the new humanity which Christ has established through his incarnation, death, and resurrection has not yet been fully realized in the life of the Church, despite being established by Christ. Thus, Bonhoeffer performs what Mawson calls "a delicate balancing act."[69] On the one hand, the fragmentation caused by the fall which results in humanity being "in Adam" (Bonhoeffer refers to the whole of humanity as the "*kollektivperson*") is *really* overcome in Christ; the new humanity, the *kollektivperson* which the Church is, is "in Christ" and Bonhoeffer insists that Christ has "really" and "objectively" established reconciliation. On the other hand, Bonhoeffer is also clear that the Church remains an historical entity which is capable of sin.

This brings us to the "actualizing" role of the Holy Spirit. In what respect can the Church be said to be "in Christ" if it continues to be capable of sin? By the Holy Spirit. It is the Spirit's work to continually actualize the Church "in Christ";

65. "For Luther, as for Bonhoeffer, the limit of philosophy is that it tries to understand the human being formally or *a priori*, apart from its standing before God as creature, sinner, and as reconciled in Christ. The insight that theology contributes, then, is that there is no such standpoint or no human being as such; there is only ever the one who has been created, has fallen into sin, and is reconciled." Mawson, "Theology and Social Theory—Reevaluating Bonhoeffer's Approach," 76.

66. Which Bonhoeffer describes as follows: "in Christ … humanity has been brought once and for all—this is essential to real vicarious representative action—into community with God." Bonhoeffer, Dietrich, *Sanctorum Communio*, 1:146.

67. Bonhoeffer, Dietrich, 1:62. Echoes of *Creation and Fall* may be discerned in this theological anthropology.

68. Mawson, "Theology and Social Theory—Reevaluating Bonhoeffer's Approach," 76.

69. Mawson, "Christ, Spirit, and Church," 132.

to continually turn the Church from sin and to Christ.[70] Therefore, what Christ "establishes" is a new reality for humanity which is fully reconciled to God, and what the Holy Spirit "actualizes" is this status of being "in Christ," as opposed to falling back into sin, and this is a continual work of the Spirit.

This pneumatology, it must be admitted, is only nascent. The Spirit's role seems, for the most part, to be an ancillary one, providing a buffer to distinguish between Christ and the Church or a bridge to connect them. At various points the original dilemma of a close approximation of Christ and the Church seems to have been replicated and replaced by the close approximation of Christ and the Spirit or the Church and the Spirit. Nevertheless, even though this pneumatology appears primarily as serving to improve Bonhoeffer's ecclesiology by avoiding an overly close identification of Christ and the Church, what this description of the Spirit's work achieves should not be passed over too quickly.

We can see that Bonhoeffer's pneumatology in *Sanctorum Communio* ameliorates his participative ecclesiology by helping him to align Christ and the Church as closely as possible without their being collapsed into each other. It does so without undermining the constitutive role Christ has in forming the Church but, instead, strengthens the distinctiveness of Christ and the Church without threatening their connection. In this way, Mawson's interpretation has advantages over those who recognize the role of the Holy Spirit in Bonhoeffer's account of the Church but underplay its importance by insufficiently distinguishing between Christ and the Spirit.[71]

Christologically speaking, this pneumatology allows Bonhoeffer to express Christ's identity both in the Church, as a reality of revelation to the world, and as risen and ascended Lord. Through this pneumatology Bonhoeffer can contend that Christ has completed the work of redemption through his incarnation, death, and resurrection and so has really established a new humanity.

70. Mawson puts it this way: "The Spirit's work is continually to actualize Christ's presence in the church. And this work of the Spirit is necessary because the church itself remains in Adam and part of sinful humanity." Mawson, "Christ, Spirit, and Church," 147. And again: "While the church is indeed a reality of God's revelation, it is so only in relation to sin and its overcoming. This means that the church can be understood as a reality of God's revelation only in terms of how it is continually being turned by the Spirit from sin and to Christ." Mawson, "Christ, Spirit, and Church," 132.

71. For instance, although Clifford Green acknowledges the "actualizing" role of the Holy Spirit, he does not always maintain its distinction from Christ, occasionally calling it the "Spirit of Christ." On the one hand he differentiates between the two when he describes the church as "grounded in the activity of the Holy Spirit who actualizes the community of the new humanity which is real in Christ's lordship of love"; on the other hand, he fails to distinguish the Spirit of Pentecost from the risen and ascended Lord Jesus when he writes: "the life and spirit of the church is continually in historical encounter with the person and Spirit of Christ." Green, "Human Sociality and Christian Community," 54–5.

Ecclesiologically speaking, this pneumatology allows Bonhoeffer to describe the ongoing reality of sin in the Church in which a people exist who are simultaneously being transformed. The work of the Spirit in continually actualizing Christ in the Church means that the Church is held accountable to the judgment of God. Furthermore, this distinction not only points to the ongoing reality of sin in the Church but also to the possibility of a fuller transformation. In this way, the Church is a place of unparalleled hope which both shares in the brokenness of the world and also points to and enacts a transformation that is yet to be fully realized.

In the following final section of this chapter, I will examine more closely what the Spirit concretely actualizes in the church community according to Bonhoeffer and, in so doing, I will return to the participative ecclesiology discussed earlier in this chapter and show the difference that a pneumatology makes to it.

Christian Formation through the Holy Spirit

Having demonstrated that Bonhoeffer does, in fact, describe the role of the Holy Spirit in his account of the Church and having demonstrated that this account of the Spirit enhances the interrelationship of Christ and the Church by overcoming the intractability of the claim that "Christ exists as church-community," I will now briefly consider a more positive dimension of Bonhoeffer's account of the Church as it is shaped by the Spirit. This will show how the pneumatology in *Sanctorum Communio* further clarifies the concept of *Stellvertretung* (already discussed in this chapter) by distinguishing Christ's action from that of the Church in vicarious representation.

Under the rubric "The Holy Spirit and the Church of Jesus Christ: The Actualization of the Essential Church" in Section 2 of the final chapter (itself entitled "Sanctorum Communio"), Bonhoeffer specifically addresses the relationship between the Spirit, Christ, and the Church in concrete terms. Here he discusses the term *Stellvertretung* at length, describing it as both "being-with-one-another" (*Miteindander*) and "being-for-one-another" (*Füreinander*).[72] He goes on to outline three ways in which the Church genuinely acts in love by "being-for-one-another."[73] These are: "self-renouncing work for the neighbour," intercessory prayer, and mutual forgiveness of sins.[74]

72. Bonhoeffer, Dietrich, *Sanctorum Communio*, 1:182.

73. "This being-for-each-other must now be actualized through acts of love." Bonhoeffer, Dietrich, 1:184.

74. Bonhoeffer does not spell out the Spirit's role in each act of love though he repeatedly uses the term "actualized" (for instance, he writes: "This being-for-each-other must now be actualized through acts of love"). That we must assume he understands the Spirit to be involved in this action is confirmed by his description of the Church in relation to the Spirit (for instance, when he states: "It is evidently a mistake, therefore, to attempt to reflect

Taking intercession as an example, we can see that Bonhoeffer understands the ethical role of the Church in *Stellvertretung* as something important, and related to, but also distinct from, God's action. Bonhoeffer writes about intercession: "In the church each one bears the other's burden and only by recognizing that intercession is *a God-given means for realizing God's purpose can we acknowledge and practice it as something meaningful*."[75] Intercession, he stipulates, should be viewed from two standpoints: that of humanity and that of God. In intercession humanity's action and God's will both distinctly operate.[76]

Human action in intercession is a manifestation of the members of the church community belonging together. The one who intercedes really does enter into the sins and afflictions of the one for whom they pray, though this is not achieved by strength of feeling (Bonhoeffer is clear that empathy is not required and "psychologism" is not the power which answers prayer).[77] As the Christian intercedes he is the vicarious representative of his neighbor, even drawing his neighbor into the body of Christ because when one person prays, the whole church community "which actually means Christ existing as church-community" participates.[78] The potential of this is greater than we can possibly comprehend, Bonhoeffer emphasizes, because we will never know what has been achieved for us by the prayers of strangers.[79]

From God's standpoint, intercession looks like "individuals organizing themselves to realize the divine will for others, to serve the realization of God's rule in the church-community."[80] Understood from this angle, intercession is no less

on the objective work of the Holy Spirit independently of the church-community. The Spirit is only in the church-community, and the church-community is only in the Spirit"). Bonhoeffer, Dietrich, 1:184; 144. This is a point with which Clifford Green agrees when he observes that it is the Holy Spirit who actualizes these ethical behaviors in the Church "It [the *Geistgemeinschaft* as *Liebesgemeinschaft*] is grounded in the activity of the Holy Spirit who actualizes the community of the new humanity which is real in Christ's lordship of love." Green, "Human Sociality and Christian Community," 55.

75. Bonhoeffer, Dietrich, *Sanctorum Communio*, 1:188–9. Italics original.

76. "For the positive form of intercession has a positive meaning: intercession must be viewed from two angles, namely *as human action and as divine will*." Italics original. Bonhoeffer, Dietrich, 1:186.

77. "A third person is drawn into my solitary relationship with God, or rather, in intercession I step into the other's place and my prayer, even though it remains my own, is nonetheless prayed out of the other's affliction and need … I really enter into the other, into the other's sin and affliction … Here, all psychologism has to vanish." Bonhoeffer, Dietrich, 1:186–7.

78. Bonhoeffer, Dietrich, 1:189.

79. "Our strength comes to us from the church-community, and we will never know how much our own prayer accomplished, and what we gained through the fervent intercession of people unknown to us." Bonhoeffer, Dietrich, 1:187.

80. Bonhoeffer, Dietrich, 1:188.

than "God's most powerful means for organizing the entire church-community toward God's own purpose."[81] Intercession relies on human action, but it only becomes effective and meaningful by God's will.

Taking this account of intercessory prayer as a case study of *Stellvertretung*, with the pneumatology we have examined in *Sanctorum Communio* fully in view, it is possible to reexamine Bonhoeffer's participative ecclesiology and the question of how Christ's agency and that of the church's or Christian's interact. Bonhoeffer's description of *Stellvertretung* with respect to intercessory prayer clearly ascribes action to God and also to the Church; both human activity and the divine will are necessarily involved. While Christ is closely related to the Church here,[82] Christ is not simply identified with the Church, thanks to the Holy Spirit who "actualizes" Christ's vicarious representative action in the Church. The Church carries out the ethical task of intercession in light of Christ as *Stellvertretung*, but their intercession is not simply equivalent to Christ's *Stellvertretung*.

It follows that *Stellvertretung* is characterized by a certain provisionality. Bonhoeffer underscores this by saying that not every act of love is a purely vicarious action.[83] This means that there is divine liberty to act or not through the works of the Church. The Holy Spirit's role in distinguishing the Church from Christ means that the Church can perform these acts of love in faith and in Christ's mode of being for the other and, simultaneously, the extent to which *Stellvertretung* has taken place will rely on God's sovereign decision to act through the Spirit. The other side of the coin of the provisional nature of *Stellvertretung*, in which the church's action cannot guarantee the Spirit's action (to actualize what Christ establishes), is that the Spirit's work is effective even where it is not recognized.[84] The Church carries out its ethical *Stellvertretung* in faith.

This is a subtle but important distinction from Williams's reading of *Stellvertretung*, examined above with respect to Bonhoeffer's ecclesiology.[85] This account of *Stellvertretung* in intercessory prayer in *Sanctorum Communio*

81. Bonhoeffer, Dietrich, 1:188.

82. "In our intercession we can become as Christ to our neighbor." Bonhoeffer, Dietrich, 1:187.

83. "Even if a purely vicarious action is rarely actualized, it is intended in every genuine act of love." Bonhoeffer, Dietrich, 1:184.

84. A point Mawson makes, too, when he writes: "This new existence is a reality in the fullest sense, irrespective of whether we as human beings and sinners recognise and acknowledge this to be the case, and irrespective, too, of the fact that this work requires continual actualisation through the work of the Holy Spirit." Mawson, "Christ, Spirit, and Church," 130.

85. Interestingly, on the first occasion Bonhoeffer discusses *Stellvertretung* in *Sanctorum Communio* at any length he particularly distinguishes it from "solidarity" (*solidarität*) which, as we have seen, is Williams's preferred term for describing Christ's mode of being toward humanity. Bonhoeffer writes: "Death can still completely separate past and future for our eyes, but not for the life that abides in the love of Christ. This is why the

would seem to challenge Williams's analysis that the primary value of vicarious representative action lies in "the patterns of connectedness" in which human relationships display Christ's mode of existence. This, we saw, appeared to relegate Christ's ongoing presence to the background of human relationships. Despite Williams's insistence that human patterns of relating are dependent on Christ's transforming work, this can, and it seems must, be further qualified.

It is Bonhoeffer's account of the Holy Spirit which enables him to secure the unique place of Christ's incarnation, atoning sacrifice and resurrection as a complete work already established, together with Christ's ongoing work in relating through the Church but also *to* it.[86] The living, animating force of Christ's action in the Church is made possible by the Holy Spirit whose living, animating force maintains the difference between Christ and the Church, so that true relationship is possible.

This account of the Church formed by Christ through the Spirit is reconcilable with many important aspects of Williams's interpretation of Bonhoeffer. For instance, we can still say that patterns of human relationships unfold from a Christological origin and continue to manifest Christ to the world. Likewise, we can affirm the implicit challenge Williams's reading of Bonhoeffer makes to the institutionalized Church in its approbation of power instead of service to the world still stands; so, too, the promotion of the Church as a place which engages in practical works of love, standing with (and standing in for) those who are judged and oppressed. These interpretations of Bonhoeffer's participative ecclesiology are by no means overturned by giving greater attention to his pneumatology. Rather,

principle of vicarious representative action [*Stellvertretung*] can become fundamental for the church-community of God in and through Christ. Not 'solidarity' [*solidarität*], which is never possible between Christ and human beings, but vicarious representative action [*Stellvertretung*] is the life-principle of the new humanity. True, I know myself to be in a guilty solidarity with the other person, but my service to the other person springs from the life-principle of vicarious representative action." It seems to me that Bonhoeffer draws a dialectic with solidarity to show that *Stellvertretung* is not only being with the other in their suffering or despair, as Williams suggests, but also by bringing hope through such works of love as he has described and as we have outlined in this chapter. Is this not what he means by "life-spring" in contrast to "guilty solidarity" (*solidarität*)? Life-spring describes Christ's involvement in the situation in addition to human solidarity alone which, after all, is sinful without Christ.

86. On this basis, Christian formation through the Holy Spirit is more accurately described as participation in Christ than solidarity, drawing on a distinction made by Mark Knight. Knight puts it thus: "The lives of individuals in the church 'with and for one another' thus flow expressly from Christ's own Stellvertretung and are characterized not by 'solidarity' so much as participation in Christ's vicarious action, of which he remains the living, animating force (DBWE 1: 147). In this way, what Christ has enduringly realized for humanity in relation to both God and neighbour is actualized in a way that is constitutive for the church." Knight, "Sin and Salvation," 218. Knight proceeds by quoting *Sanctorum Communio* and the Holy Spirit as "actualising." Ibid.

with this pneumatology in view, the relationship between the Church and Christ is given greater clarity; Christ is present to the Church without being collapsed into the Church, and through the Church Christ's presence to the world is deepened.

Conclusion

To conclude: in this chapter I have examined the ethics and ecclesiology which are tied most intricately to Christology, for Bonhoeffer, who envisages an integral relationship between Jesus Christ and the Christian. Consequently, Christian formation for Bonhoeffer is first and foremost the work of Christ conforming the Christian to himself; the incarnate, crucified, and risen one forming the Christian who is made human, judged, and transfigured. Bonhoeffer underlines the importance of preserving both the unique form of Christ and the Christian ("the real human being")[87] in this account, but how he achieves this and also maintains the relationship between them, we saw, is not always clear.

Upon further examination, the value of Bonhoeffer's Christologically inflected ecclesiology was particularly evident in Rowan Williams's interpretation. This demonstrated the significance of Bonhoeffer's use of the formulation *Stellvertretung* and emphasized how the church's ethical actions extend Christ's activity in the world; a "participative ecclesiology" in which the Christian who has been transformed by Christ enacts Christ's mode of being to the world. Nevertheless, we saw that the very close approximation of Christ and the Church appeared to erode the distinction between them.

This led us to further investigate Bonhoeffer's ecclesiology in *Sanctorum Communio*, his academic treatise on the Church, in which he adopts the phrase "Christ existing as church-community" (*Christus als Gemeinde existierend*). In that text, I argued, Bonhoeffer relies upon pneumatology to secure the enduring relationship between Christ and the Church in a way that respects the distinct integrity of each. This pneumatology, while only nascent and often underappreciated, sharpens Bonhoeffer's account of Christian formation. The "actualizing" work of the Spirit differentiates the Church from Christ in such a way that the Church remains an historical entity in which sanctification occurs as both the reality of sin is present as well as the reality of Christ's revelation. Furthermore, Christ is both present to the Church, and through it to the world, and also distinct from the Church. Christ is not the possession of the Church and the two are not collapsed together. This pneumatology, thereby, ameliorates the relationship between Christ and the Church, in this way strengthening Bonhoeffer's Christology and ecclesiology.

87. "Formation according to the form of Christ includes, therefore, two things: that the form of Christ remains one and the same, not as a general idea but as the one who Christ uniquely is, the God who became human, was crucified, and is risen; and that precisely because of the form of Christ the form of the real human being is preserved, so that the real human being receives the form of Christ." Bonhoeffer, *Ethics*, 6:99. See above, p. 97.

Part III

SPACE FOR THE HOLY SPIRIT

In Part I we examined Bonhoeffer's musico-theology, demonstrating how his musical imagination profoundly influences his theological one. We saw that his musico-theological musings in *Letters* reached their most focused treatment with his *Fündlein*, polyphony, through which he explores the relationship between earthly love and love of God, as well as between Christ and the world. Within these discussions we noted, on occasion, suggestive references to the Holy Spirit, both in the form of Bonhoeffer's own musings, as well as in some interpretations of his musico-theology.

In Part II, I focused on Bonhoeffer's Christology on the basis that he also assigns meaning to polyphony as an image of the Christological Definition. I argued that polyphony provides a positive metaphor for the Chalcedonian Definition which affirms the relationship between the natures, upholding the distinction of each as well as their interpenetration. This examination of Bonhoeffer's Christology, furthermore, demonstrated the close relationship between his Christology and his understanding of ethics and ecclesiology. I argued, with Rowan Williams, that Bonhoeffer's presentation of Christ is suggestive of an existential kenosis which can be seen to have its technical extension in the relationship between the divine and human natures, in which the integrity of the latter is supported and enabled by the former. However, we also saw that the ethics and ecclesiology which arises from Bonhoeffer's Christology entails an exceptionally close association between Christ and the Church. Bonhoeffer's Christology could also be said to have its technical extension in theological anthropology. And although, we found, he does not always adequately differentiate between Christ and the Church, in *Sanctorum Communio*, at least, pneumatology helps him to safeguard against an overidentification of the two.

In Part III we aim to thread together the arguments which have been laid out so far by showing how musical imagery helps us to reimagine Bonhoeffer's view of reality in Christ as it is brought about by the Holy Spirit: a musico-pneumatology.

Chapter 5

A MUSICO-PNEUMATOLOGY

Introduction

In this chapter I explicitly relate Bonhoeffer's pneumatology with his use of musical metaphors. In so doing, I extend the line of argument introduced in the previous chapter, but now stated here in plainer terms: Bonhoeffer's Christology and theology of Christian formation are most successfully realized through the incorporation of his pneumatology. In addition to this, I show that this pneumatology is implicit in his use of musical metaphors. These metaphors help him describe "reality" with granularity and in a way that mirrors his description of the work of the Spirit.

First, I examine evidence of Bonhoeffer's pneumatology as it is expressed in his final academic work, *Ethics*. I evaluate David Ford's argument for the presence of a pneumatology in *Ethics*, and I conclude that the evidence for a pneumatology is even greater than Ford acknowledges. In continuity with the pneumatology of *Sanctorum Communio*, Bonhoeffer's view of Christian formation in *Ethics* is shown to be one in which the Holy Spirit "actualizes" the work of Christ in the Christian's life. What is distinctive in *Ethics* is that Bonhoeffer has come to formulate this in terms of "reality" (*Wirklichkeit*), which is "revealed" in Christ and which "becomes real" in the Holy Spirit.

Second, upon further examining Bonhoeffer's view of reality in *Ethics* we identify his frustration regarding what he calls "static spatial" metaphors for their inability to adequately express one reality in Christ, whereby God and the world are both united but also differentiated. Moreover, he inquires as to what metaphorical language might serve as a suitable alternative. On this basis, I argue that the acoustic-spatial metaphor polyphony as it is employed in *Letters* provides the solution to the problem he raises in *Ethics*. The metaphor of polyphony provides an alternative to the visually bounded images which are so ill-suited to Bonhoeffer's understanding of reality. It is used by Bonhoeffer to translate and texturize the relationship between God, the world, and the Church as they are held together in Christ. Therefore, polyphony echoes, and is comparable with, the role of the Holy Spirit as articulated by Bonhoeffer in a number of important ways. Both the musical metaphor and his appeal to the agency of the Holy Spirit are vital in his portrayal of reality in which the distinct integrities of God, Christ, the

Church, and the world are essential. I thus contend that Bonhoeffer reimagines reality in Christ through a musico-pneumatology.

I conclude that Bonhoeffer's use of musical metaphors both relies on and also shapes his understanding of reality as a "shared space" between God and the world as it is established by Christ and actualized by the Spirit; that is, polyphony as it is used to articulate the shape of Christian formation in *Letters* resonates with Bonhoeffer's description of the work of the Holy Spirit in Christian formation as it is described in *Ethics.* And although he does not explicitly link his use of musical metaphors with a pneumatology, this relationship is strongly implied by his express rejection, in *Ethics*, of visual-spatial metaphors for conceptualizing reality.

The "Indirect but Pervasive Pneumatology" of Ethics

As we saw in the previous chapter, although students of Bonhoeffer have not traditionally looked to his works for a developed theology of the Holy Spirit, the notion that a pneumatology is virtually absent from his theology, or present but thoroughly inadequate, is ill-conceived, and a position which has been challenged by a number of important scholars in recent years.[1] David Ford, writing almost two decades before many of these scholars, was something of a lone voice in the wilderness. His generative and constructive discussion of the Spirit in Bonhoeffer's thought takes the form of a broad discussion of spirituality in the essay "Holy Spirit and Christian Spirituality," which is itself founded on a longer essay entitled "Bonhoeffer, Holiness and Ethics."[2] But, with respect to *Ethics*, he offers a close reading of a pneumatology which, he calls, "indirect but pervasive."[3]

Ford's argument regarding Bonhoeffer begins with the same quotation in both essays, taken from Bonhoeffer's description of reality in the *Ethics* manuscript

1. Those who positively affirm Bonhoeffer's description of the Spirit's role in ecclesiology, especially with respect to *Sanctorum Communio*, we saw in the previous chapter, include: Holmes ("The Holy Spirit"), Garcia ("Bonhoeffer and Reformation Ecclesiology"), Greggs ("Ecclesiology"), Mawson ("Christ, Spirit, and Church"), and Tietz ("Christology").

2. The main line of argument is the same for each essay, and both will be discussed in what follows. See: Ford, "Holy Spirit and Christian Spirituality," 269–90; Ford, "Bonhoeffer, Holiness and Ethics," 361–80.

3. Ford, "Holy Spirit and Christian Spirituality," 274. As an example of the breadth of Ford's claims concerning the subject of spirituality in Bonhoeffer's writings, Ford positions *Life Together* alongside *Letters* "as a classic exposition of what it means to cope 'in the Spirit' with the realities of suffering without despairing." Additionally, he identifies evidence of a postmodern pneumatology in *Act and Being*, as he writes of that text that it: "offers what is vital for any postmodern pneumatology concerned with wisdom and truth: an epistemology and a treatment of theological rationality." Ford, "Holy Spirit and Christian Spirituality," 274. Although, this last point is less convincing to my mind, since Bonhoeffer does not discuss the person of the Spirit in *Act and Being*.

"Christ, Reality and Good. Christ, Church and World." There, Bonhoeffer writes of the relationship between Jesus Christ and the Holy Spirit:

> The *subject matter of the Christian ethic is God's reality revealed in Christ becoming real* [Wirklichwerden] *among God's creatures*, just as the subject matter of doctrinal theology is the truth of God's reality revealed in Christ. The place that in all other ethics is marked by the antithesis between ought and is, idea and realisation, motive and work, is occupied in Christian ethics by the relation between reality and becoming real, between past and present, between history and event (faith) or, to replace the many concepts with the simple name of the thing itself, *the relation between Jesus Christ and the Holy Spirit*. The question of good becomes the question of participation in the divine reality which is revealed in Christ.[4]

This is the first occasion in which the Holy Spirit is discussed in *Ethics*, and it is strongly reminiscent of Bonhoeffer's description of the relationship between Christ and the Spirit in *Sanctorum Communio*. In this statement Bonhoeffer declares that the reality of God revealed in Jesus Christ only "becomes real" by the Holy Spirit. It is "the relation between Jesus Christ and the Holy Spirit" that allows him both to differentiate and also connect past history and present event; everything that *ought* to be done because of Jesus Christ, who is the ground and purpose of all ethical activity, *is* done by the Holy Spirit who enables active participation in Christ. As Clifford Green observes in his introduction to *Ethics*, the new humanity God creates in Jesus Christ "becomes a social and historical reality in the church-community by the action of the Holy Spirit."[5] Put slightly differently, Bonhoeffer is saying that participation in Christ is equivalent to participating in reality itself, and this requires the work of the Holy Spirit. This reminds us of the distinction between Jesus Christ and the Holy Spirit made in *Sanctorum Communio*; we could say with respect to this passage in *Ethics* that the Holy Spirit "actualizes" what Jesus Christ "establishes." As in the previous chapter, the distinct roles of the Spirit and Christ are crucially important in this passage, also, as they enable Bonhoeffer to differentiate Christ from the Church. However, in *Ethics* Bonhoeffer has widened the focus beyond the Church to reality itself, offering "a theological account of reality … which clearly draws ethics into coincidence with holiness," as Ford puts it.[6]

This passage is essential to Ford's overall argument, and he describes it as Bonhoeffer's "programmatic statement" in *Ethics*.[7] Ford further underscores its importance by writing that this statement "encourages one to read the rest of the *Ethics* as unfolding the implications of *the reality of Jesus Christ* being

4. Bonhoeffer, *Ethics*, 6:49–50. Emphasis mine.

5. Bonhoeffer, *Ethics*, 6:9.

6. Ford, "Bonhoeffer, Holiness and Ethics," 367. Bonhoeffer's understanding of "reality" is discussed further, below, under the subheading "Space and the Spirit in *Ethics*."

7. Ford, "Holy Spirit and Christian Spirituality," 274.

realized through the Holy Spirit."[8] From this point of departure Ford develops four pneumatological concepts based on his reading of Bonhoeffer's *Ethics*. We will look at each in turn. Outlining each of these will provide a good platform from which to analyze Bonhoeffer's pneumatology in *Ethics*.

The Realization of the Reality of Jesus Christ versus Two Spheres[9]

In his first key concept Ford accounts for the Spirit's work by differentiating it from that of Christ's as that which enables the "performance" of that which Christ has brought about. He states:

> The first key concept is therefore that of the Holy Spirit as the gift of the possibility of participation simultaneously in the reality of God and in the reality of the world in ways which "perform" the continuing realization of the world as sustained, accepted, and reconciled through being united with God in Christ.[10]

In the previous chapter, I examined Bonhoeffer's tri-formative pattern of Christian formation as expressed in "Ethics as Formation," in which he relates Christ's incarnation, death, and resurrection to our becoming human, being judged and being transformed. In the above passage Ford identifies this pattern of formation with the work of the Holy Spirit. Through the gift of the Spirit the Christian "participates" in "the reality of God" and "the reality of the world" because of the Christ-event which results in, Ford writes, the world as "sustained, accepted and reconciled." Although Bonhoeffer's view of "reality" is discussed further below, it is helpful to observe at this point that this is Bonhoeffer's alternative to the Lutheran concept of two kingdoms or "two-sphere thinking."[11] This contributes to Ford's own constructive thoughts on a theology of the Holy Spirit in a postmodern age, as he goes on to suggest that an appropriate postmodern *locus communis* for life in the Spirit is "being transformed before the face of Jesus Christ."[12]

8. See: Ford, "Holy Spirit and Christian Spirituality," 275. Emphasis original. He writes much the same thing in the other essay: "It is … appropriate to read the rest of the *Ethics* as unfolding the implications of the reality of Jesus Christ being realised through the Holy Spirit; and that also may serve as an initial definition of Christian holiness." Ford, "Bonhoeffer, Holiness and Ethics," in *Holiness Past and Present*, ed. Stephen C. Barton, 368.

9. Ford does not distinguish between the manuscripts in his essays. For clarity I will indicate which manuscripts are under discussion. References under this heading are all from the manuscript "Christ, Reality and Good. Christ, Church and World."

10. Ford, "Holy Spirit and Christian Spirituality," 276.

11. "He describes two-sphere thinking as so ingrained that it is extremely difficult to abandon. His main therapy is to 'direct our gaze to the picture of the body of Christ Himself, who became man, was crucified and rose again.'" Ford, "Holy Spirit and Christian Spirituality," 276.

12. Ford, "Holy Spirit and Christian Spirituality," 276.

Realization as Transformative Conformation to Christ

Ford's second pneumatological idea is that formation as conformation to Christ is "the main way" that realization of the reality of Christ as enabled by the Spirit takes shape. In the first pneumatological concept, Ford has already discussed the affirmation, judgment, and transformation of the world in relation to Christ incarnate, crucified and resurrected.[13] This idea focuses on "transformation" as the means by which formation occurs. Developing his *locus communis* further, Ford argues that this transformation has a relational component; the Holy Spirit's work brings about the fellowship which results from living before the face of Christ: "What happens before the face of Christ is transformation into a fellowship of the Holy Spirit."[14] Conformation to Christ, then, has an ecclesial dimension.

Differentiation: Ultimate and Penultimate

The concept of the "ultimate-penultimate" is formalized in the *Ethics* manuscript "Ultimate and Penultimate Things," though according to Bethge it was present in Bonhoeffer's thought long prior to this manuscript.[15] The ultimate may be understood as justification by grace and faith in Christ which flows from his incarnation, death, and resurrection; and the penultimate is everything which prepares the way for this. As Ford points out, the formulation should be understood to have both qualitative and temporal significance: the ultimate is final in qualitative terms as God's free word which is not necessitated by history and which determines the significance of the penultimate; yet it is also ultimate in temporal terms, as it is always preceded by the penultimate.[16] According to Bonhoeffer, the ultimate-penultimate must not be split apart and taking either one without the other results in the dangerous extremism of either radicalism or compromise.[17]

13. Ford, "Holy Spirit and Christian Spirituality," 276.

14. Ford, "Holy Spirit and Christian Spirituality," 276.

15. Bethge, *Dietrich Bonhoeffer: Theologian, Christian, Contemporary*, 375.

16. "First, it is final qualitatively, 'by the nature of its contents.' It is God's free word, not necessitated by anything in history or to be achieved by following any method. Second, it is final in temporal terms, and so always in fact is preceded by penultimate things; there is a preparation for it. These penultimate things are not such in themselves, but only through being directed toward the ultimate." Ford, "Holy Spirit and Christian Spirituality," 277.

17. As Bonhoeffer writes: "Radicalism hates time, and compromise hates eternity.
Radicalism hates patience, and compromise hates decision.
Radicalism hates wisdom, and compromise hates simplicity.
Radicalism hates moderation and measure, and compromise hates the immeasurable.
Radicalism hates the real, and compromise hates the word." Bonhoeffer, *Ethics*, 6:156.

Ford perceives two pneumatological features of the ultimate-penultimate formulation. The first concerns the temporality of the ultimate-penultimate, in which relation to Christ is enabled by the Holy Spirit. As Ford puts it: "Time is therefore also built into the dynamics of transformative conformation to the living Jesus Christ, whose ultimacy blesses the penultimate that prepares the way for it. The whole structure is simultaneously Christological and pneumatological, integrating the eschatological dimension of the Holy Spirit."[18] This connection between the Holy Spirit and the ultimate-penultimate distinction is not made by Bonhoeffer—there is no mention of the Holy Spirit in the manuscript "Ultimate and Penultimate Things," a point to which I will return in my critique of Ford's analysis.

The second pneumatological feature of the ultimate-penultimate formulation, according to Ford, is that it integrates theological epistemology and the ethic of holiness. Ford argues that through the ultimate-penultimate, Bonhoeffer forges a way through the ills of modernity and the pitfalls of postmodernity.[19] In this regard, it seems to be the combination of looseness and formalization that makes this a "Pentecostal concept," and, as such, makes it useful for understanding the nature of theological discernment: it "is structured and normative but affirms both divine and human freedom, and insists on the continual need for ethical and political discernment in one concrete situation after another."[20]

The Structure of Responsible Life

Finally, the fourth pneumatological concept is the idea of responsible living. This is the visible, ethical result of transformative conformation to Christ which Ford calls "the culminating *gestalt* of the *Ethics*."[21] The passage which Ford cites for his argument is found in the manuscript "History and the Good [2]," the only manuscript for which we have a second draft. Bonhoeffer writes the following about living responsibly:

> The structure of responsible life is determined in a twofold manner, namely, by life's bond to human beings and to God, and by the freedom of one's own life. It is this bond of life to human beings and to God that constitutes the freedom of our own life. Without this bond and without this freedom there can be no

18. Ford, "Holy Spirit and Christian Spirituality," 278.

19. "His affirmation of the penultimate insists on the continuing importance of rationality and philosophical rigor, and avoids dogmatism, fideism, foundationalism, nihilism, and positivism. He also stands as a warning for theologians who, in reaction against forms of rationality and philosophy that dismiss the reality of God, take refuge in philosophies which renounce rational and ethical norms." Ford, "Holy Spirit and Christian Spirituality," 278.

20. Ford, "Bonhoeffer, Holiness and Ethics," 376.

21. Ford, "Holy Spirit and Christian Spirituality," 279.

> responsibility. Only the life that, within this bond, has become selfless has the freedom of my very own life and action. The *bond* has the form of *vicarious representative action* and *accordance with reality* [*Wirklichkeitsgemäßheit*]. Freedom exhibits itself in *my accountability* [*Selbstzurchnung*] for my living and acting, and in the *venture* [*Wagnis*] of concrete decision. This, then, is the framework within which we have to consider the structure of responsible life.[22]

Living responsibly, we can see from this, concerns the relationship between freedom and being bound. Ford therefore explicates his fourth pneumatological concept through the lenses of "freedom" and *Stellvertretung*. Although Ford does not explain why freedom is a "pneumatological theme," he cites Ann L. Nickson's work at this point, specifically with regard to Bonhoeffer's discussion of the Holy Spirit in *Creation and Fall*: "It is the Spirit who operates on both sides of the divine/human relationship, creating and sustaining a dynamic unity of difference between God and humanity, and enabling the fully human creation to relate in freedom to the Creator."[23]

Ford recognizes the mediation of the Holy Spirit in the relationship between God and humanity as having a generative quality, since responsible living demands risk-taking. He writes:

> The notion of the venture (*Wagnis*) of concrete decision is an appropriate keystone for this ethical spirituality. It hints at that striking feature of holiness at its liveliest: its generativity, its unpredictability, its combination of newness and rightness—rightness in relation to God, to other people, to the realities of history, and to self. Yet, as Bonhoeffer was well aware, rightness is by no means apparent as the risk is being taken, and his meditation on the acceptance of guilt is the other side of the venture of free responsibility.[24]

We have already explored the second aspect of responsible life, *Stellvertretung*, in some detail in the previous chapter. We saw there that *Stellvertretung* combines the ethical outworking of conformation to Christ to the person of Christ, as our actions and Christ's correspond. In view of Bonhoeffer's understanding of responsibility in *Ethics*, we might add that his view of *Stellvertretung* can help to further clarify the structure of responsible living; responsible living originates in and takes its impetus from the one who first takes responsibility for us, much like *Stellvertretung*.

Living responsibly, then, combines both freedom and *Stellvertretung*; the freedom to "stand in" for others without any certainty of this action being right. Bonhoeffer's view of freedom is highly specialized, as Nickson demonstrates,

22. Bonhoeffer, *Ethics*, 6:257.

23. Nickson, *Bonhoeffer on Freedom: Courageously Grasping Reality*, 60. This refers to: Bonhoeffer, *Creation and Fall*, 3:64. Ford, "Holy Spirit and Christian Spirituality," 279.

24. Ford, "Holy Spirit and Christian Spirituality," 280.

because it is a freedom which binds the Christian to others; it is not freedom *from* but freedom *for* others and equates to taking risks and taking on guilt. By Ford's (and Nickson's) assessment, it is the Spirit mediating this freedom who enables us to take responsibility for others in Christ.

In evaluating Ford's argument, the first critical point to make concerns the importance he places on the role of the Holy Spirit in *Ethics* on the basis of the first passage we discussed. Of the passage, quoted above, in which Bonhoeffer describes the relation between Christ and the Spirit, Ford writes: "Bonhoeffer is sometimes criticised for saying little about the Holy Spirit, but here he *begins* his *Ethics* by making the relation of Jesus Christ and the Holy Spirit *the theological key to all that follows*."[25] As the freight of Ford's argument for a pneumatology rests on this passage, which he calls the "theological key to all that follows," it is surprising that he does not offer a clear explanation of its importance and position in *Ethics*. In particular, he does not clarify the reason for this passage and manuscript appearing at the beginning of *Ethics*.

Such an explanation is important because, as we have seen, its positioning in the opening section of *Ethics* was not necessarily Bonhoeffer's intention.[26] As discussed in the previous chapter, the intended order of the *Ethics* manuscripts is unknown (*DBW* and *DBWE* place them in the order in which they were thought to have been *written*). Therefore, the fact that this statement appears in the opening manuscript cannot solely be grounds for its being considered "programmatic." But as Ford does not discuss the editorial process and the resultant position of the manuscripts, he seems to give undue weight to this "programmatic statement."

Indeed, since he also acknowledges that *Ethics* is the culmination of Bonhoeffer's theological work in his discussion of the importance of this passage, he appears to overcompensate for the traditional neglect of Bonhoeffer's pneumatology by placing this allusion to the Holy Spirit at the zenith of his thought. We must admit that while the arrangement of the *Ethics* manuscripts is advantageous in making a discussion of the Holy Spirit more accessible to the reader (so that this manuscript becomes, to a certain degree, orienting for all that follows), it should not be assumed that this was Bonhoeffer's vision for the finished project. I am not denying the importance of this passage, which I will also discuss further in the wider context of the manuscript, merely pointing out that it is not at all self-evident why this passage should be pivotal for understanding the whole of *Ethics*.

This leads to my second critical point which is that Bonhoeffer's pneumatology in *Ethics* is only nascent. Acknowledging this need not diminish the importance of pneumatology in Bonhoeffer's thought but, instead, allows us to clarify the real achievement of his theology of the Holy Spirit. The relatively limited use of the title "Holy Spirit" in *Ethics* (which is deployed just five times in the main body

25. Ford, "Bonhoeffer, Holiness and Ethics," 368. Emphases mine. See also: Ford, "Holy Spirit and Christian Spirituality," 275.

26. In our introduction to the manuscript "Ethics as Formation" in Chapter 4. See p. 94.

of the text) itself indicates that there is not a *developed* account of the Holy Spirit here.[27] Having said that, it is curious, and problematic, that Ford addresses only one of these references to the Spirit in his defense of a pneumatology in *Ethics*. Admittedly, two of these references are only passing.[28] But, in addition to Ford's so-called programmatic statement, there are two references to the Holy Spirit contained in Bonhoeffer's discussions of the relationship with Christ and the world which are more developed. These appear in the manuscripts "Christ, Reality and Good" and "Ethics as Formation." It is unfortunate that Ford fails to address these because, as we will see, they offer further support for his claims regarding Bonhoeffer's pneumatology in *Ethics*.

Before I examine these references, it would be prudent to point out the peculiar strength of Ford's reading of a pneumatology in *Ethics*; it unearths the role of the Spirit where it is most subtle and indirect, and yet, it seems to me, assuredly present. That is, despite insufficiently explicating the importance of the original Bonhoeffer passage and failing to provide an exegesis of other crucial references to the Spirit, Ford's overall argument is, I find, compelling; in particular, because he shows how, for Bonhoeffer, the Christian's ethical behavior is a work of the Spirit even though the Spirit is not always mentioned explicitly.

This is relevant also to the third and fourth pneumatological ideas (concerning the ultimate-penultimate, and the structure of responsible life). Bonhoeffer does not explicitly relate these ideas to the Holy Spirit. However, Ford shows how they proceed from, and rely upon, the first and second pneumatological ideas. The first and second ideas sit close together as an account of reality in Christ as a work of the Spirit, in which the Christian is transformed by Christ and through the Spirit. The third and fourth pneumatological ideas describe the ethical behavior which proceeds from this transformation.

Ford thus effectively sees Bonhoeffer's pneumatology as emerging from his discussions of reality, in which Bonhoeffer clearly mentions the Spirit's role. As a result, he associates the description of the Holy Spirit in realizing, and shaping, reality in Christ with the present and visible outworking of this in Christian formation; the Holy Spirit modulates the relationship between the ultimate, ontological, and unseen reality in Christ, on the one hand, and the penultimate, visible reality of responsible relationships with the creation, on the other. Ford's fourth pneumatological idea regarding freedom and responsible living becomes another iteration of the dynamic between the ultimate-penultimate: the Holy Spirit

27. The index lists nine, but four of these are editors' notes.

28. Bonhoeffer, *Ethics*, 6:135; 290. The first is an editor's note quoting *Sanctorum Communio* in which the Holy Spirit is mentioned. The second reference occurs in a discussion of encounter with Jesus Christ as an experience of divine grace, and "the Holy Spirit" is included in the second part of a clause (" … in the word about Jesus Christ that the Holy Spirit brings.") Neither the absence nor the inclusion of these references to the Spirit seems to be anything other than incidental.

translates the freedom which has been established by Christ from the ultimate into the penultimate, by actualizing this freedom in the responsible actions of Christians.[29] I will now examine further the importance of Bonhoeffer's concept of reality and the Spirit's role in this.

Space and the Spirit in Ethics

In what follows I will address the two significant references to the Spirit which Ford does not examine and I will also further appraise the content of the statement of Bonhoeffer's that Ford calls "programmatic." I will argue, in broad agreement with Ford, that there is a pneumatology in *Ethics,* but it is even more developed than Ford permits. I begin by examining the wider discussion of "reality" in the manuscript "Christ, Reality and Good. Christ, Church and World," in which the first of these significant references to the Spirit in *Ethics* occurs.

The Spirit in "Christ, Reality and Good. Christ, Church and World"

In "Christ, Reality and Good" Bonhoeffer offers an account of "reality" as determined by Christ and which is crucial to his understanding of Christian ethics. He writes:

> It is a denial of God's revelation in Jesus Christ to wish to be "Christian" without being "worldly," or [to] wish to be worldly without seeing and recognizing the world in Christ. Hence there are not two realms, but only *the one realm of the Christ-reality [Christuswirklichkeit]* in which the reality of God and the reality of the world are united.[30]

There is one reality, in Christ, according to Bonhoeffer.[31] As such, Bonhoeffer rejects the Lutheran understanding of two kingdoms (as Ford observes in relation

29. Another advocate of Bonhoeffer's pneumatology in *Ethics* has pointed out: "In Bonhoeffer's view the thrust of the work of the Spirit in ethics is toward forming responsible human beings with the commitment to fulfill their daily responsibilities and the courage to engage in concrete actions that address the most pressing issues of the day." Brocker, "Creating Anew Responsible Human Beings: The Work of the Holy Spirit in Bonhoeffer's Ethics." My gratitude to Mark Brocker, former president of the International Bonhoeffer Society, for sharing his paper with me.

30. Bonhoeffer, *Ethics*, 6:58. Emphases original.

31. "There are not two realities, but *only one reality*, and that is God's reality revealed in Christ in the reality of the world. Partaking in Christ we stand at the same time in the reality of God and the reality of the world." Bonhoeffer, *Ethics*, 6:58.

to the first of his pneumatological concepts).[32] Two-sphere thinking is problematic because, having set up all kinds of false dichotomies which can loosely be branded secular/sacred divisions (God versus the world, the sacred versus the profane, the supernatural versus the natural, the Christian versus the unchristian), it "splits" reality.[33] Such dichotomies do not reflect reality in Christ, says Bonhoeffer, but rather the existence of those who are alienated from God.[34]

Such an account of reality runs the risk of being read as advocating for a monistic view (in which there is no distinction between God and the world). However, Bonhoeffer's emphasis is on the "shared reality" of God and humanity over and against the "necessary identity of the two."[35] That is, the shared reality of God and the world which are united in Christ in a "differentiated unity," as Ulrik Nissen points out: "Neither is understood separate from the other or identified with the other. Rather, it is an appreciation and affirmation of both realities in the same reality at the same time."[36] The dilemma Bonhoeffer faces, therefore, lies precisely in the difficulty of holding together both the relatedness of God and humanity, on the one hand, and their distinction, on the other.

This is not easy to explain and presents Bonhoeffer with a conceptual challenge. This is expressed in his concern to find suitable imagery which can convey this differentiation while avoiding a return to "two-sphere" thinking:

> This belonging together of God and world that is grounded in Christ *does not allow static spatial boundaries*, nor does it remove the difference between

32. Bonhoeffer sets out the problem as follows, intimating a spatial aspect to this thinking: "Since the beginnings of Christian ethics after New Testament times, the dominant basic conception, consciously or unconsciously determining all ethical thought, has been that two realms [Räume] bump against each other: one divine, holy, supernatural, and Christian; the other worldly, profane, natural, and unchristian." Bonhoeffer, *Ethics*, 6:55–6.

33. "[R]eality as a whole splits into two parts, and the concern of ethics becomes the right relation of both parts to each other." Bonhoeffer, *Ethics*, 6:56.

34. As Bonhoeffer writes in the manuscript "God's love and the disintegration of the world": "Now, for human beings in disunion from God, everything splits apart—is and ought, life and law, knowing and doing, idea and reality, reason and instinct, duty and inclination, intention and benefit, necessity and freedom, the hard-won and ingenious, the universal and the concrete, the individual and the collective; and even truth, justice, beauty, and love conflict with one another just as do desire and aversion happiness and sorrow." Bonhoeffer, 6:308–9.

35. As Charles Marsh puts it: "It is the 'shared reality' of God and humanity that Bonhoeffer emphasizes, not the necessary identity of the two. Similarly, this shared reality, mediated by Christ alone, militates against all conceptions of totality as self-mediated, as he affirms nowhere more elegantly than in the theme of the recapitulation of the world in Jesus Christ." Marsh, *Reclaiming Dietrich Bonhoeffer: The Promise of His Theology*, 105–6.

36. Nissen, "Letting Reality Become Real: On Mystery and Reality in Dietrich Bonhoeffer's Ethics," 325.

> church-community and world. This leads to the question of how to think about this difference without falling back into spatial images.[37]

On the one hand, we see here the difficulty of conceptualizing reality without relying on "static spatial boundaries" (i.e., spatial thinking and concepts which convey fixed and impermeable boundaries). He further reflects on spatial analogies and argues for the necessity of such images as biblical and, therefore, appropriate.[38] The spatial imagery of the New Testament leads him to the incarnation:

> When God in Jesus Christ claims space in the world—even space in a stable because "there was no other place in the inn"—God embraces the whole reality of the world in this narrow space and reveals its ultimate foundation. So, also, the church of Jesus Christ is the place [*Ort*]—that is, the space [*Raum*]—in the world where the reign of Jesus Christ over the whole world is to be demonstrated and proclaimed.[39]

Because Christ embodied God's presence on earth in a spatially restricted way, and continues to do so in the Church through which he is still taking up space, such imagery cannot simply be discarded.

On the other hand, he apparently rejects the delimitations which such images convey. Bonhoeffer observes that the Church must not compete for space but takes up space *for* the world, as he writes: "The space of the church is not there in order to fight with the world for a piece of its territory, but precisely to testify to the world that it is still the world, namely, the world that is loved and reconciled by God."[40] Bonhoeffer is clear that there are no distinctly sacred spaces annexed off for pious purposes; even the most desolate corners of the world have been loved and accepted by God in Christ. It is noteworthy that even here where the emphasis is on the church's relationship with the world rather than its distinction from it, and where spatial thinking is problematized for its potential to lead to territorialism, it remains clear that Bonhoeffer is concerned that the "world" is

37. Bonhoeffer, *Ethics*, 6:68. Emphasis mine.

38. He writes, in a move which suggests he himself has fallen prey to the kind of thinking he rejects (by equating the unseen with the spiritual): "Without doubt there are statements about the church in the New Testament that use spatial analogies; one thinks of the church described as a temple, a building, a house, and also as a body. It is clear from this that where the church is to be described as the visible church community of God on earth, spatial images cannot be avoided. In fact, the church occupies a certain space in the world that is determined by its worship, its order, and its congregational life, and this very fact is the point of departure for thinking in terms of realms in general. It would be dangerous to overlook this, to deny the visibility of the church, and thus to devalue it into a purely spiritual entity." Bonhoeffer, *Ethics*, 6:62.

39. Bonhoeffer, *Ethics*, 6:63.

40. Bonhoeffer, *Ethics*, 6:63.

distinctly the world (not the Church). The Church must witness to the world "that it is still the world."[41]

At this point the first of the two additional significant references to the work of the Holy Spirit in *Ethics* is of relevance. Bonhoeffer describes the church's responsibility to the world as fighting for the world by being a witness to the world. He goes on in the same manuscript to argue that this is a work of the Spirit in the Church:

> The church can only defend its own space by fighting, not for space, but for the salvation of the world. Otherwise the church becomes a "religious society" that fights in its own interest and thus has ceased to be the church of God in the world. For this the Holy Spirit equips those to whom the Spirit comes. Of course, it is presupposed that such a witness to the world can only happen in the right way when it comes out of sanctified life in God's church-community. Nevertheless, true sanctified life in the church-community of God is distinguished from any pious imitation by the fact that it leads the believer at the same time into witness to the world. Where the witness has become silent it is a sign of inner decay in the church-community, just as failure to bear fruit is a sign that a tree is dying.[42]

Here pneumatology is being employed to negotiate the relationship between the Church and the world, as it is the Spirit who is said to equip the Church to be a space for the world. In order to convey the relationship between God and the world in Christ, Bonhoeffer must be able to distinguish between them. At this juncture, with respect to the Church and the world, it is the role of the Spirit that allows him to do this; as he appeals to an account of the Spirit to effectively modulate the relationship between the Church and the world. Bonhoeffer's thinking here is similar to that on the subject of responsible living: the Spirit mediates freedom for the Church in such a way that self-interest is displaced by concern for the world.

This line of thought is a development of his earlier thinking at Finkenwalde in which the Spirit is described as creating a space around the Church to set her apart from the world.[43] In *Ethics* the relationship between the Church and the world is

41. This is further underscored in the same manuscript where Bonhoeffer writes: "This belonging together of God and world that is grounded in Christ does not allow static spatial boundaries, nor does it remove the difference between church-community and world. This leads to the question of how to think about this difference without falling back into spatial images." Bonhoeffer, *Ethics*, 6:68.

42. Bonhoeffer, *Ethics*, 6:64.

43. "The church-community's claim to a space of its own within this world, and the concomitant separation from the space of the world, attests that the church-community is in the state of sanctification. For the seal of the Holy Spirit seals off the church-community from the world." Bonhoeffer, *Discipleship*, 4:261. Italics mine. In a lecture series on "The Visible Church in the New Testament," also at Finkenwalde, he explores the Holy Spirit's work in the early Church and in the contemporary community. He writes: "The Spirit

reimagined; the Church does not vie for space, but is the Church *for* the salvation of the world with *its* own space. This is, likewise, reminiscent of Bonhoeffer's Christology as it was described in Chapter 3 and of his Christological ethics as examined in Chapter 4. The existential kenoticism through which Christ who is *pro nobis* greets the world in humility and vulnerability provides the *modus operandi* for the Church who is, likewise, for the world. These "patterns of connectedness," as Rowan Williams described them, which are carried out by the Church, and extend Christ's influence in the world, are—we read now in *Ethics*—enabled by the Holy Spirit.

Through this discussion we see, with Ford, that Bonhoeffer rejects two-sphere thinking in favor of thinking in terms of a "shared reality" between God and the world, divinity and humanity, a reality which is held together in Christ ("in whom all things hold together"), and brought about as a result of the work of the Spirit. The inclusion of a further reference to the Holy Spirit's work in this discussion confirms the veracity of Ford's opening statement upon which he builds his argument as being "programmatic." However, this analysis has further underscored the importance of Bonhoeffer's pneumatology by demonstrating that, according to Bonhoeffer in *Ethics*, the Holy Spirit not only "realizes" or "actualizes" reality in Christ (Ford) but also *differentiates* God–world, or Church–world. It is the inclusion of a pneumatology that allows Bonhoeffer to nuance reality as the "differentiated unity" of God and the world in Christ.

As Bonhoeffer's commitment to this "Christ-reality" results in a conceptual tension for him, in which he attempts to imagine the "space" for the Church as nonterritorial and yet also distinct from the world, we find, surprisingly perhaps, that it is not Bonhoeffer's commitment to preserve the sanctity of the Church which drives this, but rather his commitment *to* the "world" ("to testify to the world that it is still the world").[44] The claim that the Church is to be *for* (the salvation of) the world is reminiscent of Bonhoeffer's Christology with its emphasis on the preservation and distinct integrity of the human nature (discussed in Chapter 3) and his Christological ethics (Chapter 4)—as God in Christ is for us so we are to be for one another. In addition to Ford's observation that the Spirit turns people to face Christ in a way which brings them into fellowship with one another, we find that, "at the same time," they are sent out into the world. The Spirit's work also realizes Christ, therefore, by forming the Church in Christ's image which requires a movement out into the world as witness.

creates a space for itself in the world with visible signs accompanying its own coming … The Spirit draws attention to the church-community before the world. It immediately becomes the city on the hill, the city that is not hidden." Bonhoeffer, *Theological Education at Finkenwalde: 1935–1937*, 14:439.

44. Bonhoeffer, *Ethics*, 6:63.

The Spirit in "Ethics as Formation"

The second significant reference to the Holy Spirit in *Ethics* which Ford does not discuss appears in the manuscript "Ethics as Formation." It is notable that Clifford Green, in his introduction to *Ethics*, compares Bonhoeffer's argument in this manuscript to *Sanctorum Communio* (discussed in the previous chapter) remarking on the Holy Spirit's role in actualizing the real and complete ontological reality in Christ in temporal and social ways.[45] As we saw in the previous chapter, this manuscript focuses on the tri-formative shape of Christian formation (the Christian is made human, judged and transformed by being conformed to Christ who became human, was crucified and resurrected). When Bonhoeffer writes that those who are conformed to Christ as risen Lord are transfigured, he includes the role of the Holy Spirit in this formation: "In bearing it [judgement] willingly, they show themselves as those who have received the Holy Spirit and are united with Jesus Christ in incomparable love and community."[46]

Although this reference to the Spirit is probably less significant than the previous one (there is no extensive description of sanctification, for instance), given what we have seen in this chapter and the previous, it is still noteworthy. Including the role of the Holy Spirit in a description of Christian formation in the reality of Jesus which results in "incomparable love and community" is strongly reminiscent of the distinction Bonhoeffer makes between the Spirit actualizing what Christ establishes, both in the *Ethics* manuscript "Christ, Reality and Good" and in *Sanctorum Communio*.[47] By also prefacing it with the statement that those

45. "This argument parallels the similar one in his dissertation, where Bonhoeffer was also dealing with the new humanity. In *Sanctorum Communio* he argued that the Church as the new humanity was real and complete as an ontological reality in Christ, and that its social and temporal actualisation resulted from the action of the Holy Spirit, who enables individuals to appropriate new humanity in personal faith." Bonhoeffer, *Ethics*, 6:7n24.

46. Bonhoeffer, *Ethics*, 6:95.

47. In *Ethics*, as we saw above, he puts it this way: "The place that in all other ethics is marked by the antithesis between ought and is, idea and realisation, motive and work, is occupied in Christian ethics by the relation between reality and becoming real, between past and present, between history and event (faith) or, to replace the many concepts with the simple name of the thing itself, the relation between Jesus Christ and the Holy Spirit." Bonhoeffer, *Ethics*, 6:49–50. In *Sanctorum Communio* he similarly describes the Holy Spirit as building the Church by "gathering individuals": "In order to build the church as the community-of-God [*Gemeinde Gottes*] in time, God reveals God's own self as Holy Spirit. The Holy Spirit is the will of God that gathers individuals together to be the church-community, maintains it, and is at work only within it. We experience our election only in the church-community, which is already established in Christ, by personally appropriating it through the Holy Spirit, by standing in the actualized church." Bonhoeffer, Dietrich, *Sanctorum Communio*, 1:143.

who are Christians "often differ very little from other people" except that they are not concerned with self-promotion but rather promotion of Christ, we see a consistent thread in Bonhoeffer's pneumatology: the Spirit builds up the Church in time, by uniting individuals to Christ who, in turn, manifest Christ's mode of being and, in this way, form the church community.[48]

The foregoing discussion of two further references to the Holy Spirit in *Ethics* has deepened and clarified our understanding of Bonhoeffer's pneumatology in that text. In keeping with Ford's analysis of Bonhoeffer's pneumatology, we see that Christian formation is grounded in Christ but it is the Spirit who "actualizes" this ontological reality in social and temporal ways; the Spirit mediates the freedom that has been won by Christ in the life of the Christian so that she acts responsibly for others. In this respect, the Spirit causes Christ's actions to be ethically effective in the Church. This is no less than transformation in Christ, grounded in Christ's mode of being as self-othering; the Spirit turns believers away from their own interests and outward in Christian fellowship and as witnesses to the world.

Moreover, having further examined Bonhoeffer's idea of reality in *Ethics* in his first manuscript we have seen that the Spirit helps Bonhoeffer describe reality in which God and the world are held together in Christ. It is the Spirit who both creates the relationship between, and differentiates, the Church and the world. The pneumatology of *Ethics* shares with the pneumatology of *Sanctorum Communio* an important function in differentiating Christ and the Church, but Bonhoeffer now incorporates the world into this relationship. His concern with respect to conceptualizing this idea of reality is clearly in view in his demurral of static spatial thinking; such metaphors promote a division he wants to overcome and, yet, he is unable to throw them off entirely because of their capacity to demarcate boundaries which ensure the distinct integrity of God, the world, Christ and the Church.

Having established that a pneumatology is present in *Ethics*, I will now elucidate how this pneumatology is implicit in Bonhoeffer's appeal to musical concepts in *Letters*, bringing us full-circle back to the material discussed at the very start of this book, to show how musical metaphors can help to further articulate a pneumatology that is nascent in Bonhoeffer.

Musico-Pneumatology

Does the metaphor of polyphony provide Bonhoeffer with a solution to the question he raises in *Ethics* regarding suitable spatial imagery?[49] I will contend that not only does polyphony help Bonhoeffer reimagine and redescribe reality as he

48. Bonhoeffer, *Ethics*, 6:95.

49. "This belonging together of God and world that is grounded in Christ does not allow static spatial boundaries, nor does it remove the difference between church-community and world. This leads to the question of how to think about this difference without falling back into spatial images." Bonhoeffer, 6:68. Also quoted above.

has come to understand it in *Ethics*, but it does so in a way which corresponds to a pneumatology in that text. The connection between Bonhoeffer's effort to locate a means of appropriately conceptualizing his view of reality, as expressed in *Ethics*, and the acoustic metaphor, polyphony, has not been widely observed. Indeed, to my knowledge, the only other thinker who relates Bonhoeffer's criticism of a visual construal of space, in *Ethics*, with his later employment of musical concepts, in *Letters*, is Barry Harvey.[50] Harvey accurately perceives a connection between the two when he observes: "Bonhoeffer's rejection of the division of reality into separate domains readily lends itself to a dynamic and complex construal of space from an acoustic standpoint."[51] I agree with Harvey's observation. In what follows, I will explain how polyphony functions to a significant degree as a metaphor specifically for the Spirit for Bonhoeffer.

According to Bonhoeffer, a visually informed construal of space (what he refers to as "static spatial boundaries") implicitly reinforces divisions between Christianity and the world which, as we have seen, he has come to reject as a result of his Christological commitments.[52] This kind of two-sphere thinking undermines God's reconciling work in Christ. Although Bonhoeffer includes within his criticism of such thinking "spatial images" more broadly, what is missing in *Ethics* is an exploration of the notion of acoustic space in particular. It is my contention that the polyphony metaphor includes and relies for its effectiveness on just this.

As we saw in Chapter 2, Bonhoeffer alights on his "little invention" in order to express the closest possible relationship for the Christian between loving God and the world.[53] Polyphony provides a means of conceptualizing this interrelatedness with precision, so that God and the world retain their respective, distinct integrities. It, therefore, avoids the pitfalls of "static spatial" thinking which reinforce the autonomy and independence of the world (the kind of thinking we have seen

50. In view of his perspicacious account of Bonhoeffer's musical imagination, which also recognizes the role of the Spirit, it should be noted that Harvey does not develop an account of Bonhoeffer's pneumatology and Christology in relation to polyphony at great length. His approach is not exegetical but rather interweaves Bonhoeffer's work with his own highly constructive thinking. For this reason, notwithstanding the significant insights discussed here (as well as in Chapter 2) he is not addressed further in this chapter.

51. Harvey, *Taking Hold of the Real: Dietrich Bonhoeffer and the Profound Worldliness of Christianity*, 255.

52. Harvey puts it thus: "When the world establishes itself as an autonomous space, it denies the fact of its being accepted in Christ and of its grounding in the reality of revelation (*Offenbarungswirklichkeit*). When this occurs the world is not seen as reconciled by God in Christ, but as a sphere that is either subject to the extrinsic demands of Christianity, or as a domain that opposes its own law against the laws of Christ." Harvey, 256.

53. In that chapter we gently queried Harvey's assertion that "God does not stand alongside other creatures, for God's 'space' is not ours." Harvey, *Taking Hold of the Real: Dietrich Bonhoeffer and the Profound Worldliness of Christianity*, 240.

Bonhoeffer clearly reject in his view of reality in *Ethics*). The musical imagery[54] is laced with descriptive potential for presenting the work of the Holy Spirit in the life of the Church.

In this way, the metaphor of polyphony and related musical casts of mind help Bonhoeffer to conceive and articulate reality as he has come to understand it: that is, as held together in Christ and actualized by the Holy Spirit who, through Christ, both unites Christians to God and differentiates between them. In particular an acoustic understanding of space and the phenomenon of musical resonance inherent to it means that it is possible with the help of the metaphor polyphony to imagine the capaciousness of the relationship between God and the world, and their interpenetration. In this important respect, polyphony evokes Bonhoeffer's description of the work of the Holy Spirit by articulating the closest possible relationship between Christ, the Church, God and the world, while also preserving their distinct identities.[55]

As I have already intimated, this link between polyphony and a pneumatology in Bonhoeffer's theology has all too rarely been observed (and has never been explored in detail prior to this work, as far as I am aware). However, David Ford comes closest to explicitly recognizing this connection. Exploring Bonhoeffer's own life as polyphonic in a chapter of *Self and Salvation: Being Transformed*,[56] Ford discusses polyphony with regards to *Letters* and explores a similar trajectory to his essays on Bonhoeffer's pneumatology with respect to *Ethics*.[57] A brief examination of this will not only show the close proximity between polyphony

54. A musical metaphor is not, of course, strictly speaking an "image" because an image pertains to the visual field, yet, insofar as it is an imaginative metaphor, polyphony is loosely speaking an image. Nevertheless, I have largely avoided ascribing this term to polyphony.

55. Harvey comes close to this view in his reading of Bonhoeffer when he apparently acknowledges the actualizing role of the Holy Spirit in Bonhoeffer's concept of reality, together with the "tensile formation of complex space" (which I understand to mean "acoustic space"). He writes: "A performative construal of time also enters into the tensile formation of complex space, as the reconciliation of the realities of God and the world in Christ 'repeats itself, or, more exactly realizes itself again and again in human beings.' The sacramental site of this nonidentical repletion (a hallmark of Western music) is the work of the Holy Spirit in the Church. If we are to see 'reality as it is,' to see 'into the depths of things,' says Bonhoeffer, we must recognise that 'the world of things receives its full freedom and depth only where it is seen as oriented toward the world of persons in is origin, essence, and goal.'" Here Harvey is quoting from the manuscripts "Christ, Reality and Good" and "Ethics as Formation," which have been the primary focus of this chapter. Harvey, *Taking Hold of the Real: Dietrich Bonhoeffer and the Profound Worldliness of Christianity*, 256.

56. Ford, "Polyphonic Living: Dietrich Bonhoeffer," 241–65.

57. Indeed, the connection between polyphonic living and his attempts to unearth a pneumatology in Bonhoeffer's last academic work is such, for Ford, that he describes his foray into Bonhoeffer's spirituality, including attempting to unearth a pneumatology in *Ethics*, as a continuation of his own chapter on polyphonic living. See: Ford, "Bonhoeffer,

and pneumatology in Ford's assessment of Bonhoeffer, but in Bonhoeffer's thinking itself. It will, therefore, further substantiate my argument that polyphony corresponds to a pneumatology in helping Bonhoeffer to conceive a shared space between God and the world with precision.

Ford explores Bonhoeffer's theology in *Letters* through his use of polyphony by parsing it according to grammatical moods: as *the interrogative*, the *cantus firmus* concerns the question "Who is Jesus Christ for us today?"; the polyphony of Christian life is conceived of in *the imperative* to love God and love the world; *the optative* is palpable in the desire for God and the world; and *the vocative*, the most significant of these moods, "embraces and orients" all the others.[58] The vocative concerns prayer and worship. It is exemplified in Bonhoeffer's poetry, his many references to hymns and his musical casts of mind (which we discussed in Chapter 1). Of the vocative tendency, Ford asserts: "So worship is the fundamental imperative, corresponding to loving God with the whole heart, and inseparable from a life of responsibility in the world."[59]

To be fully immersed in God and the world is to live a life of "holy selfhood," according to Ford, who remarks: "Polyphony is a good image for this version of Luther's *simul*: completely in the arms of God and completely in the world."[60] He clarifies the value of the concept further in a footnote where he adds: "The imagery of sound allows much more clearly and without inappropriate paradox for a simultaneity in which one theme can be more 'constant' while yet being in essential reciprocity with others."[61] Furthermore, he also uses polyphony to conceptualize the tension of the simultaneously justified and sinful Christian: "Together these [the *cantus firmus* and counterpoint] make up the life of free responsibility before God."[62] The simultaneity and tension which Ford here describes by means of polyphony are strongly reminiscent of his description in the essays on spirituality of Bonhoeffer's pneumatology in *Ethics*, especially with respect to the ethical behaviors the Spirit enables the Christian perform.[63]

Holiness and Ethics," 362. But the closest Ford comes to explicitly linking polyphony and a pneumatology is when he refers to the musical term in the context of discussing Bonhoeffer's view of transformative conformation to Christ in the Spirit in his essay on holiness. Under the rubric of evidence for a pneumatology, Ford writes: "[First] the language of *gestalt* is well suited to Bonhoeffer's concern for the whole of life and the whole of Jesus Christ. It even has an aesthetic dimension, which is most marked in his musical imagery of *cantus firmus* and 'polyphony' in the *Letters and Papers from Prison*." Ford, 374.

58. Ford, "Polyphonic Living: Dietrich Bonhoeffer," 257.

59. Ford, "Polyphonic Living: Dietrich Bonhoeffer," 258.

60. Ford, "Polyphonic Living: Dietrich Bonhoeffer," 260.

61. Ford, "Polyphonic Living: Dietrich Bonhoeffer," 260.

62. Ford, "Polyphonic Living: Dietrich Bonhoeffer," 257.

63. The third and fourth pneumatological ideas described above concerning the ultimate-penultimate and responsible living.

The absence of the subject of the Holy Spirit in Ford's discussion, therefore, feels like an oversight. Although he understands polyphony to be a salutary way of articulating Bonhoeffer's view of Christian formation (or "holy selfhood," as he calls it), and while he has also demonstrated in two separate essays that Bonhoeffer depends upon a pneumatology for his understanding of Christian formation, he does not make the connection. Yet, it is precisely here—in Bonhoeffer's description of the dynamic of living freely before God and the world by frequently drawing close to Christ in prayer and worship—that the inclusion of a description of the work of the Holy Spirit would be appropriate. Instead, in a move that is highly suggestive of how well the two correspond, we see that Ford substitutes the musical concept of polyphony for the role of the Holy Spirit. Or, rather, we might say that it is Bonhoeffer who, in addressing the same themes in *Letters* as he does in *Ethics* (relationship with God and the world in Christ; the tension between being justified by Christ and also a sinner who must take responsible action with no certainty of rightness), substitutes the metaphor of polyphony for the Spirit. This may be best described as a musico-pneumatology.

Conclusion

In this chapter I have shown, with David Ford, that a pneumatology plays a vital role in Bonhoeffer's final academic theological work, *Ethics*. The work of the Spirit supports Bonhoeffer's structure of Christian formation, transforming the Christian into Christlikeness by "actualizing" the work of Christ in her life in social and temporal ways, turning her outward into fellowship with others. Moreover, a pneumatology also functions in Bonhoeffer's conception of "reality" itself. By appealing to the work of the Spirit in his account of "reality" as shared by God and the world in Christ, Bonhoeffer secures the all-sufficient reconciliatory work of Christ which unifies God and the world while also maintaining the distinction between God, the Church, and the world. Such a construal of "reality" calls for a spatial image which avoids the implication of static boundaries and can hold together both the necessary relation of God and humanity, on the one hand, and their distinction, on the other. I have contended that the acoustic metaphor of polyphony provides Bonhoeffer with a dynamic means of conveying both this unity and the preservation of distinct boundaries without diminishing this relationality. As this corresponds to Bonhoeffer's pneumatological commitments it may be correctly described as a musico-pneumatology.

Chapter 6

A SPIRIT CHRISTOLOGY ACOUSTICALLY DEFINED

Introduction

In this constructive development of my overall argument, I want to show that Bonhoeffer's account of the Spirit in the life of the Christian can be expanded and strengthened, though in a way that remains consonant with his commitment to a Chalcedonian Christology. I propose that a "pneumatic Chalcedonianism" of the sort provided by Ian McFarland provides a firmer foundation for a theology of Christian formation than we have seen in Bonhoeffer because it situates the work of the Spirit as integral to the life, death, resurrection, and ascension of Christ. By refining a Chalcedonian Christology so that it relies on a pneumatology to secure the humanity of Christ, McFarland's pneumatic Chalcedonianism offers a clear basis for the Spirit's role in our own lives. This retains the Chalcedonian core of Bonhoeffer's Christology while also improving upon aspects of his pneumatology, in particular deepening his account of the Spirit by situating it in a Trinitarian context. However, while a pneumatic Chalcedonianism benefits my reading of Bonhoeffer, I argue that the opposite is also the case: the account of the Spirit in relation to the Son as outlined in a pneumatic Chalcedonianism, itself, greatly benefits from musical metaphors such as those employed by Bonhoeffer. Acoustic-spatial patterns of thought provide a valuable means of articulating an orthodox Spirit Christology.

In showing how Bonhoeffer could have further developed his pneumatology by positioning it in a Christological framework, it must be acknowledged that I am addressing an ontology of Christ, the kind of discussion which he expertly resists and explicitly rejects. Nevertheless, I will show that such an exercise is worthwhile because providing an account of the Spirit in the person of Jesus of Nazareth not only results in a more clearly defined pneumatology but, arguably, also a more accurate Christology and account of Christian formation; the distinction Bonhoeffer makes between Christ and the Spirit in the twin loci of ecclesiology and anthropology is grounded in a Christological and Trinitarian framework. Furthermore, while attention to the hypostatic union can sometimes become over-abstract and esoteric, the end result of a pneumatic Chalcedonianism conforms with Bonhoeffer's own conviction: that what really matters is the person of Christ who meets and transforms us, rather than an exposition of divine and human natures considered as abstract entities.[1] The Spirit Christology discussed here, while focusing specifically on the locus of Christology—that is, upstream doctrinal theology—carries abundant implications for Christian formation; comprehending it thereby entails an invitation to the kind of Christian life which was inaugurated by Jesus of Nazareth.

In what follows, I first explore how McFarland's pneumatic Chalcedonianism conforms to an orthodox Spirit Christology (that which upholds a Chalcedonian Christology) by successfully integrating a pneumatology with Christology without undermining the identity of the Son. Upon further examining McFarland's understanding of the divine nature, I find that this account not only relies on a pneumatology but also on a Trinitarian framework. Additionally, by grounding the Spirit's role in Christian formation in Christology it strengthens the connection between the biblical accounts of Jesus of Nazareth and the Christian today in a way which is both compatible with Bonhoeffer's view of formation as conformation to Christ and more comprehensible. However, I argue that such a Spirit Christology suffers from a deficit of suitable analogical and metaphorical language. In my final, and most constructive, section I show how acoustic-spatial metaphors overcome some of the challenges presented by alternative visually defined spatial metaphors and offer a compelling way of describing the work of the Spirit.

Pneumatic Chalcedonianism: An Orthodox Spirit Christology

In his essay "Spirit and Incarnation: Toward a Pneumatic Chalcedonianism" Ian McFarland offers an appraisal of Chalcedon, which we will now examine. We also draw on his wider study of the incarnation, *The Word Made Flesh*, at various points for clarification. In his essay McFarland indicates the two questions which Chalcedon attempts to answer, as follows: "(1) In what does Jesus' status as the Son of God consist? and (2) Where do we see it displayed?" Of the first, Chalcedon establishes that Jesus' identity as Son of God is secured by his having a divine hypostasis. But the second question, he finds, is not so clearly or adequately addressed. This is also apparent in the *Tome* of Leo the Great, contemporaneous with Chalcedon, in which the influential statement regarding the divine and human natures appears: "One shines forth with miracles; the other succumbs to injuries."[2] McFarland makes the important case that this statement effectively undermines the full humanity of Christ and, also, mistakenly assumes that the divine nature is visible as such in the life of Christ. To associate the divine nature

1. As Bonhoeffer warns us, we must resist thinking of the divine and human natures as objects before us in isolation and instead focus on Jesus as God. Bonhoeffer, "Lectures on Christology," 350.

2. Cited by McFarland, "Spirit and Incarnation: Toward a Pneumatic Chalcedonianism," 147.

with the miraculous, focusing on "special powers" which mark Jesus out as divine, is inconsistent with the biblical witness: miracles are performed in the Old Testament by those who are clearly not divine, and Jesus himself claims that his followers will perform even greater miraculous displays than he did. Additionally, to imagine that the divine nature might be observed in Christ's actions is further inconsistent with the biblical witness: the only divine property actually described by Chalcedon, that of impassibility, Jesus categorically and emphatically fails to evince.[3]

McFarland accepts the basic tenets of Chalcedonian Christology which describes Christ as being in two natures: "the doctrine that in the incarnation two natures—the infinite, uncreated divinity of the Godhead and the finite, created humanity shared by all the world's people—are united in the one divine hypostasis of the Word" and "in this union each nature retains its full integrity: though united, they are not changed into or confused with each other."[4] Additionally, he follows the clarifications made after Chalcedon, that the one "person" (hypostasis) in two natures is to be identified as the eternal Word of God. A pneumatic Chalcedonianism, then, is one which first depends on identifying the hypostasis of Christ as the Second Person of the Trinity, the Son or the Word of God, who is the locus of the union between Christ's divine and human natures.[5]

The distinctiveness of McFarland's position is borne out in how he views the relationship, or more accurately the difference, between the hypostasis and the natures. McFarland draws a distinction between "who" Christ is and "what" he is; the unique identity of Christ, his *whoness*, on the one hand, and his human nature which concerns all the attributes, properties, and qualities ("his intellect, personality, self-consciousness and will, along with whatever other traits one might be inclined to include as distinctively human") his *whatness*, on the other.[6] On this interpretation everything done by Christ is done in his human nature: although the subject who wills and acts is the Word, "within the realm of time

3. "Indeed, the one divine property to which reference is made in the conciliar documents—impassibility—is precisely the one that Jesus, who was crucified, died and was buried, fails to exhibit (and in rather spectacular fashion!)" McFarland, "Spirit and Incarnation: Toward a Pneumatic Chalcedonianism," 156.

4. McFarland, "Spirit and Incarnation: Toward a Pneumatic Chalcedonianism," 145.

5. "The Chalcedonian position came to be that the one Word of God, who eternally hypostatizes the divine nature, also hypostatizes human nature in and as Jesus of Nazareth. In other words, through the incarnation the Son or Word is the subject of two distinct natures, so that from the moment of his conception the Second Person of the Trinity lives simultaneously through his divine and human natures, each nature maintaining its own ontological integrity throughout." McFarland, "Spirit and Incarnation: Toward a Pneumatic Chalcedonianism," 145.

6. McFarland, "Spirit and Incarnation: Toward a Pneumatic Chalcedonianism," 150.

and space the Word's willing and acting are properties of his human nature."[7] This means that when Jesus of Nazareth acted in the world he did so in his human nature, not his divine nature, and yet at the same time those who touched him, touched the Son of God.

While the hypostasis is the subject of Christ, it is not causative of anything Christ does in his human nature. The *whoness* of Christ is not a dictate of his *whatness*; it is not "an efficient cause" of his being or doing.[8] Or, alternatively put: his identity is not in what he does. Thus, nothing that he *did* was out of the divine nature, only the human ("For although a human being's hypostasis is manifest in his or her attributes, it is not constituted by them").[9] To smuggle in divine causation in such a way that displaced human causation would be to vitiate the integrity of Christ's human nature and differentiate Jesus' virtues at their very root, says McFarland, devaluing them as goals for our human existence.[10] While this distinction might seem to suggest that Jesus' human nature, therefore, operates independently of the divine, McFarland is quick to point out that Jesus, like all other humans, is absolutely dependent on God. By appeal to the doctrine of creation ex nihilo, he points out that all of creation is dependent on God who sustains it: including Jesus of Nazareth.[11]

The explication of the relationship between the hypostasis and the natures is absolutely critical to McFarland's case, as through it he engages those who attack Chalcedon on the grounds that a divine hypostasis (a Logos Christology) impugns the human nature.[12] But if the "who" of Jesus is answered by the hypostasis, the

7. McFarland ingrains this distinction by observing Aquinas who writes in *Summa Theologiae*, 3.7.7.2: "Thus, insofar as Christ is the eternal Son of God 'he does not need grace but is rather the one who bestows grace. But he did need to have grace in his human nature'" (trans. McFarland's own). McFarland, "Spirit and Incarnation: Toward a Pneumatic Chalcedonianism," 152.

8. "Nor, contrariwise, is Jesus' divine hypostasis the power behind his human attributes, as if it were the real engine of his human life." McFarland, 151.

9. McFarland, "Spirit and Incarnation: Toward a Pneumatic Chalcedonianism," 151.

10. McFarland, "Spirit and Incarnation: Toward a Pneumatic Chalcedonianism," 153.

11. "It must immediately be added that this claim does not mean that Jesus' human nature operates independently of God; it is merely a reminder that this (absolute!) dependence on God is not a function of Jesus's status as the Word made flesh. Because human nature is created from nothing, every human life subsists only as it is continually sustained and empowered by God the Creator." McFarland, "Spirit and Incarnation: Toward a Pneumatic Chalcedonianism," 152.

12. As McFarland claims: "The divinity of his hypostasis does not impugn his humanity because, again, the hypostasis is not some human trait—even a trait like personality or self-consciousness that we may conceive as intimately connected with one's hypostatic 'whoness'—but simply names an individual human being as the one who exhibits a particular set of human traits." McFarland, "Spirit and Incarnation: Toward a Pneumatic Chalcedonianism," 150.

Logos, and the "what" is answered by the human nature, then we have to enquire as to how the divine nature is accounted for in this description of Chalcedon. In answer, and in continuity with Chalcedon, McFarland holds that the divine and human natures are united in a single hypostasis, the Word, but remain distinct in their properties and in their operations. The implications of this are that McFarland can uphold the doctrine of impassibility: "what the Word does humanly (e.g. suffer death) is, with respect to the nature in and through which it is done, distinct from what the Word does divinely (e.g. sustain the universe in existence)."[13]

At this juncture, with weakness and suffering reserved for one nature and not the other, it could feel a little like McFarland has fallen foul of Leo the Great's dictum, reserving different behaviors for each nature. But the difference between the natures is more carefully nuanced than that. While McFarland describes the divine nature as distinct from the human so that the Son does not suffer as divine, it does not follow that he is thus ascribing to the divine nature the miraculous deeds done by Christ. Yet, as these are not typical operations of humanity they must be accounted for; and so we come to the "pneumatic" part of this Chalcedonianism.

The Incarnational Role of the Spirit

Having established that Jesus' actions are not caused by the hypostasis, McFarland must still account for those actions which are not typical human behaviors, such as non-sinful acts and the miraculous. He identifies the divine causality at work in the life of Jesus with the Holy Spirit. It is the Holy Spirit who enables Jesus to "live a life of faithful obedience and perform[s] miraculous deeds."[14] This is supported by the biblical witness which affirms Jesus' identity as Son but resists invoking this identity as the source of divine causality.[15] For that, McFarland points out, there is extensive evidence of the Spirit's work through Christ in

13. McFarland, "Spirit and Incarnation: Toward a Pneumatic Chalcedonianism," 151.

14. McFarland, "Spirit and Incarnation: Toward a Pneumatic Chalcedonianism," 153.

15. In referring to the biblical testimony McFarland is consistent with his overall approach, focusing on the identity of the Son before turning to the Spirit. He first points to the witness about the Son and how the biblical testimony suggests that the Son is not the reason for divine causality (for instance, in Matthew 4 where Jesus' temptations are to fulfil miraculous deeds as an affirmation of his identity as the Son of God). Only then does he turn to the role of the Spirit in the divine activity expressed through Jesus' life. Thus, he does not follow the usual pattern of Spirit Christologies which primarily appeal to the extensive descriptions of the Spirit's work in the Scriptures. See, for example, Myk Habets description of orthodox Spirit Christologies: Habets, "Spirit Christology: The Future of Christology?" Though it may seem to be a small point, it is striking that by focusing on the Son in the biblical witness and clarifying what might be said about Christ, the work of the Spirit is unavoidable in a pneumatic Chalcedonianism.

the Gospel accounts.[16] Here he is careful to tease out the difference between a pneumatic Chalcedonianism and certain types of Spirit Christologies. As he states: "And yet in sharp contrast to both ancient and modern Spirit Christologies, if it is by the Spirit that Jesus completes the work of salvation, this is not because the Spirit establishes Christ's divinity, but rather because he enlivens and enables his humanity."[17] On the basis of a solid Logos Christology, the work of the Holy Spirit concerns neither the divine nature nor the hypostasis but rather acts on the human nature.

On these grounds, the claim that Jesus became flesh is more satisfactorily understood, says McFarland, because Christ's identity as Son remains the hypostasis but filled with the Spirit it is the human nature that is affected by this divine action, seen in the miraculous events performed by Christ. From here, McFarland can draw a distinction between Christ's humanity and our humanity, and between the biblical witness in which Christ performs miraculous deeds and those performed by the apostles, because of the Spirit's work in and through them. There are differences, too, with regard to Christ's identity: In the case of

16. "from beginning to the end of their portrayals of Jesus, the evangelists emphasize the role of the Spirit as active in his conception (Mt. 1:20; Lk. 1:35), baptism (Mt. 3:16 and pars.; Jn 1:33), ministry (Lk. 4:1 and pars.), miracles (Lk. 11:20; Acts 10:38), death (Heb. 9:14), and resurrection (Rom. 1:4; 1 Tim. 3:16; 1 Pet. 3:18), empowering his life and work from beginning to end." McFarland, "Spirit and Incarnation: Toward a Pneumatic Chalcedonianism," 153–4.

17. McFarland, "Spirit and Incarnation: Toward a Pneumatic Chalcedonianism," 154. According to McFarland, the other thinkers who successfully incorporate a Chalcedonian Christology with a robust account of the Holy Spirit are limited to John Owen, Kathryn Tanner and Ivor Davidson. See: McFarland, 144. But this overlooks a number of important thinkers who, over the last three decades, have been faithfully advocating for an orthodox Spirit Christology. See: Coffey, "'Spirit Christology and the Trinity'"; Congar, *The Word and the Spirit*; del Colle, *Christ and the Spirit: Spirit Christology in Trinitarian Perspective*; Habets, "Spirit Christology: The Future of Christology?"; Höhne, *Spirit and Sonship: Colin Gunton's Theology of Particularity and the Holy Spirit*; Peppiatt, "New Directions in Spirit Christology: A Foundation for a Charismatic Theology"; Smail, *The Giving Gift: The Holy Spirit in Person*; Yong, *The Spirit Poured Out on All Flesh: Pentecostalism and the Possibility of Global Theology*. McFarland's allergy to the title "Spirit Christology" can be partly explained by the form this can sometimes take, namely as a kind of adoptionism, in which the Spirit replaces the divine nature in Jesus. Even those who endorse Spirit Christology as complementing a Chalcedonian Christology find themselves resorting to the same term to speak of two very different doctrines, one they affirm and one they reject. Tom Smail, for instance, advocates for a "Spirit Christology" which complements a Logos Christology (as supplied by John's Gospel) and, in the same passage, suggests that a modern "Spirit Christology" (such as that endorsed by Geoffrey Lampe) competes with Chalcedonianism. See: Smail, *The Giving Gift: The Holy Spirit in Person*, 92–3.

Christ who is the Word of God, the Spirit can be called "his Spirit," but is never *our* Spirit, just as Christ is the Son of God *by nature* and we are children of God *by adoption*.[18]

While these differences must be borne in mind, there is also a strong corollary between the life of Christ and that of Christians. McFarland puts it this way:

> Whether the person in question is Jesus, the Word made flesh, or the least distinguished of the saints, it is the gift of the Holy Spirit rather than any intrinsic property of human nature that makes possible human life active in faith and love.[19]

We have seen that McFarland's pneumatic Chalcedonianism consists, first, in establishing that the identity of the hypostasis as Logos does not compromise the integrity of the human nature; a distinction between *who* Christ is, as the hypostasis, and *what* he does in his human nature allows him to endorse the full humanity of Christ. However, we have seen, second, that reimagining the hypostatic union in this way is only possible by attributing the divine causality in the life of Jesus of Nazareth to the Holy Spirit, rather than the divine nature.

In what follows I will evaluate this pneumatic Chalcedonianism. By further clarifying some of McFarland's arguments regarding the divine nature in relation to his understanding of divine presence and his focus on the relationship between the hypostasis and human nature (rather than divine and human natures) I will draw attention to some particular strengths of his argument: first, how he avoids talking about the divine nature in abstraction and, second, how he positions Chalcedon in an account of the Trinity. Before turning to what musical thinking can offer this argument, I will also show how this leads ineluctably to a Christian anthropology which Bonhoeffer would support.

Divine Nature and Divine Presence

Through this analysis, the question which arises and sharpens with every passing mention of the humanity of Christ and the identity of the hypostasis is: What about the divine nature? Since the Son of God, the hypostasis, is *who* Jesus is and

18. "If it is by the Spirit that Jesus no less than the rest of us are claimed as children of the Father, it remains the case that as the Word, eternally begotten of the Father, Jesus is Son by nature while the rest of us are daughters and sons by grace. And this difference has a corollary: the Spirit who rests on Jesus of Nazareth is *his* Spirit, to the extent that it can be called indifferently the Spirit of God or the Spirit of Christ (Rom. 8:9; cf. Acts 16:7; Phil. 1:19; 1 Pet. 1:11). By contrast, although we, too, depend on that same Spirit to lead us in lives of faith and obedience, the Spirit is never ours." McFarland, "Spirit and Incarnation: Toward a Pneumatic Chalcedonianism," 155. Italics original.

19. McFarland, "Spirit and Incarnation: Toward a Pneumatic Chalcedonianism," 155.

the human nature is everything that is observable of Christ, all the *whatness*, we are left asking: What about the attributes, properties, and characteristics which must be proper to the divine nature? While the human nature is everything that is "up front," the properties, attributes, and characteristics of the divine appear to be backstage, apparently occluded by the human nature.

McFarland is resolute that the divine nature remains imperceptible and inscrutable, even in the hypostatic union.[20] But by, seemingly, side-lining discussion of the divine nature in its particular relationship with the human nature in the person Jesus of Nazareth (and instead privileging discussion of the relationship between hypostasis and human nature), it appears that he eschews a Chalcedonianism without reserve.[21] If the properties of the divine nature are not somehow evident through Jesus of Nazareth, how can it make sense to call him the primary ground of our knowledge of God?[22]

In his wider study, *The Word Made Flesh*, we find that McFarland's description of the divine life of God prefaces his description of the divine nature in Christological terms, setting the scene for how the divine nature should be understood in that context. In order to illustrate the conceptual difficulties of the incarnation, McFarland characterizes God (or "the divine life") via the communicable perfections of divine love (divine goodness, patience, and holiness)[23] and the incommunicable perfections of divine presence (divine unity, omnipotence, and glory).[24] Each perfection is explored in terms of the Trinitarian relations. For

20. "Moreover, since the divine nature transcends space and time, it is not a possible object of our experience of Jesus: what can be seen, heard and touched of him is simply and exclusively his humanity." McFarland, "Spirit and Incarnation: Toward a Pneumatic Chalcedonianism," 151. And: "Chalcedon affirms that Jesus is fully divine, but since the divine nature is invisible and ineffable, it cannot be shown or seen and so cannot be treated as an observable property of Jesus." McFarland, "Spirit and Incarnation: Toward a Pneumatic Chalcedonianism," 156.

21. As McFarland even acknowledges in his conclusion: "this account leaves the question of where Jesus' divinity is displayed unanswered." McFarland, "Spirit and Incarnation: Toward a Pneumatic Chalcedonianism," 156.

22. Which McFarland does, beginning and ending his study by quoting Luther ("whoever wishes to deliberate or speculate soundly about God should disregard absolutely everything except the humanity of Christ" and "If the Word is God, and the Word became flesh and lived among us in Jesus, then Jesus' flesh—his earthly, temporal existence—is the measure of all our claims about who the Word is, and thus about who God is.") McFarland, *The Word Made Flesh: A Theology of the Incarnation*, 213.

23. McFarland, *The Word Made Flesh: A Theology of the Incarnation*, 27–33.

24. McFarland, *The Word Made Flesh: A Theology of the Incarnation*, 34–42.

instance, to say that God is love is to acknowledge the Trinitarian relations, as the mutual love of Father, Son and Spirit are what it means for God to be God.[25] This is not a comprehensive doctrine of God but is intended as a means of showing the difficulty posed by the incarnation, in God becoming flesh; that is, especially, a difficulty in conveying "what Christians mean by divinity."[26]

The perfection of divine presence, it seems to me, is particularly important for McFarland's understanding of the divine nature. In choosing to speak in terms of divine *presence* rather than divine *freedom*,[27] he places the emphasis on God's presence to creation rather than God's distinction from it. This means that while he emphatically iterates the transcendence of God (God, he insists, can only be described analogically), he also, simultaneously, emphasizes God's commitment to be with creation.

Because God's divine presence is already sustaining creation, the incarnation does not pose a problem concerning the measure of divine presence in creation (the hypostatic union is not a quantitative increase of divine presence in creation) and additionally the incarnation is not overcoming an ontological breach between God and creation (because God is already sustaining the creation). It is the incarnation which *reveals* the radical incommensurability of Creator and creation.[28]

This description of divine presence provides certain conditions for understanding the divine nature in the hypostatic union as follows: the divine nature is not uninvolved with creation or removed from it, but is already sustaining it by the divine presence and is, therefore, sustaining all humanity; the divine nature in Christ does not overwhelm the human nature, just as the divine presence does not overwhelm or threaten the integrity of creation (which can be

25. The goodness of God is expressed in the generous abundance of life shared by the Father, Son and Spirit "sharing divinity freely, unstintingly and inexhaustibly"; but this sharing is not an overwhelming but rather a witness to distinctiveness, says McFarland in describing the divine patience; divine patience is further qualified by divine holiness, which is the culminating perfection of divine love because it is the steadfastness of God's being, its integrity.

26. Although he applies "divinity" and "humanity" to the two natures (see: McFarland, *The Word Made Flesh: A Theology of the Incarnation*, 2n3), "divinity," "divine nature," "divine life" and "divine presence" are virtually interchangeable terms for McFarland.

27. He follows the pattern of Barth in looking at the perfections of divine loving and divine freedom, but has renamed the latter "divine presence." McFarland, *The Word Made Flesh: A Theology of the Incarnation*, 27.

28. "The bridging of Creator and creature in Jesus is therefore not a response to a logically prior divide, but rather the ground of that very distinction." McFarland, *The Word Made Flesh: A Theology of the Incarnation*, 12.

appreciated on the grounds that Father, Son, and Spirit while eternally present to one another are also different from one another); the divine nature is, nevertheless, completely transcendent, ontologically other.

A Trinitarian Clarification

To address the radical incommensurability between Creator and creature, McFarland explicitly refocuses attention from the two natures onto the relationship between the hypostasis and the human nature.[29] In doing so he makes a Trinitarian clarification: the divine nature in the hypostatic union cannot be isolated from the divine life of the three hypostases.

The hypostasis is not another "thing," but the divine Word subsisting in two natures, McFarland reminds us.[30] That is, it is the divine *identity* or person, an identity which needs to be set in a Trinitarian context: the Son of God, the Second *Person* of the Trinity, is the hypostasis who subsists as (hypostatizes) the divine and human natures.[31] This understanding of hypostasis is complicated by our modern view of "person" as individual. By contrast to this, the Trinitarian hypostases are not three centers of consciousness. The divine hypostasis, the Son, eternally coexists in interdependence with the Father and the Spirit.

The divine nature, then, is not some*thing* other than (or prior to) the Father, Son, or Spirit. Rowan Williams puts it well when he says:

> The divine hypostasis of the Word is not one of three examples of divinity … Or, to put it as succinctly as we can, there is no divine nature independent of its actualization in Father, Son and Spirit; so that it cannot be right to think of the three divine hypostases as "countable" examples of a kind of life that we could independently identify as divine.[32]

Thus, the divine nature is not something extra to the hypostasis, the Son, and is not identifiable with only one person of the Trinity, either. Although McFarland

29. "To answer this question [of how the divine and human natures come together in the incarnation, incommensurable as they are] … it is necessary to shift the theological focus from Jesus' two natures considered in themselves to the distinction between nature and hypostasis." McFarland, *The Word Made Flesh: A Theology of the Incarnation*, 72.

30. "The hypostasis is not any kind of 'thing' at all apart from the natures, but just the particular one who subsists in and as the natures, so that, in the words of John of Damascus, 'the two natures are one in Christ, and the one Christ is two natures.'" McFarland, *The Word Made Flesh: A Theology of the Incarnation*, 90.

31. Defining the terms, he writes: "nature refers to the *whatness* of an entity, as defined by its constitutive qualities or attributes … By contrast, hypostasis or person applies to entities that have rational or spiritual natures, and which therefore take individualized forms as *whos*." McFarland, *The Word Made Flesh: A Theology of the Incarnation*, 7.

32. Williams, *Christ the Heart of Creation*, 87–8.

does not put it so bluntly, he is effectively saying that there is no divine nature apart from the three hypostases of the Trinity.

It follows that while the Son of God (the hypostasis) must *assume* a human nature he does not assume a divine nature, rather the Son *remains* divine.[33] Therefore, we do not have to account for the divine nature in the same way as we do the human nature by distinguishing it from the hypostasis. Because the hypostasis, the Son (the "who") who is met through the human nature of Jesus of Nazareth is not distinct from the divine nature in the same way as from the human nature, the divine nature and hypostasis are, for the purpose of trying to understand how the incommensurables of "divinity" and "humanity" are united in the Son, set on a par.[34] The divine nature understood as the divine life of God in Trinitarian terms is what allows McFarland to integrate the person of the Spirit in this Christology; it is also what inhibits his willingness to discuss the divine nature in distinction from the human.[35]

Having effectively reinscribed a Chalcedonian Christology to focus on the relationship between the hypostasis and the human nature, does McFarland adequately secure the union between the divine and human natures "without division or separation"?[36] On the face of it, the way that McFarland explicates this relationship between the hypostasis and human nature (when we perceive Christ,

33. "Thus, [if] the Word assumes a human nature as one who from eternity subsists in the divine nature ..." McFarland, *The Word Made Flesh: A Theology of the Incarnation*, 90.

34. Though McFarland does not explicitly identify the hypostasis and the divine nature, he leans on another who does by quoting the following to underscore his point: "If the hypostasis of the λόγος has been truly and really imparted to the assumed flesh, undoubtedly there is a true and real presence between the divine and human nature, *since the hypostasis of the λόγος and the divine nature of the λόγος do not really differ*." Quenstedt, *Theologica Didactico-Polemica*, 3:85. Italics mine.

35. This commitment to the divine nature as Trinitarian entails a commitment to divine transcendence in a way which noticeably muzzles what McFarland will say about the divine nature. The influence of McFarland's *Doktormutter* is detectable here. Kathryn Tanner goes so far as to say that proper attention to divine transcendence means that the only nature Christ has is a human one. See: McFarland, *The Word Made Flesh: A Theology of the Incarnation*, 89n38.

36. One way in which McFarland attempts to account for the unity between the natures is by the analogy of "'incarnation' as 'inscription.'" His description of an author (the hypostasis) who can be omniscient, for instance, while the character (Jesus of Nazareth) is not, well articulates the communication of attributes. But while this effectively illustrates how the distinct attributes of each nature can be preserved while the subject is essentially the same—it is not clear how the character relates to the author. Admittedly, McFarland acknowledges that this analogy (which he credits to Dorothy Sayers) is particularly useful for conveying the relationship "without confusion or change." McFarland, *The Word Made Flesh: A Theology of the Incarnation*, 80.

we perceive no one other than the divine Word and *nothing* other than a created substance, Jesus' humanity)[37] apparently preserves the distinction of each at the expense of their union. But if that is the case, how can we be sure that Jesus is God and an index for the divine life?

The argument for the unity between the natures goes as follows: Because Jesus is hypostatically divine (because of "*who*" he is) he is also *essentially* divine, which means that there can be no human *activity* of Jesus that is not divine, says McFarland.[38] McFarland then leans on the Eastern orthodox understanding of divine energies ("a given nature's characteristic modes of operation") which allows him to avoid saying that the human nature is or becomes divine.[39] Participation in the divine nature would entail change in a creature into what is divine—it would threaten the integrity of the creature and, in the case of Christ, it would vitiate a Chalcedonian Christology by bringing change to the human nature. But participation in the energies can occur without change.[40]

The upshot of this is that the human being Jesus of Nazareth participates in the divine energies through the gift of the Holy Spirit.[41] Thus, it is through the Spirit

37. McFarland, *The Word Made Flesh: A Theology of the Incarnation*, 8.

38. "Thus, if the Word assumes a human nature as one who from eternity subsists in the divine nature whatever communion exists between the divine person and the human nature must include the divine nature as well. In other words, because a hypostasis may be named divine only as it shares in the one divine essence, it is impossible to confess that Jesus is hypostatically divine without also confessing that he—the human son of Mary—is also divine essentially. This is not to say that the assumed human nature is or becomes divine, but it is to insist that if it is indeed true that in Jesus 'the whole fulness of deity dwells bodily,' then there is no human activity of Jesus that is not also divine." McFarland, *The Word Made Flesh: A Theology of the Incarnation*, 90.

39. McFarland explains what the divine energies are as follows: "Specifically, energy refers to a given nature's characteristic modes of operation, such that while an entity's energy is not the same as its nature, energy corresponds to nature, such that a being's energies are, so to speak, symptoms of its nature." McFarland, *The Word Made Flesh: A Theology of the Incarnation*, 91.

40. Participation in the energies without participating in the nature is like exhibiting symptoms of a disease without actually having the disease itself, McFarland suggests. McFarland, *The Word Made Flesh: A Theology of the Incarnation*, 92. This illustration is odd, for while it is clear that one can be asymptomatic, having a disease without the symptoms, it is not at all clear that the reverse is possible. A better illustration is the more common analogy of light, as Vladimir Lossky has it: "The sun's rays are different from the solar disk, but they are inseparable from it, since they are the natural energies of this luminous disk." Lossky, "The Doctrine of Grace in the Orthodox Church," 77.

41. "This is especially clear in the case of Jesus, for whom the entirety of his earthly career from his conception (Matt. 1:18; Luke 1:35) to his baptism (Matt. 3:16 and pars.), to his sojourn in the wilderness (Matt. 4:1 and pars.), to his teaching (Luke 4:14-18; 10:21) and

that the characteristics of the divine life of God become perceptible, as McFarland writes (quoting Vladimir Lossky):

> Thus, although the divine nature remains invisible in the incarnation, its characteristics nevertheless become visible in Jesus' humanity through the Spirit's power: "The Son shows his person and hides his nature. The Spirit hides his person and shows the divine nature by pointing to the Son."[42]

This is the same Spirit who makes participation in the divine energies possible for all humans. But only in the case of Jesus of Nazareth does his human activity always participate in the divine energies. This is only possible because his will is deified. In this respect, Jesus differs from other human beings. McFarland points to the importance of his will being deified, because it is by means of a deified will that Jesus is fully human and yet also does not sin.[43] While this appears to smuggle in a structural change in Jesus, in which the divine nature modifies his humanity thus making him unlike other humans in a fundamental way, McFarland seeks to allay this concern by pointing out that a deified will is only distinct from a non-deified will by its mode of operation.[44]

miracles (Matt. 12:28; cf. Acts 10:38), to his death (Heb. 9:14) and resurrection (Rom. 1:4; 1 Tim 3:16; 1 Pet 3:18) is ascribed to the Spirit." McFarland, *The Word Made Flesh: A Theology of the Incarnation*, 92–3.

42. McFarland, *The Word Made Flesh: A Theology of the Incarnation*, 93.

43. "If Jesus' will is deified, however, it follows that none of his humanly willed actions involve any deviation from God's will for him." McFarland, 95. Interestingly, on the same matter of securing Christ's sinlessness, McFarland elsewhere suggests that Christ is sinless because his nature and hypostasis are not inseparable, as they are in all other human beings: "Therefore, whereas in all other human beings the nature and hypostasis are inseparable (so that if the former is fallen, the latter is sinful), the divine hypostasis of Christ pre-exists—and thus is not bound by—his human nature by virtue of its eternal subsistence in the divine nature. … A careful analysis of the question of Christ's human nature allows a clear distinction to be drawn between fallenness and sinfulness as predicates in relation to the Chalcedonian categories of nature and hypostasis, respectively.… A nature can be damaged (and thus fallen); but a nature cannot sin, because sin is ascribed to agents, and thus is a matter of hypostasis." McFarland, "Fallen or Unfallen? Christ's Human Nature and the Ontology of Human Sinfulness," 412–13.

44. He clarifies that a human will is a matter of *agency* rather than *control*, stating: "to have a will is to experience oneself as an 'I' who owns one's actions (viz. '*I* did them') rather than as some power by which an essentially disembodied 'I' exercises control over the body." McFarland, *The Word Made Flesh: A Theology of the Incarnation*, 95n62. Maximus the Confessor (from whom McFarland derives this understanding of the deified human will of Jesus) helpfully draws on Jesus in the garden of Gethsemane to illustrate the point: while Jesus wants the cup of suffering to be taken from him, he aligns himself to the will of God. See also: "By contrast (and as Maximus takes pains to insist), to speak of Christ's

It is here, it seems to me, in this close analysis of the relationship between the hypostasis and human nature that the two distinct agencies of the Spirit and the Son come into sharpest relief with respect to this Christology. While Jesus is hypostatically divine because he is the Son of God, it is the agency of the Holy Spirit who makes participation in the divine energies possible for Jesus of Nazareth. The integrity of the human nature is preserved from any change that would be entailed by participation in the divine nature via the hypostasis of the Son.[45]

This, again, is better understood within a Trinitarian context. As the divine nature pertains to all three hypostases, it has been possible for the human nature of Jesus of Nazareth to be in relationship with the divine nature via two persons, the Son and the Spirit: Jesus is hypostatically divine because of the Son, but any divine causation results from the Spirit.

To make this plainer still, if we consider the three hypostases of the Trinity to be "unique activations" of the divine nature,[46] then there are two activations of the divine nature in this account, through the Son and the Spirit. The divine nature is "in" Jesus who is the Son of God who assumes a human nature; and is, additionally, *active* in his human nature by virtue of the Spirit. On this reading, the union between the divine and human natures is fully realized only through the Holy Spirit. Put slightly differently we could say that the divine nature, which is latent in Jesus through the Son, is "actualized" in him by the Spirit by virtue of the energies.

Of course, McFarland would resist this means of clarification: the divine nature is both imperceptible and inseparable from the full Trinitarian life of God.

will as deified does not imply any such structural alteration: as a piece of human nature, the deified will differs from the non-deified will only in its relationship to God (i.e. in its mode of operation)." McFarland, "Fallen or Unfallen? Christ's Human Nature and the Ontology of Human Sinfulness," 410.

45. "In other words, because a hypostasis may be named divine only as it shares in the one divine essence, it is impossible to confess that Jesus is *hypostatically* divine without also confessing that he—the human son of Mary—is also divine *essentially*. This is not to say that the assumed human *nature* is or becomes divine, but it is to insist that if it is indeed true that in Jesus 'the whole fullness of deity dwells bodily,' then there is no human *activity* of Jesus that is not also divine." McFarland, *The Word Made Flesh: A Theology of the Incarnation*, 90.

46. This expression offers a means of clarifying what McFarland is saying. The expression is used by Rowan Williams to summarize a positive idea from Christopher Beeley. It relates to Williams's statement that "there is no divine nature independent of its actualization in Father, Son and Spirit." He goes on to describe "the eternal hypostasis, which is the divine nature in one unique activation of its eternal life, entering into the state of being the organizing or unifying reality of a human individuality …" Williams, *Christ the Heart of Creation*, 87–8.

Presenting it in terms of how it is "activated" by members of the Trinity might seem to undermine the extent of the Trinitarian corrective to a Chalcedonian Christology which he is providing. Thus, McFarland writes: "And because the divine nature remains invisible and inaccessible even in the incarnation, the divine may only be experienced as present to the world hypostatically, in the person of the Son, sent into the world by the Father in the power of the Spirit to live a human life."[47]

This pneumatic Chalcedonianism might not satisfy all advocates of a Chalcedonian Christology. The way that McFarland has secured the unity between the natures by the deified will of the human Jesus means that there is, seemingly, a point at which the extent of the union abjures the parameter "without confusion or change." In keeping with his analogy of "'incarnation' as 'inscription,'" a deified will means that the "character" Jesus of Nazareth is conscious of his identity as "author" (self-conscious to the degree that he understands he is the Son of God).[48] And although in this account, Jesus is a "reliable index" of the divine, the divine activity that is disclosed to us through Jesus comes from the Spirit (as the Son remains hidden by the human nature). Beyond the recitation that Jesus is "hypostatically" and "essentially" divine because the Word assumed a human nature, it is still somewhat unclear that the divine nature is united to the human nature *in* the Second Person of the Trinity (though McFarland calls the Son "the locus" of this union): it is only in an account of the relationship between Jesus of Nazareth and the Holy Spirit that this hypostatically divine human nature is divine in any practical or observable way.

This line of criticism, however, magnifies the problem Chalcedon poses in abstract terms and eclipses the solution on offer. The Trinitarian theology required to understand this Christology is what makes it more convincing, not less; as the Son hypostatizes the human nature and the Spirit activates the divine energy in that nature, we have a Christology which integrates an orthodox account of God, on the one hand, and an account of Christian anthropology, on the other.[49] While, on the face of it, expounding the definitions of hypostasis and natures appears to be an abstract exercise, we are left with a study of the incarnation which forms a compelling basis for understanding how humanity can participate in the divine life of God. We come now to our final analysis of McFarland's Chalcedonianism.

47. McFarland, *The Word Made Flesh: A Theology of the Incarnation*, 74.

48. But, according to McFarland, does Jesus understand this within his being, as the Son, or does this knowledge come to him via the Holy Spirit? It seems to be a combination of the two, as a deified will means that Jesus of Nazareth is fully obedient to God, but this obedience is exercised through the Holy Spirit.

49. "And so attention to the Spirit's role as that which defines the character of Jesus humanity also gives shape to a properly Christian anthropology." McFarland, "Spirit and Incarnation: Toward a Pneumatic Chalcedonianism," 158.

Spirit Christology for Christian Formation

Having further interrogated McFarland's pneumatic Chalcedonianism, we can see that it corroborates with the claims of other orthodox Spirit-Christologies: it offers a convincing account of the agency of the Holy Spirit in the life of Jesus of Nazareth while also effectively securing a Logos Christology. We are now in a position to make a number of direct claims concerning how this account of the Spirit in relation to a Chalcedonian Christology strengthens and develops Bonhoeffer's pneumatology; where it correlates with it and where it can improve upon it.

First, this pneumatic Chalcedonianism is underpinned by an account of the Trinity. This is unlike Bonhoeffer's theology which is famously criticized for offering no developed discussions of the Trinity.[50] By contrast, McFarland's pneumatic Chalcedonianism relies heavily on an orthodox Trinitarianism. As the agency of the Holy Spirit is the divine causality in the life of Jesus of Nazareth, a Trinitarian context needs to be drawn out: Jesus is a reliable index not only of the Son but of the divine life of God which he shares with the Spirit and the Father.[51] As such, the Christian anthropology which results from this is one in which we are brought into relationship with the Father (who is now *our* Father) by the Son and the Spirit.

Second, this orthodox Spirit Christology prioritizes the person of Jesus of Nazareth in such a way as to result in a stronger account of Christian formation. By unencumbering the human nature of Christ from exclusive associations with suffering (which McFarland calls "the Leonine temptation"[52]), emphasizing the unavailability of the divine nature to our objective inquiry and reinforcing the distinction between hypostasis and nature—so that the actions of Jesus of Nazareth which are evidently divine in origin are better regarded as the direct

50. Although Christopher R. J. Holmes observes of Bonhoeffer's morning prayer for prisoners written in Tegel that Bonhoeffer clearly understood the Spirit in a Trinitarian context rather than as a "free-floating Spirit," Bonhoeffer rarely wrote about Christ and God in the Trinitarian terms of Son and Father. Of his "notable reticence regarding the doctrine of the Trinity," Philip Ziegler remarks: "Bonhoeffer most certainly does not say everything one might want to say in a Christian doctrine of God." Ziegler, "God," 148.

51. McFarland affirms that in Jesus we see what God is like without having an exact model for God: "Consequently, because Jesus is the particular person he is (viz., the second person of the Trinity), all Jesus' human actions participate in the divine energies, making them reliable indices of the divine that allow us to affirm, on the basis of the attributes revealed in those actions, that the divine nature is merciful, compassionate, righteous, and so forth." McFarland, *The Word Made Flesh: A Theology of the Incarnation*, 96.

52. This refers to the *Tome* of Leo the Great and the pithy summary of Chalcedon, mentioned above ("One shines forth with miracles; the other succumbs to injuries."). "The Leonine Temptation," McFarland tells us, is the habit of ascribing divinity to an aspect of Jesus, a temptation which should be resisted because it renders that element of Jesus qualitatively different from the rest of humanity. McFarland, "Spirit and Incarnation: Toward a Pneumatic Chalcedonianism," 146–9.

work of the Spirit—McFarland draws a line of continuity between Christ's actions in his humanity and our own.[53]

Emphasis on the incarnation, as inimitably and uniquely the locus of a restored relationship between humanity and God, is redolent of Bonhoeffer's account of Christian formation which is concentrated on the person and works of Jesus Christ; in this sense, a pneumatic Chalcedonianism chimes with the Christological keynote of Bonhoeffer's theology.[54] But the connection between Christ and the Christian today is made more resilient by appeal to the work of the Spirit in the life of Jesus of Nazareth.

By identifying the Spirit as the power by which Jesus of Nazareth was demonstrably divine, a Christian anthropology arises which better accounts for the Spirit's work in sanctifying Christians without losing the Christological focus. From the description of the agency of the Spirit in the life of Christ we glean how the agency of the Spirit can act in us, too. Because Jesus did what he did through the Spirit, and not as a result of his identity as the Word, so we can do the same. With Christ, we are children of God, sharing the same Spirit and inheritance which is Christ's by right and ours by gift: we are adopted sons or daughters.[55] By the Spirit we are conformed to the likeness of the Son and are united to God the Father.

We are left with an account of humanity and creation in which the *telos* is not limited to a view of salvation in terms of rescue (from sin, death, and separation from God, an emphasis which is often associated with Protestant-Evangelicalism), but is also cast in terms of "participation" in the divine life of God (*theosis*), realized in the Son and by the Spirit. Moreover, in this account the *telos* is already realized, to some extent, in the life of creation as it is, by the very fact of its existence which is sustained by the divine life.[56] A Chalcedonianism

53. It should be observed that this line is also drawn by Rowan Williams in his account of what we called Bonhoeffer's "existential kenosis," in which Christ's mode of being corresponds to our own. Except that Williams does this without the all-important pneumatology we have been defending.

54. Recall Bonhoeffer's description of the *tri-formative* pattern of Christ's earthly life (in his incarnation, death, and resurrection) and how the Spirit actualizes our transformation into Christlikeness as an ongoing, simultaneously realized process of "becoming human, being judged and renewed." Bonhoeffer, *Ethics*, 6:93–5.

55. "from a purely formal perspective (i.e. as it moves his humanity into a life of faith, hope and love before God) the Spirit works upon him in the same way as upon any other human being." McFarland, "Spirit and Incarnation: Toward a Pneumatic Chalcedonianism," 158.

56. So, for example, McFarland can explicate his Christology through an illustration pertaining to other human lives, describing how the unique value of "who" a person is lies in his hypostasis and not his personality. For instance, he writes: "If it seems odd to distinguish hypostasis from personality or self-consciousness, consider that to do so makes it possible to maintain that a person who through traumatic brain injury or dementia or mental illness experiences severe diminishment or loss of these traits does not cease to be who they are." McFarland, 150. It is in being *created* that human value is located.

refined by a pneumatology clarifies how the humanity of Christ is the grounds of our own human condition and this results in an elevated view of humanity as a consequence of the incarnation.[57]

In these ways, a Spirit Christology such as McFarland's pneumatic Chalcedonianism shores up Bonhoeffer's pneumatology and his theology of Christian formation. Grounding the relationship between the Spirit and the Son in the incarnate life of Jesus of Nazareth, and grounding this in the *intratrinitarian* life of God, we are provided with a more developed and nuanced understanding of the relationship between Christ, the Holy Spirit, and the Church. The clarification of the distinct persons of the Son and the Spirit and the explanation of the Trinitarian life of God as the context for a Chalcedonian Christology, in turn, provides a stronger account of the unity between the persons of the Trinity which is the basis for our own unity as a Church. This Trinitarian core gives a much-needed depth to pneumatology, where the Spirit's role has, at times, seemed more functional (as a means of clarifying Bonhoeffer's ecclesiology).

Acoustic Space for the Spirit

In what remains I will develop the findings of this research with respect to a musico-pneumatology by demonstrating what musical casts of mind and language have to offer to understanding the dual agency of the Son and Spirit as just outlined. So far, I have been contending that Bonhoeffer's pneumatology can be usefully expanded through a Spirit Christology in the vein of a pneumatic Chalcedonianism. I will now show that a Spirit Christology which seeks to be orthodox, likewise, can be beneficially expanded via musical casts of mind and language such as those employed by Bonhoeffer which have been the subject of this book.

McFarland's pneumatic Chalcedonianism faces an implicit challenge shared by all accounts of the Spirit in relation to Christology: how we can speak of multiple agencies actively engaging with each other in such a way as they can both establish and enhance each other without their particularity and integrity being diminished. The difficulty with negotiating the relationship between the distinct persons of the Spirit and the Son in the hypostatic union is exemplified in Oliver Davies's remarks concerning the "space" McFarland's pneumatic Chalcedonianism opens up for the Spirit in the distinction between the Logos-hypostasis and human Jesus. As Davies writes:

> The decisive shift away from thinking that features of Christ's humanity are effectively divine to the recognition that his divinity lies in "who" he is rather than in "what" he is, opens *a space for the Holy Spirit* to be the dynamic presence of God within the human life of Jesus Christ himself. It is *the Spirit who is the*

57. This corresponds with Bonhoeffer's emphasis on "becoming human" in his *tri-formative* pattern of Christian formation. See: Bonhoeffer, *Ethics*, 6:93–5.

> *point of contact between the divine hypostasis and the humanity of Jesus*, and that Jesus receives the Spirit, and is informed by the Spirit, testifies to the integrity and authenticity of his humanity.[58]

In this excerpt, Davies describes the Spirit as requiring space in order to be "the point of contact" between the hypostasis and human nature of Jesus. By mistakenly reading McFarland as saying that the Spirit's role in the hypostatic union involves being "the point of contact" between the divine hypostasis and the humanity of Jesus (McFarland makes no such direct claim),[59] Davies inadvertently illustrates the intractability of discussing the Son and the Spirit in the hypostatic union.

The problem is further exemplified by Oliver Crisp in his critique of John Owen's Spirit Christology.[60] Crisp identifies the problem with this Spirit Christology in trying to preserve the agency of the Son along with that of the Spirit, and to account for how both can be active through the human nature simultaneously. He draws an analogy between a hand surgeon who makes himself a new hand which is facilitated by a special membrane: the surgeon (the Word) wills to move his hand (the human nature), an action which is enabled by the membrane (the Holy Spirit).[61] He, rightly, points out that while this analogy has the advantage of conveying the direct actions of the Son in his human nature, this is unsatisfactory because it suggests that the Spirit has no agency, but is rather merely an interface.[62] As Crisp's analogy makes clear, conveying the mutual agency of the Spirit and the Son is anything but straightforward.

The risks include making the Spirit too impersonal (a mere interface) or giving the Spirit too much agency (putting the Spirit in the driving seat and relegating the Son to the backseat). Crisp objects in stark terms to the Spirit's involvement in the hypostatic union which, he says, amounts to "a denial of the efficacy of the Son's assumption of human nature" and introduces "an illegitimate cleavage

58. Davies, "Holy Spirit and Mediation: Towards a Transformational Pneumatology." My emphasis.

59. With the exception of affirming Jesus Christ's conception by the Spirit in Mary, McFarland's discussion of the Spirit is limited to the observable features of the Spirit in the life of Jesus, *ad extra*. Although it might be possible to infer the Spirit's involvement in Christ *in se* with respect to the deification of the human will of Jesus (arguing, for instance, that the mode of activity which corresponds to a deified will is enabled by the Holy Spirit and this pertains to the relationship between the Son and the human nature in the union), this is not explicitly described by McFarland.

60. Crisp, "John Owen on Spirit Christology."

61. "When he wills to move his hand, or one of his digits, this bodily action is enabled via the membrane between the arm and the new hand of the surgeon." Crisp, 23.

62. In an alternative analogy he compares a humanoid robot in a spacesuit which is synched to an astronaut to the Holy Spirit's power in the human nature which is controlled by the Son. See: Crisp, 15.

between the immediate agency of the Son and his human nature."[63] But this interpretation seems to rest, in the main, upon the idea that the efficacy of the Son is somehow threatened by the presence of the Spirit or that the distinct identity of the Spirit is compromised by being too closely associated with the Son.[64] Crisp seems to come close to trading off the agency of the Spirit against the Son in favor of the Son.

At this point, our theological language is hard pressed and must be brought under scrutiny. Crisp speaks critically of a "cleavage"—too great a degree of separation between the Logos-hypostasis and human nature, as a result of the Spirit; Davies, on the other hand, affirms the "space" opened up for the Holy Spirit between the Logos and human nature.[65] In both instances (whether conveying "space" in positive terms or "cleavage" in negative terms) the metaphorical language attempts to convey the discrete integrity ("distinction" or "difference") of the subjects under discussion while they are, simultaneously, in relation. With both thinkers we must acknowledge that preserving an understanding of the distinct identities of the subjects under discussion (whether the Son and the Spirit or human nature) is of vital importance in order to uphold orthodox Trinitarian and Chalcedonian Christology.

As we might expect by now, it is my contention that this discussion can greatly benefit from alternative metaphorical language. By inculcating our theological imaginations with acoustic-spatial concepts we can provide a better account of the "space" for the Spirit to which Davies alludes. Through musical language and

63. In full: "It amounts to a denial of the efficacy of the Son's assumption of human nature, and introduces an illegitimate cleavage between the immediate agency of the Son and his human nature that is unsustainable given the intimate relation that must obtain between his divine and human natures in order for the hypostatic union to be maintained." Crisp, 22.

64. It is not entirely clear whether McFarland's pneumatic Chalcedonianism would satisfy Crisp, whose essay is the earlier of the two. On the one hand, Crisp concludes by proposing an alternative to Owen's Spirit Christology which upholds a Chalcedonian Christology together with a "robust pneumatology." On the other, McFarland's insistence that divine causality in the life of Jesus of Nazareth comes from the Spirit, and his equal insistence that it does *not* come from the Son, would seem to correspond with Crisp's criticisms of Owen, that the Spirit's role removes the *immediate* action of the Son upon the human nature. See: Crisp, 22.

65. Though he does not recognize the metaphorical aspect of speaking about "space" being opened up for the Holy Spirit, in the same essay Davies is acutely aware of the problems with metaphorical language. He writes: "Christian revelation is more coherently conceptualized by stripping away the metaphoricity which is largely a residue from the old 'enchanted' universe of scriptural tradition, which structured the human–divine relation three-dimensionally, within a geo-centric universe." Davies, "Holy Spirit and Mediation: Towards a Transformational Pneumatology," 160.

conceptuality, it is possible to reimagine the dynamic work of the Holy Spirit in relation to the Son and describe the Spirit's work in sustaining the hypostatic union while making clear that this does not override the Son.

Acoustic-spatial patterns of thought provide a valuable means of articulating an orthodox Spirit Christology in which the agency of the Holy Spirit sustains the divine hypostasis and human nature. In the language of polyphony, this metaphor imaginatively articulates the Chalcedonian definition by conveying how the distinct voices of the human nature and divine hypostasis are attuned by the Holy Spirit, remaining discrete while also fully relating ("without confusion or change, without division or separation").[66] By conceptualizing the work of the Spirit as "attuning" the distinct voices of the Son and the human nature to one another, "modulating" the human nature to the divine Son and creating resonance between them, we can imagine the Spirit's work without obscuring the Son or the human nature. The polyphony of Christ is a work of the Holy Spirit who, we can imagine, not only attunes the human nature to the Son, but also the Son to the Father in the *intratrinitarian* life.[67]

A musico-pneumatology which inherently relies on an acoustic perception of space, therefore, can bring about a subtle but important shift in our understanding of how the Holy Spirit is integrated with the Son in an orthodox Spirit Christology. Through such patterns of thought we can postulate the Spirit's agency at the level of the hypostatic union (Christ *in se*) without threatening a Logos Christology *or* denying the presence and role of the Son. Being able to thus articulate the agency of the Holy Spirit in the relationship between the divine hypostasis and human nature in Christ has the potential to overcome possible criticisms of McFarland's pneumatic Chalcedonianism; in particular those criticisms pertaining to the apparent "independence" or "decoupling" of the divine hypostasis and human nature through the apparent caesura between the "who" and "what" of Jesus, in which the human nature might be seen to operate "independently" of the divine

66. "The two are 'undivided and yet distinct,' as the Definition of Chalcedon says, like the divine and human natures in Christ." Bonhoeffer, *Letters and Papers from Prison*, 8:394.

67. In this way the economic trinity is the immanent trinity and, vice versa, because what has been recognized of the Spirit and Son's relationship in testimonies to the life of Jesus of Nazareth is reflected back onto what we say about the immanent trinity. With respect to McFarland's pneumatic Chalcedonianism, I am not claiming that the conceptual language he employs has blocked a more developed account of the *intratrinitarian* relations; only that there is potential to reimagine these relations more fruitfully with a different understanding of "space." The potential is evident when McFarland observes, strikingly, that the persons of the Trinity do not compete for space: "Within the Godhead one person does not subsume the other; *neither do the three compete for a common space*; rather, each sustains the others in and through their mutual presence in one another in love: the Father by begetting the Son in the Spirit, the Son by receiving the Father's gift of divinity in the same Spirit, and the Spirit, as the Spirit of the Father and the Son, as inseparable from either." McFarland, *The Word Made Flesh: A Theology of the Incarnation*, 37.

hypostasis. Although, to my mind, articulating the Holy Spirit's work in the hypostatic union as "attuning" simply makes plainer what is already implicit in McFarland's account: the hypostatic union is only possible because of the Spirit.

Furthermore, this musico-pneumatology eschews Crisp's idea that a Spirit Christology denies the efficacy of the Son's assumption and creates an "illegitimate cleavage"; accusations which seem to result, to a not insignificant degree, from a series of analogies which rely on a visually informed understanding of space. As opposed to viewing a Spirit Christology as placing the Son and the Spirit in competition, musical metaphors allow us to imagine multiple agencies interrelating in a noncompetitive way.

A further benefit of musical casts of mind and categories derived from them is in the area of Christian formation, as we re-imagine our own polyphonic relationship with God and the world. Although I will not explore this at length, I can briefly indicate how a musico-pneumatology could begin to be developed for more downstream discussions of Christian formation. The Spirit Christology discussed in this chapter, I have argued, inexorably generates a theology of Christian formation on the basis of the claim that Jesus of Nazareth was sanctified by the Spirit; a sanctification which, in turn, grounds all human sanctification by the Spirit. Musical terms like polyphony can be employed interchangeably in discussions of the Spirit's work in Christology and Christian formation. Just as we can say that the Spirit attunes the Son to the Father, or the human nature to the Son, we might also speak of the work of the Spirit in attuning us to the Son and, through the Son, to the Father. A particular benefit of being able to easily transfer these terms is that it reflects the consonance of Christology and Christian formation and reinforces the importance of the incarnation as the basis of our formation.

In line with this, this musico-pneumatology could be further developed as a heuristic device for spiritual discernment, in which musical ideas form an imaginative tool for understanding and actively participating in our formation as Christians. This would be an extension of Bonhoeffer's original intention in first employing polyphony to help a Christian regulate how he engages with God and the world, but with the addition of a greater emphasis on the Spirit's role in this process. In the sanctifying process, we can imagine our individual identity, unique and irreplaceable, as a distinctive melody; a particularity which is maintained even while Christ lives in us and we in Him. Just as we experience music inwardly without seeing it, this musico-theological imagination can help us to engage with the Spirit, who helps us to listen, and attunes us, to the call of Christ in our lives.

Conclusion

In the final analysis of what I have been able to achieve in this last chapter, I have endeavored to show what difference it makes to articulate an orthodox Spirit Christology by employing musical metaphors. We have seen that a pneumatic

Chalcedonianism provides a compelling basis for the work of the Spirit in Christian formation which shores up Bonhoeffer's pneumatology, providing a Trinitarian context for the relationship between the Spirit and the Son in the person of Jesus of Nazareth. In turn, however, musical patterns of thought and language, such as those Bonhoeffer employs, can help to further clarify this account of the agency of the Holy Spirit in sustaining the hypostatic union without obscuring the Son. Articulating the dual agency of the Son and the Spirit through musical metaphors offers a refined description of the collaborative actions of the Son and the Spirit in the life of Jesus of Nazareth. The Holy Spirit causes God and the world to resonate in Christ by attuning the human nature to the Son and, through the Son, to the Father. As the basis of our attunement to God through Christ, our own voices are gathered into this greater polyphony of life.

CONCLUSION

This treatment of Dietrich Bonhoeffer's musico-pneumatological imagination and language yields a number of important benefits, both for the field of Bonhoeffer studies and for contemporary theology more widely. In this conclusion, I want to draw attention to four.

First and foremost, an interrogation of Bonhoeffer's musico-theology has elucidated the important role of the Holy Spirit in his theological appeal to musical ideas. Where polyphony, and other musical references, have traditionally been evaluated as having an exclusively Christological significance, I have argued that the work of the Spirit is also implicit in this musical language. By discovering in his musico-theological imagination and language an inherent pneumatology, a subtle doctrine of the Spirit has been thrown into relief; one which has all too often gone unrecognized. As such, this study acts as a mild corrective to those who have identified in Bonhoeffer a complete lack of attention to the Holy Spirit, and could potentially be useful for further developing insights into his theology of the Spirit.

Following on from this, second, this implicit pneumatology is highly compatible with the Christological focus of Bonhoeffer's thought, and even enhances it. On my reading, Bonhoeffer's Christology and his corresponding account of Christian formation are greatly strengthened through developing this nascent theology of the Holy Spirit. This is because pneumatology, where it is employed, safeguards against an overidentification of Christ and the Church, thereby enriching the kind of ecclesiology Bonhoeffer is advocating. The Spirit is not in competition with Christ or the Christian but helps to establish their relationality without undermining their distinct identities, as the acoustic metaphors beautifully disclose.

Third, Bonhoeffer's musical imagination profoundly and unquestionably informs his theological one, and vice versa. His own "aesthetic existence" is long in evidence in the evolution of his anti-racist actions in the 1930s, which find expression in his embrace of African American spirituals and also in his warning against sung worship without corresponding acts of justice. But this "aesthetic existence" begins to be formalized in his prison letters, in which musical casts of mind help Bonhoeffer express otherwise seemingly contradictory aspects of his Christian experience. His self-professed *Fündlein* brings this musico-theology to its fullest expression. The "polyphony of life" stands alongside the formulations "religionless Christianity" and "world come of age," as a dynamic means of articulating his "new theology" in which the Christian lives fully with God in the world because of Christ.

Finally, we come to the implication of all this for contemporary theology more widely, and it is this: Acoustic-spatial metaphors provide a potent means of articulating the work of the Holy Spirit and Christ in the life of the Christian. These metaphors, with their reliance on an acoustic perception of space, enable a subtle, but important, shift in thought. They allow us to articulate an orthodox Spirit Christology, a noncompetitive relationship between the Son and the Spirit in which their relationality is not presented as a threat to their distinct integrities. Consequently, it is possible to imagine the sanctifying work of the Spirit in the person of Jesus of Nazareth as the basis of the Christian's, and the church's, life in the Spirit.

I began this book with a quotation from Bonhoeffer in which he compares the greater beauty entailed by music when recollected though unheard to Christ's "new body." We can finally say with more certainty what this means. A familiar piece of music, even though unheard, is comparable to the new body of Christ, who is unseen, because it inhabits us in such a way that exceeds mere remembrance; it pervades our being just as Christ, also, lives in us by the Holy Spirit. For Bonhoeffer, music infuses his life, occupies his thoughts, and penetrates his being in a way that is analogous to the Holy Spirit who lives in him and attunes him to the risen Christ.

BIBLIOGRAPHY

Adkins, Imogen Helen. "Sound, Space and Christological Self-Giving." University of Cambridge, 2013.

Barth, Karl. *Church Dogmatics*. Edited by G. W. Bromiley and T. F. Torrance. vol. IV.2. Edinburgh: T&T Clark, 1958.

Begbie, Jeremy. *Resounding Truth: Christian Wisdom in the World of Music*. London: SPCK, 2008.

Begbie, Jeremy S. *Music, Modernity and God: Essays in Listening*. Oxford: Oxford University Press, 2013.

Begbie, Jeremy S. "Room of One's Own? Music, Space and Freedom." Oxford Scholarship Online, 2014.

Begbie, Jeremy S. and Steven R. Guthrie, eds. *Resonant Witness: Conversations between Music and Theology*. Grand Rapids, MI and Cambridge: Eerdmans, 2011.

Bethge, Eberhard. *Dietrich Bonhoeffer: Man of Vision, Man of Courage*. Edited by Edwin Robertson. Translated by Eric Mosbacher, Peter and Betty Ross and Frank Clarke. New York: Harper & Row, 1970.

Bethge, Eberhard. *Dietrich Bonhoeffer: Theologian, Christian, Contemporary*. Edited by Edwin Robertson. Translated by Eric Mosbacher, Peter and Betty Ross, Frank Clarke and William Glen-Doepel. St James's Place: Collins, 1970.

Bonhoeffer, Dietrich. *Act and Being*. Edited by Wayne Whitson, Floyd Jr. Translated by H. Martin Rumscheidt. vol. 2. DBWE. Minneapolis: Fortress Press, 1996.

Bonhoeffer, Dietrich. *Life Together*. Edited by Geffrey B. Kelly. Translated by Daniel W. Bloesch and James H. Burtness. vol. 5. DBWE. Minneapolis: Fortress Press, 1996.

Bonhoeffer, Dietrich. *Prayerbook of the Bible: An Introduction to the Psalms*. Edited by Geffrey B. Kelly. Translated by James H. Burtness. vol. 5. DBWE. Minneapolis: Fortress Press, 1996.

Bonhoeffer, Dietrich. *Creation and Fall*. Edited by John W. de Gruchy. Translated by Douglas Stephen Bax. vol. 3. DBWE. Minneapolis: Fortress Press, 1997.

Bonhoeffer, Dietrich. *Sanctorum Communio*. Edited by Clifford Green. Translated by Reinhard Krauss and Nancy Lukens. vol. 1. DBWE. Minneapolis: Fortress Press, 1998.

Bonhoeffer, Dietrich. *Discipleship*. Edited by Geffrey B. Kelly and John D. Godsey. Translated by Barbara Green and Reinhard Krauss. vol. 4. DBWE. Minneapolis: Fortress Press, 2001.

Bonhoeffer, Dietrich. *Ethics*. Edited by Clifford J. Green. Translated by Reinhard Krauss, Charles C. West and Douglas W. Stott. vol. 6. Works. Minneapolis: Fortress Press, 2005.

Bonhoeffer, Dietrich. *Conspiracy and Imprisonment, 1940–45*. Edited by Mark S. Brocker. Translated by Lisa E. Dahill. vol. 16. DBWE. Minneapolis: Fortress Press, 2006.

Bonhoeffer, Dietrich. *London, 1933–35*. Edited by Keith Clements. Translated by Isabel Best. vol. 13. DBWE. Minneapolis: Fortress Press, 2007.

Bonhoeffer, Dietrich. *Barcelona, Berlin, New York: 1928–1931*. Edited by Clifford J. Green. Translated by Douglas W. Stott. vol. 10. DBWE. Minneapolis: Fortress Press, 2008.

Bonhoeffer, Dietrich. *Berlin: 1932–1933*. Edited by Larry L. Rasmussen. Translated by Isabel Best and David Higgins. vol. 12. DBWE. Minneapolis: Fortress Press, 2009.

Bonhoeffer, Dietrich. *Letters and Papers from Prison*. Edited by John W. de Gruchy. Translated by Isabel Best. vol. 8. DBWE. Minneapolis: Fortress Press, 2010.

Bonhoeffer, Dietrich. *Theological Education at Finkenwalde: 1935–1937*. Edited by H. Gaylon Barker and Mark S. Brocker. Translated by Douglas W. Stott. vol. 14. DBWE. Minneapolis: Fortress Press, 2013.

Brocker, Mark S. "Creating Anew Responsible Human Beings: The Work of the Holy Spirit in Bonhoeffer's Ethics." Stellenbosch: South Africa, 2020.

Coakley, Sarah. "What Does Chalcedon Solve and What Does It Not? Some Reflections on the Status and Meaning of the Chalcedonian 'Definition.'" In *The Incarnation: An Interdisciplinary Symposium on the Incarnation of the Son of God*, edited by Stephen T. Davis, Daniel Kendall and Gerald O'Collins, 143–63. Oxford: Oxford University Press, 2002.

Coffey, Dave. "'Spirit Christology and the Trinity.'" In *Advents of the Spirit: An Introduction to the Current Study of Pneumatology*, edited by B. Hinze and D. Lyle Dabney, 315–18. Milwaukee, WI: Marquette University Press, 2001.

Colle, Ralph del. *Christ and the Spirit: Spirit-Christology in Trinitarian Perspective*. New York: Oxford University Press, 1994.

Congar, Yves. *The Word and the Spirit*. London: Geoffrey Chapman, 1986.

Crisp, Oliver D. "John Owen on Spirit Christology." *Journal of Reformed Theology* 5, no. 1 (2011): 5–25.

Dahill, Lisa E. *Reading from the Underside of Selfhood: Bonhoeffer and Spiritual Formation*. Eugene, Oregon: Pickwick Publications, 2009.

Davies, Oliver. "Holy Spirit and Mediation: Towards a Transformational Pneumatology." *International Journal of Systematic Theology* 16, no. 2 (2014): 159–76.

De Gruchy, John W. *Bonhoeffer and South Africa: Theology in Dialogue*. Grand Rapids, MI: William B. Eerdmans Publishing Company, 1984.

De Gruchy, John W. "Restoring Broken Themes of Praise." In *Christianity, Art and Transformation: Theological Aesthetics in the Struggle for Justice*, 136–68. Cambridge: Cambridge University Press, 2001.

De Gruchy, John W. "The Search for Transcendence in an Age of Barbarism: Bonhoeffer, Beethoven, Mann's Dr Faustus and the Spiritual Crisis of the Present Time." In *Polyphonie Der Theologie: Verantwortung Und Widerstand in Kirche Und Politik Auflage, Ed. 2019*, edited by Matthias Grebe and Andreas Pangritz, 161–74, first edition. Stuttgart: Kohlhammer, 2019.

DeJonge, Michael P. *Bonhoeffer's Reception of Luther*. Oxford: Oxford University Press, 2017.

Denzinger, Heinrich and Peter Hünermann, eds. *Compendium of Creeds, Definitions, and Declarations on Matters of Faith and Morals*. 43rd edition. San Francisco: Ignatius Press, 2012.

Dumas, André. *Dietrich Bonhoeffer: Theologian of Reality*. London: SCM Press Ltd., 1971.

Feil, Ernst. *The Theology of Dietrich Bonhoeffer*. Translated by Martin Rumscheidt. Based on third German edition. Minneapolis: Fortress Press, 1985.

Ferreira, M. Jamie. *Kierkegaard*. Malden, MA and Oxford, UK: Wiley-Blackwell, 2009.

Ford, David F. "Polyphonic Living: Dietrich Bonhoeffer." In *Self and Salvation: Being Transformed*. Cambridge: Cambridge University Press, 1999.

Ford, David F. "Bonhoeffer, Holiness and Ethics." In *Holiness Past and Present*, edited by Stephen C. Barton, 361–80. Edinburgh: T&T Clark, 2003.

Ford, David F. "Holy Spirit and Christian Spirituality." In *The Cambridge Companion to Postmodern Theology*, edited by Kevin J. Vanhoozer, 269–90. Cambridge: Cambridge University Press, 2003.

Ford, David F. "Humanity Before God; Think Through Scripture: Theological Anthropology and the Bible." In *The Theological Anthropology of David Kelsey: Responses to Eccentric Existence*, edited by Gene Outka, 31–52. Grand Rapids, MI: William B. Eerdmans Publishing Co., 2016.

Franklin, Patrick S. "Bonhoeffer's Anti-Logos and Its Challenge to Oppression." *Crux* 41, no. 2 (2005).

Frobenius, Wolf. "Polyphony." In *Grove Music Online*. Oxford Music Online. Oxford University Press. Accessed August 4, 2017. http://www.oxfordmusiconline.com/subscriber/article/grove/music/42927.

Fuller, Sarah. "Early Polyphony to Circa 1200." In *The Cambridge Companion to Medieval Music*, edited by Mark Everist, 46–66. Cambridge: Cambridge University Press, 2011.

Garcia, Javier. "Bonhoeffer and Reformation Ecclesiology." *Journal of Reformed Theology* 12, no. 2 (August 8, 2018): 164–89.

Gardiner, Craig. *Melodies of a New Monasticism: Bonhoeffer's Vision, Iona's Witness*. London: SCM Press, 2018.

Green, Clifford. "Human Sociality and Christian Community." In *The Cambridge Companion to Dietrich Bonhoeffer*, edited by John W. de Gruchy, 113–33. Cambridge: Cambridge University Press, 1999.

Green, Clifford J. *Bonhoeffer: A Theology of Sociality*. Grand Rapids, MI/Cambridge, UK: William B. Eerdmans Publishing Company, 1999.

Green, Clifford. "Trinity and Christology in Bonhoeffer and Barth." *Union Seminary Quarterly Review* 60, no. 1 (2006).

Greggs, Tom. "Ecclesiology." In *The Oxford Handbook of Dietrich Bonhoeffer*, edited by Philip G. Ziegler and Michael Mawson, online edition. Oxford: Oxford University Press, 2019.

Habets, Myk. "Putting the 'Extra' Back into Calvinism." *Scottish Journal of Theology* 62, no. 4 (2009): 441–56. https://doi.org/10.1017/S003693060999010X.

Habets, Myk. "Spirit Christology: The Future of Christology?" In *Third Article Theology: A Pneumatological Dogmatics*, edited by Myk Habets, 207–32. Minneapolis: Fortress Press, 2016.

Harrison, Carol. "Augustine and the Art of Music." In *Resonant Witness: Conversations between Music and Theology*, edited by Jeremy Begbie and Stephen Guthrie, 27–45. Grand Rapids, MI and Cambridge: William B. Eerdmans Publishing Co., 2011.

Harvey, Barry. "Augustine and Thomas Aquinas in the Theology of Dietrich Bonhoeffer." In *Bonhoeffer's Intellectual Formation: Theology and Philosophy in His Thought*, edited by Peter Frick, 11–29. Tübingen, Germany: Mohr Siebeck, 2008.

Harvey, Barry. *Taking Hold of the Real: Dietrich Bonhoeffer and the Profound Worldliness of Christianity*. Eugene, OR: Cascade Books, 2015.

Heaney, Maeve Louise. *Music as Theology: What Music Says about the Word*. Princeton Theological Monograph Series. Eugene, Oregon: Pickwick Publications, 2012.

Höhne, David A. *Spirit and Sonship: Colin Gunton's Theology of Particularity and the Holy Spirit*. Farnham, UK and Burlington, VT: Ashgate, 2010.

Holmes, Christopher R. J. "The Holy Spirit." In *The Oxford Handbook of Dietrich Bonhoeffer*, edited by Philip G. Ziegler and Michael Mawson, online edition. Oxford: Oxford University Press, 2019.

Janz, Paul D. *God, the Mind's Desire: Reference, Reason and Christian Thinking*. Cambridge Studies in Christian Doctrine, Cambridge: Cambridge University Press, 2004.

Jensen, Alexander. *Divine Providence and Human Agency*. Farnham, UK and Burlington, VT: Ashgate, 2014.
Jenson, Matt. "Real Presence: Contemporaneity in Bonhoeffer's Christology." *Scottish Journal of Theology* 58 (2005): 143–60.
Jenson, Robert W. "Once More the Logos Asarkos." *International Journal of Systematic Theology* 13, no. 2 (2011): 130–3.
Kelly, Geffrey B. "Kierkegaard as 'Antidote' and as Impact on Dietrich Bonhoeffer's Concept of Christian Discipleship." In *Bonhoeffer's Intellectual Formation: Theology and Philosophy in His Thought*, edited by Peter Frick, 145–66. Tübingen, Germany: Mohr Siebeck, 2008.
Kelsey, David H. *Eccentric Existence: A Theological Anthropology*. First edition. Vol. 1. 2 vols. Louisville, Kentucky: Westminster John Knox Press, 2009.
Kirkpatrick, Matthew D. *Attacks on Christendom in a World Come of Age: Kierkegaard, Bonhoeffer, and the Question of "Religionlessness Christianity."* Eugene, Oregon: Pickwick Publications, 2011.
Knight, Mark. "Sin and Salvation." In *The Oxford Handbook to Dietrich Bonhoeffer*, edited by Philip G. Ziegler and Michael Mawson, online edition. Oxford: Oxford University Press, 2019.
Lakoff, George and Mark Johnson. *Metaphors We Live By*. Chicago: University of Chicago Press, 2003.
Law, David R. *Kierkegaard's Kenotic Christology*. Oxford: Oxford University Press, 2013.
Leibholz-Bonhoeffer, Sabine. *The Bonhoeffers: Portrait of a Family*. Chicago: Covenant Publications, 1994.
Marsh, Charles. "Dietrich Bonhoeffer." In *The Modern Theologians*, edited by David F. Ford, 37–51, second edition. Oxford: Blackwell, 1997.
Marsh, Charles. *Reclaiming Dietrich Bonhoeffer: The Promise of His Theology*. New York; Oxford: Oxford University Press, 1994.
Marsh, Charles. *Strange Glory: A Life of Dietrich Bonhoeffer*. London: SPCK, 2014.
Mawson, Michael. "Christ, Spirit, and Church." In *Christ Existing as Community: Bonhoeffer's Ecclesiology*. Oxford: Oxford University Press, 2018.
Mawson, Michael. "Theology and Social Theory—Reevaluating Bonhoeffer's Approach." *Theology Today* 71, no. 1 (April 1, 2014): 69–80.
McBride, Jennifer M. "Christ's Public Presence." In *The Church for the World: A Theology of Public Witness*. Oxford: Oxford University Press, 2011.
McCormack, Bruce. "Kenoticism in Modern Christology." In *The Oxford Handbook of Christology*, edited by Francesca Aran Murphy, 15. Oxford: Oxford University Press, 2015.
McCormack, Bruce L. "Christology." In *The Cambridge Companion to Reformed Theology*, edited by Paul T. Nimmo and David A. S. Fergusson, 60–78. Cambridge: Cambridge University Press, 2016.
McFarland, Ian A. "Fallen or Unfallen? Christ's Human Nature and the Ontology of Human Sinfulness." *International Journal of Systematic Theology* 10, no. 4 (October 2008): 399–415.
McFarland, Ian A. "Spirit and Incarnation: Toward a Pneumatic Chalcedonianism." *International Journal of Systematic Theology* 16, no. 2 (April 2014): 143–58.
McFarland, Ian A. *The Word Made Flesh: A Theology of the Incarnation*. Louisville, Kentucky: Westminster John Knox Press, 2019.
McGarry, Joseph. "Formed by the Spirit: A Third Article Theology of Christian Spirituality." In *Third Article Theology: A Pneumatological Dogmatics*, edited by Myk Habets, 283–96. Minneapolis: Fortress Press, 2016.
McGarry, Joseph M. "Christ among a Band of People: Dietrich Bonhoeffer and Formation in Christ." PhD, Aberdeen, 2013.

McLaughlin, Eleanor. *Unconscious Christianity in Dietrich Bonhoeffer's Late Theology*. Lanham, Maryland and London, UK: Lexington Books/Fortress Academic, 2020.
Moseley, David. "'Parables' and 'Polyphony': The Resonance of Music as Witness in the Theology of Karl Barth and Dietrich Bonhoeffer." In *Resonant Witness: Conversations between Music and Theology*, edited by Jeremy Begbie and Steven Guthrie, 240–70. Grand Rapids, MI and Cambridge: William B. Eerdmans Publishing Co., 2011.
Nickson, Ann L. *Bonhoeffer on Freedom: Courageously Grasping Reality*. Aldershot: Ashgate, 2002.
Ott, Heinrich. *Reality and Faith: The Theological Legacy of Dietrich Bonhoeffer*. London: Lutterworth Press, 1971.
Pangritz, Andreas. *Polyphonie Des Lebens: Zu Dietrich Bonhoeffers "Theologie Der Musik."* Berlin: Alektor-Verlag, 1994.
Pangritz, Andreas. "Who Is Jesus Christ, for Us, Today?" In *The Cambridge Companion to Dietrich Bonhoeffer*, edited by John W. de Gruchy, 134–53. Cambridge: Cambridge University Press, 1999.
Pangritz, Andreas. *Karl Barth in the Theology of Dietrich Bonhoeffer*. Translated by Barbara Rumscheidt and Martin Rumscheidt. Grand Rapids: Eerdmans, 2000.
Pangritz, Andreas. "Point and Counterpoint—Resistance and Submission: Dietrich Bonhoeffer on Theology and Music in Times of War and Social Crisis." In *Theology in Dialogue: The Impact of the Art, Humanities, and Science on Contemporary Religious Thought (Essays in Honor of John W. de Gruchy)*, edited by Lyn Holness and Ralf K. Wüstenberg, 28–42. Grand Rapids, MI: William B. Eerdmans Pub. Co., 2002.
Pangritz, Andreas. "Dietrich Bonhoeffer: 'Within, Not Outside, the Barthian Movement.'" In *Bonhoeffer's Intellectual Formation: Theology and Philosophy in His Thought*, edited by Peter Frick, 245–82. Tübingen, Germany: Mohr Siebeck, 2008.
Pangritz, Andreas. *The Polyphony of Life: Bonhoeffer's Theology of Music*. Edited by John W. de Gruchy and John Morris. Translated by Robert Steiner. Eugene, Oregon: Cascade Books, 2019.
Parsons, Preston David Sunabacka. *A Friendship for Others: Bonhoeffer and Bethge on the Theology and Practice of Friendship*. PhD, The University of Cambridge, 2018.
Peppiatt, Lucy. "New Directions in Spirit Christology: A Foundation for a Charismatic Theology." *Theology* 117, no. 1 (January 2014): 3–10.
Pickstock, Catherine. "Soul, City and Cosmos after Augustine." In *Radical Orthodoxy: A New Theology*. London and New York: Routledge, 1999.
Plant, Stephen J. *Taking Stock of Bonhoeffer: Studies in Biblical Interpretation and Ethics*. Farnham: Ashgate, 2014.
Rasmussen, Larry L. *Dietrich Bonhoeffer: Reality and Resistance*. Revised edition. Louisville: Westminster John Knox Press, 2005.
Robinson, J. A. T. *Honest to God*. London: SCM Press, 1963.
Schlingensiepen, Ferdinand. *Dietrich Bonhoeffer 1906–1945: Martyr, Thinker, Man of Resistance*. Translated by Isabel Best. London: Bloomsbury, 2009.
Selby, Peter. "Christianity in a World Come of Age." In *The Cambridge Companion to Dietrich Bonhoeffer*, edited by John W. de Gruchy, 233–9. Cambridge: Cambridge University Press, 1999.
Smail, Tom. *The Giving Gift: The Holy Spirit in Person*. London: Darton, Longman & Todd, 1988.
Soskice, Janet Martin. *Metaphor and Religious Language*. Oxford: Clarendon Press, 1985.
Spence, Alan. "Christ's Humanity and Ours: John Owen." In *Persons Divine and Human: King's College Essays in Theological Anthropology*, edited by C. Schwöbel and C. Gunton, 74–97. Edinburgh: T&T Clark, 1992.

Tietz, Christiane. "The Role of Jesus Christ for Christian Theology." In *Christ, Church and World: New Studies in Bonhoeffer's Theology and Ethics*, edited by Michael G. Mawson and Philip G. Ziegler, 9–27. London: Bloomsbury T&T Clark, 2016.

Tietz, Christiane. "Christology." In *The Oxford Handbook of Dietrich Bonhoeffer*, edited by Philip G. Ziegler and Michael Mawson, online edition. Oxford: Oxford University Press, 2019.

Wannenwetsch, Bernd. "The Whole Christ and The Whole Human Being: Dietrich Bonhoeffer's Inspiration for the 'Christology and Ethics' Discourse." In *Christology and Ethics*, edited by F. LeRon Shults and Brent Waters, 75–98. Grand Rapids, MI/ Cambridge, UK: William B. Eerdmans Publishing Co., 2010.

Welker, Michael. *God the Revealed: Christology*. Grand Rapids, MI/Cambridge, UK: William B. Eerdmans Publishing Company, 2013.

Williams, Reggie L. *Bonhoeffer's Black Jesus: Harlem Renaissance Theology and an Ethic of Resistance*. Waco, Texas: Baylor University Press, 2014.

Williams, Rowan. "Word and Spirit." In *On Christian Theology*. Oxford: Blackwell, 2000.

Williams, Rowan. *Christ the Heart of Creation*. London: Bloomsbury Continuum, 2018.

Woelfel, James W. *Bonhoeffer's Theology: Classical and Revolutionary*. Nashville: Abingdon Press, 1970.

Wolff, Christoph and Walter Emery. "Bach, Johann Sebastian." *Grove Music Online*, 2001.

Wüstenberg, Ralf K. *A Theology of Life: Dietrich Bonhoeffer's Religionless Christianity*. Translated by Doug Stott. Grand Rapids, MI: William B. Eerdmans, 1998.

Wüstenberg, Ralf K. "Religion and Secularity." In *The Oxford Handbook of Dietrich Bonhoeffer*, edited by Philip G. Ziegler and Michael Mawson, 321–30. Oxford: Oxford University Press, 2019.

Yong, Amos. *The Spirit Poured Out on All Flesh: Pentecostalism and the Possibility of Global Theology*. Grand Rapids: Baker Academic, 2005.

Ziegler, Philip. "Christ For Us Today—Promeity in the Christologies of Bonhoeffer and Kierkegaard." *International Journal of Systematic Theology* 15, no. 1 (January 2013): 25–41.

INDEX

www.ingramcontent.com/pod-product-compliance
Lightning Source LLC
Chambersburg PA
CBHW051525230426
43668CB00012B/1743

* 9 7 8 0 5 6 7 7 1 3 9 4 0 *